T0305897

"We must end teaching, researching, and legitimizing business-as-usual practices that are rapidly destroying the planet's capacity to support all species. These authors tell exciting stories that inspire business schools around the world to break away from those practices to focus on activism, researching, and teaching to create a sustainable/flourishing/regenerating world. These powerful stories will inspire many to follow in their footsteps, and to share our own transformation stories."

James A. F. Stoner, *PhD, Professor Emeritus, Fordham University*

"If we are ever to overthrow the yoke of shareholder primacy, we must creatively destroy business education as we know it. This important new book provides a roadmap and narrative for making that happen."

Stuart Hart, *PhD, Professor, University of Vermont and author of* Beyond Shareholder Primacy

"We all agree that business education needs to be transformed if we are to transition towards a sustainable political economy but how exactly is this to be done? *Transforming Business Education for a Sustainable Future: Stories from Pioneers* will be an invaluable resource for anyone who is currently wrestling with this question."

Lee Matthews, *PhD, Lecturer in Business and Society, University of Nottingham*

"This book provides a deep and sincere insight into meaningful and useful practices regarding sustainability in education. The simple writing of each chapter encourages the reader to realize and encourage aspects of sustainability in work and daily life."

Respati Wulandari, *PhD, Associate Professor, BINUS Business School, Bina Nusantara University, Indonesia*

"What we are teaching in business schools today is irrelevant. Many organizations are working against an urgent timeline to change business and business education for human survival. This book takes us beyond conversations about what might be done or should be done. It offers stories from pioneers who are in action. No one has all the answers but these pioneers are on the front lines of figuring out business for a finer future."

Hunter Lovins, *JD., President and Founder of Natural Capitalism Solutions (NCS), founding professor of the MBA in Sustainability at Bard College*

"I was deeply inspired as I read the 16 chapters of this urgently needed book which is filled with well documented, positive, '*sustainability promoting*,' examples of changes that have been and are being made in business schools' courses and curricula. As an educator since 1965, I strongly endorse this book for educators, students, and business school policy makers, globally."

Donald Huisingh, *Professor and Editor-in-Chief, Emeritus,* Journal of Cleaner Production

"Education is arguably the most immediate way to drive socio-ecological change and have an impact in business/management. This book is a fantastic collection of hands-on stories from those committed to transforming business education and making a difference. It provides much-needed resources and practical insights and I am sure it will become a reference in the field."

Anne Touboulic, *PhD, Chair of the Social and Environmental Responsibility Group, Nottingham University Business School*

"The world is facing unprecedented challenges, and it is essential that our future business leaders are equipped with the knowledge, skills, and mindset necessary to navigate and address these complex issues. This book serves as a guiding light, providing a collection of success stories from pioneers who have developed innovative programs, courses, and systems that are already transforming the way business education is conducted to cope with our global sustainability challenges."

Rupert Baumgartner, *PhD, Professor of Sustainability Management University of Graz, Austria*

TRANSFORMING BUSINESS EDUCATION FOR A SUSTAINABLE FUTURE

As the impact of climate change becomes more evident and dire, business leaders, educators, students, and academic leaders are deciding what they need to change and do to survive and thrive in a new and dramatically different environment. This book sets out how to transform business education and integrate sustainability practices into curriculum and a wider academic culture.

While some universities around the globe are still teaching business practices that have contributed to human and environmental crises, pioneering educators and higher education institutions are researching, developing, and implementing programs to transform business education and practices. With stories from 26 administrators, researchers, and faculty across the globe, this book inspires business educators with innovative tools and creative solutions to address challenges in the business world and society. These pioneers are helping students and business ventures change the way they conduct business to survive and thrive in a fast-changing global environment. Their unique and personal journeys offer tools, models, lessons-learned, and inspiration for change.

The book will both inspire and guide faculty members, administrators, students, and alumni to transform business education for a sustainable future.

Linda Irwin taught Strategy and Marketing and is passionate about transforming business education for sustainability. She is the CEO of SeeComm Group and a member of Global Movement Initiative.

Isabel Rimanoczy is the convener of PRME Working Group on Sustainability Mindset and co-developer of the Sustainability Mindset Indicator. She authored/edited 28 books about sustainability, learning, poetry, and children's books.

Morgane Fritz is Associate Professor in Sustainable Supply Chain Management. She researches/teaches about sustainable and ethical supply chain management and acts as an author/editor/reviewer for various peer-reviewed journals and books.

James Weichert is a serial entrepreneur in all aspects of real estate development, the founder of www.livingconservancy.org, and a doctoral candidate in sustainable economics.

The Principles for Responsible Management Education Series

Since the inception of the UN-supported Principles for Responsible Management Education (PRME) in 2007, there has been increased debate over how to adapt management education to best meet the demands of the 21st-century business environment. While consensus has been reached by the majority of globally focused management education institutions that sustainability must be incorporated into management education curricula, the relevant question is no longer why management education should change, but how.

Volumes within the Routledge/PRME book series aim to cultivate and inspire actively engaged participants by offering practical examples and case studies to support the implementation of the Six Principles of Responsible Management Education. Books in the series aim to enable participants to transition from a global learning community to an action community.

Principles of Sustainable Business
Frameworks for Corporate Action on the SDGs
Rob van Tulder and Eveline van Mil

Transforming Business Education for a Sustainable Future
Stories from Pioneers
Edited by Linda Irwin, Isabel Rimanoczy, Morgane Fritz, and James Weichert

For more information about this series, please visit: www.routledge.com/The-Principles-for-Responsible-Management-Education-Series/book-series/PRME

TRANSFORMING BUSINESS EDUCATION FOR A SUSTAINABLE FUTURE

Stories from Pioneers

Edited by
Linda Irwin, Isabel Rimanoczy,
Morgane Fritz, and James Weichert

Global Movement Initiative, Inc.
408 W 25th St. Ste. 5FW
New York
NY 10001 USA

Routledge
Taylor & Francis Group

LONDON AND NEW YORK

Designed cover image: © Getty Images / Petmal

First published 2024
by Routledge
4 Park Square, Milton Park, Abingdon, Oxon OX14 4RN

and by Routledge
605 Third Avenue, New York, NY 10158

Routledge is an imprint of the Taylor & Francis Group, an informa business

British Library Cataloguing-in-Publication Data
A catalogue record for this book is available from the British Library

Library of Congress Cataloging-in-Publication Data
Names: Irwin, Linda, editor. | Rimanoczy, Isabel, 1956– editor. | Fritz, Morgane, editor. | Weichert, James, editor.
Title: Transforming business education for a sustainable future : stories from pioneers / edited by Linda Irwin, Isabel Rimanoczy, Morgane Fritz, and James Weichert.
Description: Abingdon, Oxon ; New York, NY : Routledge, 2024. | Series: The principles for responsible management education series | Includes bibliographical references and index. |
Identifiers: LCCN 2023036285 (print) | LCCN 2023036286 (ebook) | ISBN 9781032601472 (hardback) | ISBN 9781032591162 (paperback) | ISBN 9781003457763 (ebook)
Subjects: LCSH: Business education. | Executives—Training of.
Classification: LCC HF1106 .T73 2024 (print) | LCC HF1106 (ebook) | DDC 650.07/1—dc23/eng/20230913
LC record available at https://lccn.loc.gov/2023036285
LC ebook record available at https://lccn.loc.gov/2023036286

ISBN: 978-1-032-60147-2 (hbk)
ISBN: 978-1-032-59116-2 (pbk)
ISBN: 978-1-003-45776-3 (ebk)

DOI: 10.4324/9781003457763

Typeset in Galliard
by codeMantra

CONTENTS

CONTRIBUTORS

Celine Berrier-Lucas is Associate Professor at ISG Business School in Paris and teaches at the executive education of Paris-Dauphine PSL University. She is a co-editor-in-chief of the *Review of Responsible Organization*. She teaches CSR, organizational theory, and business models in the Anthropocene. Her research interests include historical analysis of CSR, Indigenous perspective, and CMS.

Jean-Claude Boldrini, PhD, is a Researcher in innovation management, strategic management, and transition to the circular economy. For about 30 years he was a teacher of mechanical engineering and automation in high schools. From 2011 to 2021, he was Associate Professor at Nantes Université (France). His research focuses on the management of the upstream phases of projects in cross industry exploratory partnerships, in particular the projects devoted to the transition toward the circular economy and its business models.

Nurete Brenner holds a PhD in Organizational Behavior from Case Western Reserve University in Cleveland, Ohio, an MBA from the University of Derby, an MA from Hebrew University in Jerusalem, and a BA from Bar Ilan University in Ramat Gan, Israel. She is the executive director of Lake Erie Institute, a Cleveland, Ohio-based nonprofit dedicated to ecological leadership and holistic environmental education. Dr. Brenner's previous role was Executive Director of the MBA and Business Programs at a College in Ohio, and she teaches undergrad and graduate level courses in Organizational Behavior, Communications, Ecological Economics, Sustainability, and Leadership at universities in Israel and the United States. She was among the founding team of professors at AIM2Flourish, a program at Case Western Reserve University devoted to collecting case studies about businesses addressing the UN Sustainable Development Goals. In previous roles, she was a career and life coach, and she has convened and facilitated Arab-Jewish dialogue circles. Her research and publications have focused on intercultural dialogue, women's leadership, and Eco Judaism. She is passionate about contributing toward a shift to a more peaceful, just, and sustainable world.

Miguel Cordova is Associate Professor of Management at Pontificia Universidad Católica del Perú. He is Resources Vice-Chair at Teaching & Education SIG in the Academy of International Business (AIB) and serves as Peru Country Director for the AIB Latin America and the Caribbean chapter. He is the Associate Editor of the *International Journal of Sustainability in Higher Education*. His research interests are Sustainability, Sustainable Supply Chain Management, Power and Influence in Organizations, and International Business.

Donatienne Delorme, PhD, is Associate Professor at Excelia Business School, Head of the Strategy and CSR Department. Her research and teaching topics focus on innovation management, strategy, and business models, from a sustainable perspective.

Valérie Fernandes, PhD, is Full Professor at Excelia Business School and Associate Dean of Faculty and Academic Development. Her interest in Ethics, Sustainability, and Responsibility led her to lead the CSR strategic axis as part of Excelia's strategic plan. She has published in international journals on her favorite research topics – sustainable supply chain management and circular economy.

Morgane Fritz, PhD, is Associate Professor in Sustainability Management in Supply Chains at Excelia Business School, La Rochelle, France. Her research and teaching interests include supply chain sustainability, sustainable procurement, business ethics, and stakeholder management. She publishes and acts as a reviewer and guest editor for various peer-reviewed journals.

Ruth Areli García-León, PhD, is a Lecturer and Researcher at Ostfalia University of Applied Sciences and the University of Hamburg in Germany. Her research interest focuses on Sustainability Marketing and Responsible Management Education. She is part of the steering committee of the PRME Chapter DACH (Germany-Austria-Switzerland). She holds a PhD in Education Sciences, a Master's in marketing, an M.Sc. in Communication, a Licenciate in Communication Sciences, and is a certified coach and trainer of cross-cultural competencies.

Jesus Gonzalez-Feliu, PhD, is Full Professor at Excelia Business School since 2020. He held teaching and research positions at Ecole des Mines de Saint-Etienne and CNRS (France). His main domains are interactive problem solving, group decision-making, sustainable transport planning, city logistics, humanitarian logistics, equity food systems, and sustainability evaluation.

Luciana Hashiba, PhD, is Professor and Researcher at FGV-EAESP (Fundação Getúlio Vargas), coordinator of programs for innovation at FAPESP, counselor of IPT (Technological Research Institute and Eldorado Institute), expert and consultant on innovation management, strategic management of innovation and evolution of the open innovation model in networks.

Luís Henrique Pereira, PhD, is Professor and Researcher at FGV-EAESP (Fundação Getúlio Vargas), International Management Master program coordinator, and consultant on customer behavior and marketing for large companies, International Insight of Living Brazil NGO president.

Carina Hopper is a sustainable business lecturer teaching at the Master's level at leading European business schools. She is also active in the entrepreneurship community, advising and collaborating with start-ups across Europe. She is the co-founder of Join EDuC and the nonprofit Back to School for the Planet, offering innovative lifelong learning solutions for higher education institutions.

Linda Irwin, MBA, served as Lecturer and course developer for Anderson College of Business Regis University, in strategy and marketing for 25 years. She is the CEO of SeeComm Group, a business consulting firm serving Fortune 500 companies, social enterprises, and nonprofits. She is a member of Global Movement Initiative.

Fabio B. Josgrilberg, PhD, is Professor and Researcher at the UNESCO Chair for Communications and Regional Development, at the Methodist University of São Paulo, associate researcher at Beta Laboratoire (CNRS), Strasbourg University, consultant on innovation and socioenvironmental corporate projects.

Orla Kelleher is a senior lecturer in Responsible Management and PRME lead at the College of Business, Law and Social Sciences, University of Derby, UK. She is the program leader for the MSc Sustainable & Ethical Business Management and member of PRME Sustainability Mindset, and Climate Change and Environment groups.

Jed Lindholm is a senior-level HR performance and rewards professional who teaches leadership practices for sustainability at Worcester Polytechnic Institute in Worcester, MA. As an HR leader, Lindholm is integrating competencies into workplace programs that promote sustainability by designing jobs that link individual and corporate actions to sustainable goals. He has taught at Penn State, Clark University, WPI, and internationally in China, Singapore, Israel, and Poland.

Gabriel Penagos is Associate Professor of Finance in the Department of Economics at Pontificia Universidad Javeriana de Bogotá. Main research subject: applying machine learning and stochastic calculus techniques to finance, publishing in *Journal of Modelling in Management, JEcon Interact Coord, Climate Risk Management,* and *PLoS ONE*, among others.

Lovasoa Ramboarisata is Associate Professor at the school of management of the University of Québec in Montréal. She acts as the school's PRME coordinator. She teaches CMS, grand challenges, socio-political context of businesses, and social and organizational change. Her research focuses on RME, decolonial perspectives, and CSR.

Dimbi Ramonjy is Associate Professor in strategy and CSR at Excelia Business School (France). He is also a member of the CEREGE Poitiers laboratory within the "Governance and Sustainable Development (SD)" axis. He is active in the specialized academic networks on SD & CSR (RIODD) and on Fair Trade (FairNESS).

Subhasis Ray, PhD, is Professor of Marketing and Sustainability at XIM University, India. He has taught and spoken on Sustainability in 26 countries to students of 35 nationalities. His research interests include sustainability, marketing, circular economy, and social entrepreneurship.

Luis Raúl Rodríguez-Reyes is Associate Professor of Economics and Finance at ITESO Business School, Guadalajara, Mexico. Fellow of Mexico's National Research System since 2018. Member of the *Journal of Management for Global Sustainability* Editorial Board. Main research interests are financial economics, public policy, and sustainability.

Magdalena Rusch has a background in Management & Law and Environmental Systems Sciences, with a focus on Sustainability Management and Innovation. She worked as a PhD researcher at the CD-Lab for Sustainable Product Management enabling a Circular Economy at the University of Graz, where she was and still is involved in research and teaching activities. Affiliation: Institute of Environmental Systems Sciences, Merangasse 18, 8010 Graz, University of Graz, Austria.

Ken Sagendorf, PhD, is the John J. Sullivan Endowed Chair for Free Enterprise and directs The Innovation Center and MBA in the Anderson College of Business & Computing at Regis University. He holds a PhD from Syracuse University and works to design educational environments that foster deep, transformative student learning.

Marina A. Schmitz serves as a Researcher and Lecturer in the Coca-Cola Chair of Sustainable Development at IEDC-Bled School of Management in Bled, Slovenia, as well as CSR Expert/Senior Consultant at Polymundo AG in Heilbronn, Germany. She draws on several years of work experience as a Lecturer, Research Associate, and Project Manager at the Center for Advanced Sustainable Management (CASM) at the CBS International Business School in Cologne, Germany.

Christel Tessier Dargent, PhD, ESCP Business School, is a teacher–researcher at Université Grenoble Alpes, Grenoble, France. She is responsible for Entrepreneurship, Innovation, and Creativity modules for engineering schools. Her research domains are necessity entrepreneurship and entrepreneurial education. She started her career as a process manager at a major digital transformation consulting company, working on worldwide software implementations.

Johanna Wagner is a sustainability advisor and lecturer. She is passionate about people and sustainability and teaches in leading hospitality Master's programs in Europe. She is the co-founder of Join EDuC, an impact-first company dedicated to accelerating the integration of sustainability content in higher education curricula, as well as the non-profit Back to School for the Planet.

FORETHOUGHTS

Isabel Rimanoczy, PhD

One breezy morning a few decades ago, I was sipping my coffee and going through a pile of newspaper cuttings that I collected about leadership failures: Enron, WorldCom, Volkswagen, Wirecard, Luckin Coffee, and more. What had influenced these individuals and led them to prioritize short-term financial returns or personal gain? What economic models, values, and practices were we currently teaching in business schools to support such failed decisions? What if we identified a different set of leaders who championed more sustainable initiatives, and learned from them, instead? This was in the early 2000s, and the impacts of our behaviors on the environment and society were far less visible than they are today. I gave some thought to identifying a few business leaders who were real pioneers, who were managing and transforming the standard purpose of their corporations. That was the start of my journey of exploration, trying to sort out what motivated visionary business leaders. What did they know, how were they thinking? I didn't realize it at that time, but I was entering a "Zeitgeist Zone", along with a myriad of others who were equally impatient and ready to bring about change. We just didn't see one another.

Fast forward to 2022 when a group of concerned business school professors and members of the Global Movement Initiative realized that there were "intellectual earthquakes" shaking business schools' landscape. They, too, were sorting out what topics were necessary to be taught to transform business education and foster sustainable and humanitarian business leaders. Continuing the geological analogy, some tremors were short lived, some were barely perceptible, others were stronger and more disruptive. What these events had in common was that they were questioning systems, processes, pedagogical approaches, economic models, and assumptions, and were bringing in new frameworks, starting new conversations. They were less intense at first, growing bolder as they met enthusiastic students or colleagues.

You will find in these pages the stories of these pioneers, these changemakers, and how they are transforming the purpose, pedagogies, and contents taught in business schools around the globe.

Stories of successes and of failed expectations, plus lessons learned from their journeys. "Teaching sustainability is no longer an option, but it remains a challenge in business schools," says **Subhasis Ray**. "Business schools are ground zero for forming future leaders and yet...." reflects **Nurete Brenner**. These are the landscapes that the authors of this book are shaking up. They are zeroing in on the operating system and mindset that created business behaviors that are dysfunctional, shortsighted, and unsustainable for people and ecosystems. They are aspirational: inspiring students and communities to envision the future they would like, and then inviting them to collectively find ways to make it happen.

In these pages, you will find innovative pedagogical approaches using interdisciplinary connections for systems learning to challenge our siloed thinking. **Orla Kelleher** describes how Business, Social Sciences, Law and Engineering departments at the University of Derby, UK, are connecting via the Principles of Responsible Management Education (PRME). **Jean-Claude Boldrini,** formerly with Nantes Université (France) and **Donatienne Delorme,** Excelia Business School, France, utilize a circular business model for incorporating sustainability across management disciplines. They describe a 10-year experiment they implemented particularly in capstone projects. Their goal is to prepare students to become sustainability transition champions, as well as reflective and committed citizens.

Miguel Córdova at Universidad Católica del Perú and **Marina A. Schmitz** at University of Bled, Slovenia decided to experiment by bringing ecology and the natural sciences to their management teaching. What metaphors connect fish and leadership? From Brazil, comes the story of **Fabio Botelho Josgrilberg, Luciana Hashiba , and Luís Henrique Pereira,** who led a creative academic transformative experiment. They found student self-assessment of creativity to be very low, which is a challenge considering the urgency to unleash our innovative skills to solve many unsustainable problems. They used art and even a circus as pedagogical resources, and applied design thinking, with ecological considerations in an applied, real-world project.

Subhasis Ray shares how teaching both in Europe and in developing countries made him aware of very different realities and context that impact the presence of sustainability in business schools. How can we see beyond the short-term benefits of a job market? He has some answers. Finance, Marketing, and Economy are bastions of how we think about the purpose of business. When we develop new perspectives, we can build a more resilient, flourishing future. This is what **Luis Raúl Rodríguez-Reyes and Gabriel Penagos** of ITSEO, Mexico, and Pontificia Universidad Javeriana de Bogotá, Colombia, have done creating a new introductory finance course by proposing a different paradigm for finance.

Editor **Linda Irwin** felt the urge to toss Marketing's traditional focus on "pushing consumption and profits" and replaced it with a new purpose of marketing: to serve real needs and to create a better world. She shares her journey rewriting three graduate marketing courses at Regis University, Colorado. **Ruth Areli García-León** of Brunswick European Law School, Germany, decided to use the news of the week in her marketing courses, which leads to the open discussion of sustainability concepts. **Jed Lindholm** at Worcester Polytechnic Institute, USA, realized that business-as-usual no longer reflected the world we live in, so he decided to transform his curriculum to include Sustainable Mindset Principles and the UN Sustainable Development Goals.

To foster much-needed social entrepreneurs, **Christel Tessier Dargent** at the University of Grenoble, France, introduced entrepreneurship modules to give students the practice necessary to adapt and influence today's challenges. What would happen if we brought in different voices? For example, having students interact with older alumni, who want to learn more about applicable sustainability practices? Or even invite students to design a course, influence contents that they would like to learn? **Magdalena Rusch** shares about her experience creating a student-led course in sustainability at the University of Graz, Austria, while **Carina Hopper and Johanna Wagner** tell us about their Back to School for the Planet initiative engaging alumni.

All the change makers sharing their stories in this book are using their unique skills, knowledge, and context to make the highest impact given their circumstances. The road, however, is never straight and smooth. **Nurete Brenner** moved with her family from Israel to the

USA to take on the transformation of an MBA, questioning the underlying assumptions of the textbooks and curriculum she inherited, only to have the program shut down by the administration after three years. **Ken Sagendorf** led the complete overhaul of an MBA program at Regis University, USA, so far without the expected results. Both are ready to share valuable insights about what *could have led* to success. As the saying goes – there is no trial and error: there is only trial and learning!

Lovasoa Ramboarisata at University of Québec in Montréal, **Celine Berrier-Lucas** at ISG Business School in Paris, **and Dimbi Ramonly** at Excelia Business School in France, challenge business schools to reconsider the fundamental principles of business education and consider a decolonized and broad humanitarian approach to business. Imagine an institution where strategy, management, and educators are aligned and supporting one another. **Valerie Fernandes**, Dean of faculty at Excelia Business School, France, joins **Jesus Gonzalez-Feliu**, Head of Supply Chain, Purchasing, and Project Management Department and Associate Professor **Morgane Fritz** to share how they are embedding sustainability across three campuses.

Loud and soft, broad and focused, all these stories have one message: change is happening. It is mostly around the edges; it is messy and complex and so is our reality. Besides, change never starts as mainstream.

Years ago, I wrote a Haiku:

Stand up now

Let your voice be heard

Wait no more.

This is what these pioneers are doing. Meet them and join the movement.

INTRODUCTION

As the impact of climate change and human suffering becomes more evident and dire, business leaders, educators, students, and academic program managers are considering what they need to do or learn to survive and thrive in a new and dramatically different environment. While many universities around the globe are still teaching business practices that have contributed to the crisis, some pioneering educators and higher education institutions are researching, developing, testing, and implementing programs to significantly change business education and business practices for a future that supports sustainable survival.

This book is a compilation of stories from administrators, faculty, students, and business communities who are actively working to transform business education to support a just and sustainable world. These pioneers from around the globe are helping students and business ventures transform the way they conduct business to survive and thrive in a fast-changing environment.

Each chapter begins with an abstract that enables readers to see the direction of their story. Some relate to transforming business education systems, some trial innovative and integrated ideas, and others focus on specific courses or pedagogies. These pioneers' stories offer tools, models, lessons-learned, challenges, and opportunities for others to follow. The unique and personal journeys of innovative educators offer inspiration and incentive to act.

1

SEEING SHADOWS

Unveiling Assumptions Underlying Management Education

Nurete Brenner

Abstract

Business schools are ground zero for forming future leaders of society and yet the current business school curriculum does not allow space for questioning the business systems currently in place. A system that cannot be questioned becomes an indoctrination rather than an education. Worse, the current system is one that is proving to be incompatible with the continuation of life on planet earth. Three of the assumptions embedded within the business school curriculum that need to be questioned are endless growth; the acceptance of nondemocracy in the workplace; and free markets and competition are positives. If we are to have a shot at leaving a better world for our children, indeed, if we are to maintain the possibility of an inhabitable planet, we need to make drastic changes and business schools are one of the leverage points for doing so.

Context

In 2015, I was offered a job as director of an MBA program at a teaching college near Cleveland, Ohio. The job entailed an overseas move back to the United States with my children after we had been living in Israel for five years. At the time, the move didn't seem feasible, so during the interview process, I was authentic to a fault and explained that I didn't believe in management education the way it was being taught

DOI: 10.4324/9781003457763-1

today by most schools. I have a PhD in Organizational Behavior, which is a business-school degree, and yet my values had changed to the point where I no longer believed in "business as usual." In the interviews, I expressed my belief that capitalism had become an impediment to human flourishing and an obstacle to a sustainable planet. Every MBA that I had ever heard about, read about, taught in, or been a part of took capitalism as the basic "operating system" of the economy.

Instead of "business as usual," I outlined a vision of a socially conscious business school curriculum, which put people and planet above profits. To my astonishment, they offered me the job. Now it was no longer a question of moving my kids overseas because of a job; now it was a matter of making an overseas move for a vision. And that changed everything. I accepted the job and created what I called a Socially Conscious MBA curriculum. As it turned out, the program never got past the pilot stage. The story of the short-lived Socially Conscious MBA program is one of the essential stepping-stones in my journey, and I hope that the narrative will be informative for others.

Description of Process

When I first arrived at my post as the Director of the MBA program at the College, I found that I inherited a program that didn't look much different from, say, a Harvard MBA. That sounds like a good thing, right? Just like the Harvard curriculum, my program included the familiar business disciplines of Finance, Accounting, Leadership and Organizational Behavior, Marketing, Operations, Strategy, etc. Harvard's program emphasizes global entrepreneurship, while the program I inherited in suburban Ohio centered on Project Management and Human Resource Management. I am not trying to critique Harvard's MBA nor any other MBA program, my argument is that my small local MBA was as mainstream as any other when it came to teaching the MBA basics.

One of my guiding philosophies as an educator is that there is no point in teaching something that someone can learn from reading a textbook and students should have a reason for coming to class. Therefore, when I began my tenure as the head of the MBA program, I added a discussion-driven course called The Socially Conscious Economy which was essentially a class in socio-political macroeconomics. This course encouraged students to reevaluate the entire economic system on both a macro and micro level, and it exposed the basic assumptions of business that are embedded – and rarely questioned – throughout all MBA programs and indeed the entire current global economy. These assumptions are leading us down a path that can no longer sustain life on this planet.

The Underlying Assumptions

Perhaps the current business school curriculum does not allow space for questioning the validity of the business system because many of the instructors themselves are so immersed in the system that they do not think to examine it. Or it could be because cultural sea-change is slow, and deeply entrenched paradigms are difficult to uproot. Whatever the reasons, a system that cannot be questioned becomes an indoctrination rather than an education. Worse, the current system is one that is proving to be incompatible with the continuation of life on planet earth. It really needs to be stated as starkly as that.

The first assumption that must be questioned in a business program is the idea of unlimited growth. If you think for a moment about each of the business-school disciplines I mention above: marketing, strategy, accounting, global management, operations, etc. you realize that they are all predicated on growth: growing a business, growing a corporation, growing sales, growing profits, and growing an economy. For classical, mainstream economics, growth is axiomatic. However, maverick and nonmainstream economists have been saying for years that growth cannot continue. Recently, even conventional publications such as the *New York Times* (NYT) have begun publishing articles questioning the premise of unchecked growth, although they do so with some resistance; notice the word "counterintuitive" in the following quote. In 2018, the NYT published an article about economist Herman Daly who has been promoting the idea of a "steady-state economy" since his first book *Towards a Steady State Economy* was published in 1973. His second book *Beyond Growth,* (1996) took this idea further. The NYT writes: "… Without a continually rising G.D.P., we're told, we risk social instability, declining standards of living and pretty much any hope of progress."

But what about the counterintuitive possibility that our current pursuit of growth, rabid as it is and causing such great ecological harm, might be incurring more costs than gains? That possibility – that prioritizing growth is ultimately a losing game – is one that the lauded economist Herman Daly has been exploring for more than 50 years

(https://www.nytimes.com/interactive/2022/07/18/magazine/
herman-daly-interview.html). Economic research has discovered that
GDP growth in the developed world no longer improves health, happiness, or measures of well-being.

Today there are many other economists (see Kate Raworth, *Doughnut
Economics*, Smith and Neef *Economics Unmasked*, Charles Eisenstein,
Sacred Economics among others) who question the idea of growth but
none of these books are taught in most business schools.

Each time I teach a class on our economic system, I ask the students
the following question: "What are the top ten things you do that make
you happy?" The answers are always similar. The students list things
like spending time with friends and family, caring for children, tending
to pets, playing sports, listening to, or making music, exercising, and
connecting to nature. These are the key activities that most people find
contribute to their well-being and yet these activities contribute very
little to the GDP. Thus, we have created a system in which the measure
we use for our economic well-being – GDP – does not correspond with
any of the things that make us happy in life. Instead, GDP includes
items such as hospital visits, environmental disasters, and criminal activity. The assumption that GDP growth is good allows environmental,
societal, and health problems to be ignored (or at least postponed),
since it is presumed that they will be resolved by more growth.

The MBA program that I created asked: *what if we could transition
away from an obsession with growth and from an economy in which maximizing profit is the prime mover to a socially conscious one in which maximizing human well-being is the focus?* How can we encourage this shift
if we continue teaching from the old paradigm? In the courses I taught
at the College, I invited students to envision a society in which there is
a shift from wealth creation to well-being creation, from bottom-line
transactions to bottom-up transformation, from growth at all costs to
caring for one another as the primary concern of all. I was attempting to shift the business school conversation to one that states that an
organization's first commitment is not to the growth of the business
and not to the bottom line of the accounting books, but to the health,
happiness, and well-being of the employees, the stakeholders, the communities, the planet, and future generations.

I also introduced to business students the concept of "degrowth"
which is a tenet of ecological economics and now increasingly being
given a platform at academic conferences and in the scholarly literature

but still not yet being taught in most business-school classes. The degrowth movement advocates for societies that prioritize social and ecological well-being instead of corporate profits, production, and consumption. This requires radical redistribution, reduction in the material size of the global economy, and a shift in common values toward care, solidarity, and autonomy. Degrowth means transforming societies to ensure environmental justice and a good life for all within planetary boundaries (Hickel, *Less is More: How Degrowth will Save the World*, 2022). Ecological economics recognizes that the Earth is sick from the activities of human beings living out of ecological balance. Everywhere we look we can see the living fabric of life, prairies, forests, savannas, estuaries, and swamps – the healthy tissue of the Earth's body – being replaced by trash development, buildings, stores, parking lots, factories, and roads (Haenke, https://www.resilience.org/stories/2021-04-28/david-haenke-on-bioregionalism-ecological-economics/). Growth is destroying the planet and yet we continue to teach it in business school.

Questioning underlying assumptions is crucial because business schools are the ground zero for forging future leaders in and of the world. We are sending young people out into the world to perpetuate a death machine and promising them rewards for doing so. Society then bemoans or blames business leaders who seem to succumb to greed when the system itself is created to reward greed.

The second assumption deeply embedded in the business school curriculum, and in business in general, is the absence of democracy in the workplace. Although we don't – in principle – accept tyranny in our political system, we surprisingly do accept it in the workplace. We are proud of our democratic institutions and yet rarely question the hierarchical, nondemocratic nature of the standard workplace. When I introduce the idea of democratic workplaces in the classroom, I often get intense pushback from the students. Many of them aspire to be bosses and managers in their future careers and thus feel justified in expecting to assume positions of power-over others in the workplace. They accept without question the tyranny of the hierarchical system in the workplace, which restricts your time, your attention, and forces you to conform to a circadian rhythm in line with the workplace's needs. We never question the very idea of exchanging all our working hours to survive and thus become slaves to our wages.

One of the main proponents of this idea of democratic workplaces is sociologist Richard Wolff (2012), who writes,

> If democracy is a genuine foundational social value, it ought to govern the workplace first and foremost. Yet workers in most modern capitalism corporations are required by law and / or custom to accept working conditions over which they exercise no democratic control. If they refuse, they can be fired – and the primary option available to them is to work for another employer under similarly undemocratic conditions. For most workers in capitalist systems, there is no democracy in the workplace where they spend most of their lives.... Retaining the hierarchical capitalist organization of enterprises, is, in fact, the obstruction of democratization.
> (*Wolff,* Democracy at Work: A Cure for Capitalism, *2012*)

I suggest that it's taboo in our capitalist society to expect democracy in our workplaces.

Another writer and thinker who dares to question the absence of autonomy in the workplace is Raoul Martinez in his book, *Creating Freedom* (2017). The pertinent questions that Martinez asks are:

> If democracy is something we value, why is it so often excluded from the institutions to which we devote so much of our lives? Why should workers not be able to participate in the decisions that impact them. Why should those who create profit not decide how it is spent? Why must the democratic rights of the citizen be left behind on entering the workplace?

It is interesting how these questions are not always welcomed even by the young people in our society. There is an inherent resistance to changing the status quo.

Once we allow for such questioning in the classroom, it can open a space for us to speculate on how an organization can change its structure to create a democratic workplace. Some of the ideas that are being discussed in the cultural conversation revolve around worker self-management, which becomes the preferred model for a socially conscious company because it allows the workers to control the pace, the mode of production and the direction of the company. In a truly democratic workplace, each worker is an equal member of the board and major decisions are arrived at democratically by the principle of one-person-one-vote rather than one share one vote.

Economists call this model of worker ownership "self-directed enterprises" (Richard Wolff). Workers rotate certain roles so that no one occupies the role of manager for too long and so that no one exercises disproportionate influence over discussion, debates, and decisions. In these democratic organizations, the wage gap between managers and workers is often much smaller than in the current corporate shareholder model. This model allows many workers to develop a variety of skills and abilities, leading to better decision making and a greater understanding of the business. Job rotations also prevent burnout and give people the chance to discover what they enjoy doing, what they're good at, and a chance to continue learning.

Although the predominant form of business organization today is a for-profit, shareholder-owned business, there is value in teaching students that this is not the only effective way people can work together. While some profit-making businesses have high ethical standards, the institutional framework and often cut-throat market pressure invite and encourage all businesses into an exploitative relationship with their employees. For most of the population, it is at work that they interact most closely with people other than family and work has the potential to serve the need for community. When community life weakens, anxiety in a society rises. Greater equality is equated with more cohesive communities and higher levels of trust (Wilkinson and Pickett, *The Inner Level*, 2018) and so a business that is organized around equality, participation, and shared ownership become socially conscious.

The idea of a democratic workplace is not even that radical. It has been tried and tested in various places throughout the world and has been successful. One such example is the Mondragon Corporation in the Basque region of Spain which is considered one of the most successful worker cooperatives to date. This case study is rarely taught in the business school curriculum. Mondragon is not the only such example. Worker's cooperatives are an old and tried corporate structure with the first of such organizations going back to the 19th century.

The socially conscious business school curriculum should consider business models that subvert the private, shareholder-owned company to create democratic workplaces. Today, there are many models that can be encouraged and need to be embedded in the curriculum from democratically managed, employee ownership organizations which are controlled by the workers themselves rather than outside investors; shared ownership organizations where employees own shares in the company which are a shift from business as a property to business as a working community; group-owned social enterprises whose aim is to improve the economic conditions of their community of employees and stakeholders and where leadership is rotated and shared; benevolent ownership small businesses created for the purpose of contributing to a social cause; businesses for social responsibility; B corporations or Benefit corporations which are social enterprises verified by B Lab, a nonprofit organization which incorporates the interests of all stakeholders in to the corporate charter. These models follow a fundamentally different governance philosophy that a traditional shareholder centered corporation and if we were to teach the next generation of business leaders these concepts, then we would be much further ahead in shifting our economy toward a more equitable one.

If one chooses to look beyond the "business as usual paradigm" it becomes clear that the current model of shareholder-owned business management is being tested and rejected everywhere. We hear stories about The Great Resignation where a record number of workers quit their jobs during and post the Coronavirus pandemic. Another phenomenon which is now gaining attention is that of "quiet quitting" in which workers don't resign but do only the minimum to serve the company. Quiet quitting becomes a kind of silent protest against the absence of democracy and the demoralizing conditions of the workplace. The lesson that we must teach our students in response to such social movements is not that it is wrong to protest against the workplace, but that we must examine the practices that lead to the need to do so in the first place. We must empower, enlighten, engage, beyond the common practices that have been offered by the organizational development practitioners which addresses the "lack of engagement" of workers with offerings such as mindfulness classes and motivational speakers. These offerings are not enough when instead we need to be questioning the very fundamentals of the workplace itself. This, to me, is what a business school should be teaching its students who – as a reminder – are the future leaders of the country.

The third assumption that is implicit and embedded within the business school curriculum is the belief that competition and free markets will solve our health, environmental, emotional, and social problems.

The free market and its inherent emphasis on competition has long been lauded as the key to organizing our economy. Free-market ideology claims that to help society, we must help ourselves. Since 1776 when Adam Smith (2009) suggested in *The Wealth of Nations* that if we all act selfishly the invisible hand will make everyone better off, became an inherent belief. So here we have an ideology that promotes selfishness in the name of group benefit. However, this way of thinking is a deception, which causes grave damage to social cohesion. Yet free-market thinking has beaten out many other ideologies.

In the alternative economics online magazine *Evonomics*, political economist Blair Fix (2021) writes: "Free-market ideology, I propose, is a *double lie*." First, it's a lie in the sense that its central claim is false. Acting selfishly does not maximize group well-being. Modern evolutionary theory makes this clear. Second, and more subtly, free-market thinking is a lie in the sense that it does not lead to greater freedom and autonomy. Quite the opposite. The evidence suggests that free-market thinking actually leads to greater obedience and subordination. The spread of free-market thinking goes hand in hand with the growth of *hierarchy*. The business school curriculum is not designed to question the basic tenets of free-market ideology and competition as a good.

During my teaching career, I taught both undergraduates and master's degree students. Often when I'm in a class of undergraduate business students, I find that many of them play sports and have been competing at sports since childhood. The students have been encouraged by parents, coaches, teachers, and all other adults in their lives to be competitive, to stand out from the crowd, to always strive to do better. These are not necessarily negative messages, but what is forgotten is that all team sports are essentially a cooperation rather than a competition. I ask the students to tell me what they are seeing when they watch a soccer match, or football game, or basketball tournament. Inevitably they see competition rather than cooperation. But that's what they've been taught to see. There is no team in any sport that would succeed if it did not first learn to cooperate. I suggest that they should watch for cooperation and play for cooperation rather than competition.

American author and human behaviorist, Alfie Kohn makes the case against competition even more forcefully. He says the research helps to explain the destructive effect of win/lose arrangements. When children compete, they are less able to take the perspective of others — that is, to see the world from someone else's point of view. One study demonstrated conclusively that competitive children were less empathetic than others; another study showed that competitive children were less generous. Cooperation, on the other hand, is marvelously successful at helping children to communicate effectively, to trust in others, and to accept those who are different from themselves. Competition interferes with these goals and often results in outright antisocial behavior. The choice is ours: "we can blame the individual children who cheat, turn violent, or withdraw, or we can face the fact that competition itself is responsible for such ugliness." (Alfie Kohn). Competition and free markets need to be questioned and examined in every business school curriculum.

Reflections

As I was building the curriculum and teaching these courses at the College, I had to deal too with my own doubts about the ideas I was presenting. It occurred to me that perhaps it is not fair to ask students who have chosen business as a field of study, to confront the dysfunctionality of the very system they have come to study. I got past that vague discomfort when I discovered over-and-over how much each student is suffering under the system that they can't name. In my graduate level classes, I taught mid-career students who are working in industries such as collections agencies, banking, insurance, healthcare. Once we got to a level of trust and intimacy in the class so many of them shared how much their jobs feel like an assault on their souls. One student shared how much he hated his job and getting up on Monday morning was torture to him. His peers and colleagues all told him to "suck it up; that's life" but the thought of having to live that way for the next 40 years until retirement filled him with despair. In a Business Ethics class where the students were expecting to learn case studies on how to behave ethically in specific situations in the workplace, I instead suggested that it's the entire system that is unethical. The values of the current economic system and our own individual values are so often at odds that they cannot be reconciled.

When I teach my business school classes, I feel a great deal of compassion for the young people coming up in the world. In my opinion, we should not be in despair over the thought of adulthood, nor should we be condemned to a life in which the pursuit of endless growth causes us to ignore our own inner values, one in which the tyranny of the workplace dooms us to a life of quiet despair, and the endless competition makes people ashamed when they lose. Social critic Noam Chomsky writes:

> ... This is an extremely atomized society. People are alone... The very explicit goal of the business world is to create a social order ... in which you're watching ads and going to purchase commodities. There are tremendous efforts made ... to try to induce this kind of consciousness ...
>
> *(Chatting with Chomsky)*

Our souls long for connection and to express our creativity and yet our society teaches us merely how to become consumers. The program I developed at the College taught students to see the problem but – in effect – didn't teach solutions. And that left me with a great deal of discomfort, which is one of the reasons I eventually started the Ecological Leadership Program at Lake Erie Institute.

Personal Outcomes and Recommendations

The Socially Conscious MBA program itself only remained in existence for three years. Although it was popular with students, it ultimately conflicted with the vision of the University. Even though the program that I offered was in line with the university's social-justice mission, it ended up exposing the pretense embedded within the system and the internal conflict between the University's espoused faith-based mission and its enacted rigid structure.

I also discovered that the social justice orientation of the college was not shared by many of the faculty and administrators. When I tried to introduce these questions and ideas, I met with resistance both from my faculty members and from the university administration. I was labeled too subversive; I did not fit in with the university culture. I don't even think it was completely conscious on their part, nor do I think it was a personal charge against me. I believe that the university as a system is not yet open to and certainly the business school is not yet able to contain, accept, hold space for such ideas.

I believe the institutions themselves need to evolve to a place where they are willing to embrace such ideas. For a program such as this to succeed it would need buy-in from many layers of university leadership. I believe it could possibly succeed only if the President of the College were on board to shape it, shift it, and promote it. I do believe that academic institutions are evolving, changing, and shifting and that these ideas will eventually find a home in academia as pressure points both from students and society as well as likeminded professors are pushed, and the world continues to undergo the massive changes we are currently experiencing.

It has been seven years since this experience, and I've personally grown and evolved past my original ideas of a socially conscious program and now feel that I didn't go far enough in my thinking. Subsequently, I created an Ecological Leadership program that pushes the envelope even farther. The Ecological Leadership program which is offered by a nonprofit called Lake Erie Institute rather than through an academic institution was different from the socially conscious MBA program. Freed from the constraints of the university and free to question the assumptions that I mention above plus a list of others, I was able to create a full program devoted to a new set of principles.

At the heart of the Ecological Leadership program is the emergent idea that leadership is about cocreating a new story for the world. We are living in a period of radical transformation in human and Earth history. The old myths and stories that sustained us in earlier periods are no longer serving us during this time of transformation. We need to find new ways of being and new leadership to forge the path forward. Leadership is about sensing and stepping forward into the future; Ecological Leadership thus means embracing the idea that we are all emerging into a sustainable future within an enhanced awareness of the environment.

Informed by the scholarship of ecological thinkers Joanna Macy, ecologist Thomas Berry, cultural critic Charles Eisenstein, leadership scholars Otto Scharmer, and Joseph Jaworski, systems-thinker Peter Senge, transformative education scholars Riane Eisler, Vandana Shiva, VF Cordova, and many others, this program incorporates leadership with a distinct acknowledgment of the environmental, social, and cultural changes taking place on our planet at this point in time. It questions existing notions of identity and encourages us to focus on **social justice, the value of life**, and a sense of the **sacred**. I was able to add courses such as ecological economics, which emphasizes degrowth; eco-psychology which says that our physical, psychological, and spiritual well-being is dependent and interdependent on the health of the Earth itself, and eco-entrepreneurship which is any enterprise that places the health of the planet as central to its core mission. The program is designed to prepare participants to become entrepreneurs and social entrepreneurs, managers of and for the future, keepers of community, stewards of the planet, and guardians of future generations.

Thomas Berry sees our moment in history as both a "terminal state" and a "moment of grace." "In moments of grace we take danger and turn it into opportunity. In moments of grace, we take decadence and turn it into creativity." Berry maintains that to survive our moment, we must be prepared to take a journey in to a new creative "story." He suggests that our present cultural story, exemplified in the technical-industrial values of western Eurocentric culture, is dysfunctional in its larger social dimensions even though we continue to firmly believe in it and act according to its guidance. According to Berry, we are in pressing need of a "… reassessment of our present situation, especially concerning those basic values that give life some satisfactory meaning." (O'Sullivan).

If we are to have a shot at leaving a better world for our children, indeed, if we are to maintain the possibility of an inhabitable planet, we need to make drastic changes and business schools are one of the leverage points for doing so. As I mentioned, business schools are ground zero for forming future leaders of society and it is sobering to think about the influence that management education has in the world and the potential for doing good. We as educators must continue pushing that envelope until it tears completely and the message, we deliver is one of profound structural change toward a vision of regenerative life on the planet.

References

Alfie Kohn. (2014, November 11). *The case against competition*. Alfie Kohn. Retrieved January 31, 2023, from https://www.alfiekohn.org/article/case-competition

Chatting with Chomsky. (n.d.). In These Times. Retrieved January 31, 2023, from https://inthesetimes.com/article/chatting-with-chomsky

Daly, H. E. (1973). *Towards a steady-state economy*. W.H. Freeman.

Daly, H. E. (1996). *Beyond growth: The economics of sustainable environment*. Beacon Press.

Eisenstein, C. (2021). *Sacred economics money, gift, and society in the age of transition*. North Atlantic Books.

Fix, B. (2021, February 3). *Why free market ideology is a double lie*. Evonomics. Retrieved January 31, 2023, from https://evonomics.com/why-free-market-ideology-is-a-double-lie/

Hickel, J. (2022). *Less is more: How degrowth will save the world*. Penguin Random House Ireland.

Marchese, D. (2022, July 18). *This pioneering economist says our obsession with growth must end*. The New York Times. Retrieved January 31, 2023, from https://www.nytimes.com/interactive/2022/07/18/magazine/herman-daly-interview.html

Martinez, R. (2017). *Creating freedom*. Canongate Books Ltd.

O'Sullivan, E., Morrell, A., & O'Connor, M. A. (2002). *Expanding the boundaries of transformative learning: Essays on theory and praxis*. Palgrave.

Raworth, K. (2018). *Doughnut economics*. Random House UK.

Resilience. (2021, April 28). *David Haenke on 'Bioregionalism & Ecological Economics'*. Resilience. Retrieved January 31, 2023, from https://www.resilience.org/stories/2021-04-28/david-haenke-on-bioregionalism-ecological-economics/

Smith, A. (2009). *Wealth of nations*. Classic House Books.

Smith, P. B., & Max-Neef, M. (2012). *Economics unmasked: From power and greed to compassion and the common good*. Green Books.

Wilkinson, R. G., & Pickett, K. (2018). *The inner level: How more equal societies reduce stress, restore sanity and improve everybody's wellbeing*. Allen Lane.

Wolff, R. D. (2012). *Democracy at work: A cure for capitalism*. Haymarket Books.

2

A TRANSFORMATIONAL ATTEMPT TO EMBED PRME COLLEGE-WIDE

Orla Kelleher

Abstract

This case study explores the journey of embedding Principles for Responsible Management Education (PRME) across a College, with a view to create a transformational shift across the full College provision. It highlights the importance of integrating PRME within College strategy and building relationships with a coalition of the willing. It also highlights different elements that can help to build an authentic new learning ecosystem within the College, such as cross-college collaborations, staff development, and innovative programme design. This case study example is offered for other institutions or PRME leads who wish to pioneer the integration of PRME within their business school or University, or to those who wish to create transformational change within their teaching area.

The Journey Begins

I came into Higher Education after spending over a decade working in marine science research, innovation, and strategy, and running my own learning and development training company. As a marine biologist, I was concerned about how we take care of this sacred, living planet for the long term. I came to a simple realisation at that time that we would need to transform the values we hold as a society if we are to sufficiently influence long-term policy and transforming values would

DOI: 10.4324/9781003457763-2

require a profound shift in mindset and long-view vision. When I finally took up a new senior lecturer role within the College of Business, Law, and Social Sciences (SBLSS), I saw the opportunity to develop a new Master's programme aimed at helping businesses embed environmental sustainability and social values as the new norm.

Like many others, I was the only person advocating for change. Seven years ago, there was a prevailing lack of understanding of the need for change, and the immediate response to this proposal was negative. However, I was very fortunate to have a highly supportive line manager who supported the idea until we achieved approval for validation of a MSc Sustainable & Ethical Business Management a few years later. It was this background work, along with a ground swell of initiatives from other like-minded staff and increasing external demand, that led to the formation of a 'Sustainability Champion' role for the College. At the request of my line manager, I took up this role and discovered that my first task was to prepare the College's second Principles for Responsible Management Education (PRME) Sharing on Progress (SIP) report! Once I understood the overarching scope of the PRME principles, I realised that this framework could be a key enabler in supporting a college-wide transformation.

Embedding PRME within College Strategy

Preparing my first PRME SIP report provided the first overview of all the relevant teaching and research projects happening across the College and offered college executives tangible evidence of progress. Since the report was due within the first three months of my new role, I gathered most of the input with the support from divisional heads and key staff and collating relevant marketing events and inhouse documents. I also carried out our first audit of the Business School curriculum (using an ERS keyword search) that established our first curriculum baseline. All of which helped to inform the next set of PRME reporting objectives for 2020–2021.

I realised for the next PRME SIP report, to prevent PRME simply becoming a reporting process, a more extensive stakeholder consultation and conversations would help build engagement with this agenda. Given my prior background in organisational change, I knew that if we could get PRME into our College strategy, it would ultimately provide a strong platform for college-wide transformation. A trans-disciplinary approach is fundamental to creating a responsible business landscape (Laasch et al., 2020), so I began to initiate dialogue with colleagues in Environmental Sciences about PRME, even though they were in a different College and unfamiliar with PRME. However, I had previously engaged with them in the trans-disciplinary design of the new Master's programme (MSc Sustainable & Ethical Business Management) so discussions around PRME seemed a natural progression. Once again, I was fortunate to meet a few key people, including the then Head of Environmental Sciences, who supported this aspiration.

Cross-College PRME Steering Group

After considerable discussions between both Colleges and the University Pedagogic Practice team, I was finally able to set up a cross-college PRME steering group between the College of Business, Law, and Social Sciences (CBLSS) and College of Science & Engineering (CoSE) in September 2021. Its aim is to provide an overall leadership body to direct, oversee, and track PRME implementation in alignment with university strategic priorities. It includes over 20 people from both colleges including Heads of Schools, professors, associate professors, course Directors, programme and module leaders, representatives from the University's Pedagogic Practice Team, Commercial, Research and Innovation team, Estates Management, and Union of Students.

This Steering Group prepared the PRME 2020–2021 SIP report submitted by the end of January 2023. Over a four-month period, four sub-groups worked on different aspects of the report, and I facilitated sessions and wrote the final report. The benefit of Steering Group cross-representation became clear when we finally pulled the report together. By incorporating examples from two Colleges, we demonstrated an abundance of vibrant, substantive, case studies evidencing emerging work across the University. More hands-on-deck meant we were now able to re-audit the Business School not only from an ethics, responsibility, and environmental sustainability (ERS) perspective, but now also from the 17 UN SDGs' perspective. In addition, the Built Environment from College of Science & Engineering carried out their first SDG audit of their curriculum. Working together, we carried out a joint SDG audit of research publications over 2020–2021 from both CBLSS's perspective as well as the Environmental Sustainability Research Centre (ESRC), College of Science & Engineering. These audits led to useful discussions highlighting the natural synergies between existing curriculum and research and the UN SDGs which was not previously clear in the programme and module documentation. Compared to my first experience of compiling the PRME SIP report, this cross-college PRME Steering Group offered a much better representational structure for agreeing the 2022–2023 PRME objectives in line with College and University strategic priorities.

Linking with University Strategy

The University Pedagogic Practice team successfully made the case for including Education for Sustainable Development (ESD) goals in the new University-wide learning, teaching, and assessment framework (LTAF) in line with Advance HE/QAA (2021) UK guidance. The Steering Group acted as a grassroots driving force complementing the case for ESD. While this happened more or less organically, this combination of bottom up and top-down approach is one of four recommended key enablers identified in the PRME Blueprint for SDG Integration.

The University established five strategic themes that required partnering across colleges. One strategic goal was Zero Carbon. In our college (CBLSS), a group of people including myself, were nominated to form a leadership group around this goal. Early group discussions led to creating a college theme under the broader definition of 'Sustainable Futures'. We believed this would offer a more holistic view of our objective. From my perspective, this theme enabled embedding of PRME & UN SDGs directly within college strategy.

Upon the Dean's approval of our re-definition of scope, we began the task of developing a 'Sustainable Futures' strategy for the College and consolidated our activities relating to Net Zero, ESD, PRME, accreditations such as EFMD, AACSB, Small Business Charter, and so on. In this context, we are currently discussing mainstreaming approaches, starting with defining SDG priorities and setting objectives in line with the PRME SDG compass. The intention is that we will bring the College through a consultation process to ensure engagement and feedback on this emergent strategy. From this consultation process, we will identify a clear implementation plan, leadership and governance structure, and communications plan.

Accreditations

In the capacity of PRME lead, I had responsibility to oversee embedding of ERS as a transversal standard for our application to EFMD. While I felt we were making some good progress in terms of PRME, I wanted to better understand EFMD priorities. Serendipity came into play when I saw an invitation for SDG integration training in the EFMD newsletter and I attended training in November–December 2022. The training was invaluable for several reasons. Over 20 Universities participated so there was significant peer learning. EFMD facilitators demonstrated a specific process for embedding SDGs that can be applied from organisational level right down to programme/module level. I found that particularly useful as I was able to feed that process into the development of the Sustainable Futures strategy.

One significant observation was the different priorities that a University/Business School in Africa might have from an UK institute. That led me to focus on what five SDGs would best represent the impact we as a UK College would wish to make? The training reinforced using PRME as the driving power for change because I was able to draw on the PRME SDG audits to help answer some of the questions raised. It was also clear that those Universities who had adopted PRME seemed further ahead in transformation and SDG integration.

Where Are We Now? Starting with Deeper Questions

When making the case for the new Master's programme, I reviewed literature around the new pedagogic approaches in support of ESD and integration of UN Sustainable Development Goals (SDGs). What stood out for me was David Orr's quote that the crises we face '*cannot be solved by the same kind of education that helped create the problems*' (Orr, 1992, p. 83), and that '*sustainability learning requires an appreciation of the behavioural/transformative power of a learning intervention, such as the "head, hands and heart" taxonomy of sustainability learning*' (Sipos et al., 2008). In other words, we cannot solve the problems we face from the level where these problems were created. I take that to mean that unless we can access a greater consciousness, true purposes for living, and deeper human values, we may end up with alteration of practice, but with no real human transformation.

While the SDGs represent a significant step forward in addressing essential environmental, social, and economic global goals, I feel it is important that we do not forget to question why we are facing these convergent crises in the first place. For example, why have we lost our connection and value for this extraordinary planet that gives us life? Why do we view the planet from primarily an anthropocentric as opposed to eco-centric lens? Why do we use natural resources as if there is no tomorrow? Why are we consumed with material wealth instead of human qualities, such as peace, care, compassion, reverence for life? Why are most of the ecologies we create as human beings, whether they be industrial, economical, societal even educational, unnatural in design? Why does it seem we have lost connection with deeper human universal values and higher human purpose? No matter which lens you use, it makes no sense to destroy the planet that hosts you or risk the survival of future generations. When I reflect on where we are today, it seems to point to a major disconnect in the human story, particularly in terms of its natural alignment and progression.

Despite these profoundly challenging questions, my intuition and personal stance is that this is a pivotal point in our evolution as a species. Having worked for a short time as a geologist, I see the future through the perspective of geological time which shows humans appear on this planet in relative recent times. If you then imagine travelling into the future, there is hope in the long view. We can no longer plead ignorance to what humans have created but we can reach for the humility and grace to re-evaluate, take responsibility, and course correct. Holding the long view helps me to hold the hope of a better, more humane future, and when I get discouraged, I come back to this view to renew my own motivation and resolve.

A Practical Place to Start

While ongoing philosophical questions remain, I began to consider a good practical starting point for both staff and students in terms of implementing PRME. Given ESD addresses climate change and ecological crises (IPCC, 2021), and PRME's vision is to nurture responsible leaders of the future, I began to see educating staff and students on climate change and climate emergencies as a fundamental place to start. After attending the UN PRME Carbon Literacy training led by Nottingham Trent University, I was inspired my Group project would develop a Carbon Literacy programme for our own University.

Our college Dean supported the initiative because it aligned with the college strategic focus on Net Zero. He set a college target to ensure all academic staff become Carbon Literate (CL) certified and to achieve the highest level of Carbon Literate Organisation (CLO) accreditation (Platinum status) by September 2024. This will prepare staff for moving into a new Net Zero Business School by the end of 2024. Currently, by drawing on the UN PRME Carbon Literacy training series and the Carbon Literacy programme I developed in Summer 2022, we have currently trained over 50 staff members. We started with five members of the Senior Leadership Team, including the Dean of the college as well as the University Pedagogic lead for ESD. I am delighted to say that in January of this year, they all received their Carbon Literacy certification!

By the end of 2023, we intend to have trained over 80% of all academic staff. This means we can apply for CLO status in association with the Carbon Literacy Project. Achieving CLO status requires the embedding of Carbon Literacy within the organisation's performance systems and College leadership is encouraging all staff to complete the training and support what we call a 'Sustainable Futures staff academy'. The purpose of the staff academy is to help staff to integrate carbon literacy in their curriculum and research. For now, the staff academy is resourced by me, and another equally committed associate professor in sustainable business and clean growth. But our hope is that Sustainable Futures staff academy will expand in the future. For now, we can clearly demonstrate a definitive response to one of the greatest crises of our time, climate change (SDG 13). While the immediate focus is College-wide, there are now also requests for the training coming from other parts of the University and discussions about students receiving Carbon Literacy training.

Curriculum Requires New Pedagogic Design

In preparing our recent PRME report, we conducted an SDG curriculum audit in both the Business School (CBLSS) as well as the Built Environment (CoSE). What became apparent is while there was clear activity happening in the SDG topic areas, it was not clearly represented in modules or programme documentation. The same was true for the SDG research audit. But now recently validated programmes are being designed with clear reference to the SDGs and ESD principles. The Sustainable Tourism and Hospitality discipline pioneered commitment by ensuring that all their documentation was revalidated to align to Sustainable Development and the UN SDGs.

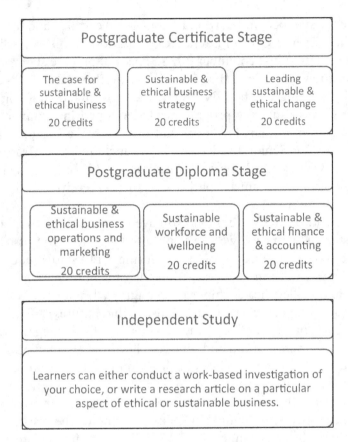

FIGURE 2.1   MSc Sustainable & Ethical Business Management programme structure.

Another example is our new *MSc Sustainable & Ethical Business Management*, where I am both programme and module leader. We designed the programme to align to ESD pedagogical approaches with programme learning outcomes based on the eight sustainability competencies identified by UNESCO Education for Sustainable Development Goals (2017). While you might typically be familiar with competencies such as critical thinking, strategic competency, and self-awareness, our new programme also includes competences such as systems thinking, anticipatory, normative, and collaborative competencies and integrated problem-solving. Each module identifies relevant SDGs in terms of both module description, learning outcomes, and assessment. In addition, the curriculum, assessment, and marking approaches allow for deeper dimensions of sustainability learning (e.g., Knowledge (Thinking),

Values and Attitudes (Being), Competency (Doing)) (Hermes & Rimanoczy, 2018).

The programme (Figure 2.1) diverges significantly from a traditional Business Master's programme given its trans-disciplinary, work-based learning, and whole person-learning approach (Jarvis & Watts, 2011). The programme enables business leaders to apply the learning directly into their own organisations through its work-based approach, and has a strong focus on experiential, problem-orientated, and transformative learning. We are embedding carbon literacy so the learners can have the option of becoming CL certified as part of the programme.

There is also a strong focus on personal growth with the PRME Sustainability Mindset model (Rimanoczy, 2020) embedded across the programme, a reflexive focus on values and purpose exploration and the aforementioned sustainability competencies as learning outcomes. We are also planning to use the Sustainability Mindset Indicator as a before, during, and after diagnostic in support of learner development. We hope that this balance of inner and outer learning supports not only the practical challenges of responsible business practice but also supports the personal transformation needed to become responsible leaders.

Where to Next? What's Working?

The wider involvement of other colleagues, particularly the cross-college PRME Steering Group and the consultation around the PRME SIP report, led to a much more meaningful process in our transformation. In terms of PRME 2022–2023 objectives, we committed to some major milestones such as relaunching the Business School curriculum as a 'Responsible Business' portfolio in tandem with moving to a Net Zero Business School. We now have a clear (measured) baseline to move forward in embedding the UN SDGs and Carbon Literacy across the Colleges portfolio, to help guide next steps in integrating the SDGs.

Collaboration with the University Pedagogic lead for ESD has been very helpful, as ESD is now a learning, teaching, and assessment theme and validates PRME. Other University activities include the successful NUS Responsible Futures accreditation and a University-wide ESD staff network, led by the University pedagogic practice team. The University strategic goal of Net Zero provided further rationale to embed Carbon Literacy and triggered a deeper discussion within our college. As a result, we are now working on consolidating all relevant PRME activities into a coherent 'Sustainable Futures' strategy that includes defining what we mean by 'Sustainable Futures' in the context of purpose, vision, and approach. Overall, these combined initiatives begin to provide evidence of a 'critical mass' moving in the right direction. This very positive status is a testament to the power of the committed individuals acting with passion and determination combined with senior leadership support.

The inclusion of ESD in the learning, teaching, and assessment strategy is providing opportunity to dialogue and share the knowledge, experience, and progress from our PRME journey. In a recent staff 'learning lunch' where I shared practical ideas and examples of how to embed the SDGs, I was heartened see the appetite and openness for this learning and it reinforced the power of the top down (ESD) and bottom up (PRME) approach.

It is exciting to see integration of PRME objectives in the emerging 'Sustainable Futures' college strategy. I believe setting and achieving these objectives will mean that PRME is more effectively integrated across the College as part of its overall strategic direction. We are planning conversations around this strategy, so staff (and hopefully students) can be involved in the co-creation of an inspiring purpose and future vision. Ideally, this strategy will then become a live brief that adapts as we navigate our way forward. Wider engagement and consultation are essential to avoid a tick-box approach to SDG integration. We continue to ask, '*What can we do to ensure this is not a tick-box exercise?*' and '*what more do we need to learn?*' so that we can begin to walk the talk ourselves, before we begin to teach students.

What's Not Working?

The emerging field of responsible management learning is '*characterised by an urgent need for transdisciplinary practices*' (Laasch et al., 2020, p. 735). While the PRME partnership between our college (CBLSS) and CoSE is truly inter-disciplinary, there are significant barriers to achieving the kind of trans-disciplinary approach needed across the entire university to ensure '*sustainability practices grounded in both corporate sustainability management and environmental management*' (Schaltegger et al., 2003 cited in Laasch, 2021).

When the Carbon Literacy training was rolled out, college staff were essentially 'told' to complete the training. Once something is mandatory, it can tend to cause a compliant, reactive, or resentful response. Through feedback, we learned the importance of ensuring there is clear justification to ask staff to do more, particularly given their already pressured workloads. I tried to explain reasons for the initiative at a college away-day and by producing a supporting brochure. Overall, I appreciate the importance of 'choice' as the better approach.

In a session on Carbon Literacy for level 5 (year 2) students, I asked the group of roughly 50 students whether they believed we could reach safe carbon limits, assuming we had resources to do so. Only four or five students agreed we could. When teaching climate science, you see all kinds of reactions: overwhelm, anxiety, optimism, rejection, determination, etc. It's an emotive subject that I try to land in a positive way. However, there is much work to do to support students (and us) in approaching the future with hope, inspiration, and confidence. I believe we need to begin to tell ourselves and our students a new story, one that offers an attractive and compelling vision of a better future.

Conclusion – Personal Reflections

It is encouraging to see the progress in our organisation compared to four years ago. There are still many challenges to address. However, it feels we now have our feet on the path, and we have started moving forward. As with all change, you need multiple levers to bring about transformation and these have started to appear, from shifts in University and College strategy to like-minded individuals coming together to collaborate and work collectively. The question I have is can we together and globally reach a new elevation in educational purpose, values, and vision for the future?

While educators have long been questioning the purpose of higher learning (Dewey, 1938) my own personal view is we need an urgent review of the purpose of higher education. What are we educating people for if it is not to ultimately serve our evolution and humanity as a species? What is it that we would want future generations to look back on and see? Would we not want them to say: '*What an extraordinary transformation they went through to ensure we survived, and that the planet thrived. What a turning point for maturing into the greater humanity we know today?*' Well, here's hoping!

Recommendations

Here's a few thoughts for any PRME pioneers!

- Take the time to work out your own position, values, and motivations in relation to leading with PRME. You will find knowing your own deeper, more authentic positions will matter for self-leadership and conversations with others.

- Also consider your unique strengths, how can you best bring them to play?
- If you are new to PRME, focus on building a strong relationship with your line manager/senior leadership, as their support is essential for this journey. The support of my line manager was invaluable in sharing the value of this work and for bridging PRME into senior leadership discussions.
- Engage and build relationships with people across the organisation and treat every meeting as an opportunity to educate, engage, and influence.
- Consider the different needs or desires of senior leadership, the organisation, and academic staff to see how PRME is of genuine value to their learners.
- Draw on examples from the PRME network to highlight leading practices to bring the message home.
- If you are further along in your PRME journey, consider how to mainstream this work so that it becomes a vehicle for genuine transformation. Stay alert for opportunities to influence College or University strategy or align with relevant accreditations.
- Make the case for wider strategic consultation and discussions with staff and students. This kind of consultation takes time and requires engagement and commitment from leadership and staff, but wider engagement is essential if we are to move beyond a tick-box mindset and build the ecology for transformation.
- It will still be an ongoing challenge to achieve authentic cultural shift in mindset, purpose, values, and practice. Consider staff development needs supported by feasible milestones for curriculum transformation, with timescales ideally negotiated by the schools and programme leads themselves.
- Make use of the supporting guidance from PRME such as the Blueprint for SDG Integration which provides a step-by-step process for mainstreaming the SDGs.
- Lastly, we need to move hearts and minds if we are to transform business education as an enabler for a truly sustainable and just future. Starting with ourselves first. Wishing you every success on your PRME journey!

References

Advance HE/QAA. (2021). *Education for sustainable development guidance.* Available at: https://www.advance-he.ac.uk/knowledge-hub/education-sustainable-development-guidance

Dewey, J. (1938). *Experience and education.* Collier Books.

Hermes, J., & Rimanoczy, I. (2018). Deep learning for a sustainability mindset. *The International Journal of Management Education, 16,* 460–467.

Jarvis, P. and Watts, M.H. (2011) *The Routledge international handbook of learning.* London: Routledge.

Laasch, O. (2021). *Principles of management: Practicing ethics, responsibility, sustainability* (2nd ed.). SAGE.

Laasch, O., Moosmayer, D., Antonacopoulou, E., & Schaltegger, S. (2020). Constellations of transdisciplinary practices: A map and research agenda for the responsible management learning field. *Journal of Business Ethics, 162,* 735–757.

Orr, D. (1992). *Ecological literary: Education and the transition to a postmodern World.* University of New York Press.

PRME: *Blueprint for SDG integration into curriculum, research and partnerships.* Available at: Blueprint for SDG Integration | uk-prme (unprme.org.uk). Accessed on Jan 31 2023.

Rimanoczy, I. (2020). *The sustainability mindset principles: A guide to develop a mindset for a better world.* Routledge.

Ivanova, E., & Rimanoczy, I. (Eds.). (2021). *Revolutionizing sustainability education: Stories and tools of mindset transformation* (1st ed.). Routledge. https://doi.org/10.4324/9781003229735

Sipos, Y., Battisti, B., & Grimm, K. (2008). Achieving transformative sustainability learning: Engaging head, hands and heart. *International Journal of Sustainability in Higher Education,* 9(1), 68–86.

UNESCO (2017). Education for sustainable development goals: Learning objectives. Available at: Education for Sustainable Development Goals: learning objectives - UNESCO Digital Library. Accessed 31 Jan 2022.

3

PLURALISM AND *"CONSCIENTIZAÇÃO"* IN THE BUSINESS CLASSROOM AND BEYOND[1]

Lovasoa Ramboarisata (she/her) Celine Berrier-Lucas (she/her), and Dimbi Ramonjy (he/him)

Abstract

We believe it is now time to decolonize the business curricula following earlier calls by critical management scholars, emancipatory pedagogues, and decolonial theorists. Decolonizing the business curricula means raising students' awareness about the reproduction of colonialism (paternalism, grabbing, exploitation, hierarchization of people, territories, and knowledges) in business models and practices and the different injustices (racial, gender, environmental, territorial, epistemic) which spurs from that. Moreover, it aims at training students to imagine alternative (non-oppressive, non-exploitative, emancipatory, inclusive) ways of organizing and interacting with humans and non-humans. In this chapter, we present our personal journeys to transform our management and CSR (corporate social responsibility) teaching and to contribute to the decolonization of our curricula. Our approach is founded on a non-dichotomous (theory/practice) ontology, pluralism, and *conscientização*, or critical consciousness developed by the Brazilian philosopher of education Paulo Freire.

The post-COVID-19 context presents an ideal opportunity for radical change, and the momentum for an overhaul of our teaching practice, as well as the disruption of the outmoded, neoliberal narrative. Today's context of sanitary and economic uncertainty, climate crisis, geopolitical conflict, and social unrest in many regions warrant the transformation of business education – helping to create a sustainable world and to heal our society.

DOI: 10.4324/9781003457763-3

Introduction

The opportunity to share our journeys to transform business pedagogy using decolonial perspectives is both rewarding and exhilarating. Within the business school community, being critical of the neoliberal narrative and displaying an acquaintance with different ontologies – such as Feminist, Decolonial, Indigenous, and Marxist perspectives – are at best not considered as a serious scientific and pedagogical endeavor, and may even be risky for one's career (Nkomo, 2021). As Clegg et al. (2011) have noted, scholars adopting a critical view of business schools are often challenged or belittled and teaching critical courses seldom translate into positive recognition (Liu, 2022; Ramboarisata, 2022).

In the right environment, however critical approaches to business education can thrive, especially where academics find themselves in a caring and intellectually stimulating community that supports their academic freedom. Those choosing this path often take comfort in collective projects such as book projects, special issues, and workshops. The opportunity to share our teaching approaches – addressing socioenvironmental justice, racism, and gender bias – gives us optimism for the future of business education's decolonization and assures us that our stories are worthy of being told.

The changes we brought to our pedagogies and courses' content were inspired by the works of French and Grey (1996), Currie and Knights (2003), Clegg et al. (2012), Perriton and Reynolds (2018) in CME (Critical Management Education); Fournier and Grey (2000), Alvesson et al. (2009), Fotaki and Prasad (2015), Contu (2020) in CMS (Critical Management Studies); and Ahmed et al. (2019), Dar et al. (2021), Banerjee and Berrier-Lucas (2022), Sauerbronn et al. (2022) in decolonial and anti-racist management education. Proposals from these authors have served as building blocks for the courses we developed in both undergraduate and graduate levels. In line with their perspectives, we hope our courses have contributed to the deconstruction of taken-for-granted yet obsolete ideas about the purpose of businesses and to the construction of a new narrative more attuned to the agenda of socio-ecological transition and justice.

The tenants of critical and decolonial perspectives raise awareness about the limitations, the biases, and the obsolescence of mainstream theories. They highlight the social and ecological hazards these theories generate once performed in actual business decision-making, especially in a globalized economy. They also call out for an additional step: the building of alternatives. This requires a discussion of "taboo" issues such as poverty, race, gender, class, colonization, structural inequalities, and ecocide; a plurality of organizing modes – social enterprises, the commons, Indigenous organizations, cooperatives, social economy, solidarity economy and the like; and diversified sources of inspiration, from other disciplines, from social and political movements, and from often sidelined philosophies such as Ubuntu and Buen vivir.[2] Using these concepts while designing and teaching our courses has reinforced our belief that the transformation of business education can be a vehicle for creating a sustainable world, and a powerful force for societal renovation (Banerjee & Berrier-Lucas, 2022; Dar et al., 2021).

We are three privileged, mid-career, French-speaking, CSR, and management academics who share a belief that decolonizing business education matters. We first crossed paths 12 years ago at a RIODD (Réseau international de recherche sur les organisations et le développement durable)[3] scientific conference. We collaborated on multiple projects with the latest being a special issue "Decolonizing CSR" in the Review of Responsible Organization, published in Spring 2022.

Let us first explain why we believe decolonizing teaching practices is imperative to achieve sustainability. Following the path laid out for us by critical researchers (Gilmore et al., 2019), we present our personal journeys to enact change in management and CSR curricula. Finally, drawing on our combined journeys, we lay out recommendations that we hope will inspire others.

A sustainable world for us is one that works for everyone with no one left out. Those left out – humans and non-humans – are at the heart of decolonial perspectives. We use decolonial perspectives as an analytical category encompassing diverse approaches such as postcolonial theory, subaltern studies, Indigenous studies, Latin-American decolonial theory, feminism in the third world, Chicana feminism, Caribbean decolonial approaches, epistemologies of the South, and environmental humanities. Each contest the universalization of Eurocentric worldviews, demonstrate the continuation of colonialism in today's social lives, (re)claim the dignity of victims of colonial violence and exclusions, and share experiences of resistance and emancipation (Mignolo, 2011; Yousfi, 2021). Originating in the Humanities and Social Sciences, they have been used in Organization and Management Theory (OMT) for the last 30 years.

Teaching from a Decolonial Standpoint

Women of the Global South, Indigenous people, the oppressed – they are the subalterns (Spivak, 1988) – the ones whose voices and systems of knowledge have been excluded or belittled. In an empirical study we conducted a few years ago (Ramboarisata, 2016; Ramboarisata & Gendron, 2019), we noticed that in CSR, the subalterns are generally caricatured as stakeholders and/or as beneficiaries of shared value. Such an assumption reinforces an essentialist narrative, legitimizing the purported civilizing effect of Western business and fails to address myriad barriers: the structural inequalities, racial and gender division of labor, and power asymmetry preventing a sustainable world.

Decolonial perspectives also address the domination of humans over nature and non-humans, and the marginalization of Indigenous wisdom. Per critical scholars, corporate environmentalism has dictated the conceptual development, the praxis, and the teaching of sustainability (Banerjee, 2003; Banerjee & Arjaliès, 2021; Banerjee & Berrier-Lucas, 2022; Ergene et al., 2021; Grove, 2010; Liboiron & Lepawsky, 2022). In environmental management courses, for example, pollution and biodiversity loss are usually presented as impacts to be managed. Such an understanding fails to address the economic and political worldviews that accept the natural world as a resource to be exploited.

The romanticized view of the relationships between the corporation and the subalterns, as well as the a-political and a-historical view of the corporate solutions to the ecological crisis are precisely the ones we deconstruct in our courses. In our view, a sustainable future will remain unattainable if solutions are designed around the very system creating such injustices, exploitation, exclusions, violence, and destruction. As we will explain more thoroughly in a subsequent section titled "Our journeys," our pedagogy offers space to learn differently, grounded in peoples' realities, histories, and struggles. With our students we nurture other possibilities, including stories of resistance and alternative building in the sectors of finance, health and social services, and mining.

A Non-Dichotomous (Theory/Practice) Approach

Decolonizing knowledge disrupts a Eurocentric assumption established since Enlightenment: the separation of areas of knowledge. Decolonial perspectives refuse to separate nature from culture and theories from practices. The experiences we will account for in the section "Our journeys" will describe how our students are made aware of the danger of rational methodologies. As we will narrate with more details in that section, our pedagogy in both our undergraduate and graduate courses let students experiment with decolonial praxis – meaning, "[...] the possibility of re-knowing multiple knowledges, thoughts, experiences, existences, cosmovisions, dissidences, and emotions from subjects and populations in positionalities that locate them as subalternized, exploited, oppressed, etc."[4] (Cariño et al. (2013, p. 524). Knowledge about the colonial matrix (Quijano, 2000) – the coloniality of gender, race, class, knowledge, and nature – is explored in our teachings through music, photography, poetry, political discourse from grassroots movement leaders, presentations from Indigenous entrepreneurs, etc. Our combined three journeys will highlight how these are adequate means to decolonize the learning and how the students react to them. We anchor our knowledge in peoples' realities and struggles and not in theories, and favor learning through discomfort by un-censoring wrath, lament, oppression, redemption, and sorority.

Courses Core "Postures"[5]

Two core notions, *conscientização* and pluralism, define our decolonial and non-dichotomous teaching "posture" without interfering with our deconstruction/reconstruction stance. Our syllabi and instructional approach follow the Brazilian theorist Paulo Freire and his philosophy of *conscientização* – developing a critical understanding of reality through action and reflection – along with problematizations and actions against the oppressive elements of reality. In his seminal book *Pedagogy of the Oppressed* (1970), he presents a political and humanistic vision that denounces the "banking" education, a concept where the teacher is the sole bearer of knowledge and "deposits" it into the heads of students. To achieve social justice and liberation from all forms of oppression (Walsh, 2015), and strongly influenced by the work of Frantz Fanon (Dei, 2016; Mignolo & Walsh, 2020; Teasley & Butler, 2020; Walsh, 2015), Freire's pedagogy is a sociopolitical practice grounded in people's realities and struggles.

Our courses also favor a pluralist view by contesting the idea of the "one best way" found in most business curriculum, including in CSR courses. Our teachings expose students to pluralism and eschew a sole framework of neoliberal capitalism and its conceptual apparatus of growth, productivity, individual meritocracy, and deregulation. We

include many varieties of capitalism developed by heterodox economists (e.g., Albert, 1991; Amable, 2003; Boyer, 2002), as well as a
diversity of coordination and governance modes, and a multiplicity of
organizational logics beyond the rent-seeking one. As we will argue in
the next section about our journeys, being taught about the plurality
of organizing modes (e.g., social economy, solidarity economy, Indigenous businesses, etc.) gives our students experience in the richness and
complexity of organizational realities.

Moreover, our physical locations also play a role. We each live and
teach in coordinated economies, France and Québec, Canada and not
in liberal market economies. Finally, following our decolonial stance,
we include often sidelined knowledges and practices from Latin-
American, African, and Aboriginal settings in our teachings.

We are aware of the limitations of the Freirian logic – a pedagogy
that finally remains Western, sexist, and anthropocentric. As bell hooks,
feminist professor and author insists, Freirian praxis and liberation-
based thought remains relevant. In *Teaching to Transgress* (1994), she
highlights the fact that educators and students can resist the "imperial-
ist white supremacist capitalist patriarchy" system of power within the
educational structure through the liberatory pedagogy of love and a
praxis of liberation as a praxis of freedom.

Our Journeys

Before sharing our individual journeys, it seems relevant to share our
own positionalities (Haraway, 1988). Celine Berrier-Lucas is a white
heterosexual mother, professor of CSR at ISG business school in Paris,
France. She also teaches at PSL-Paris-Dauphine University. She is the
coeditor-in-chief of Review of Responsible Organization, a review in the
field of Business & Society which publishes works mostly in French and
following critical perspectives. Lovasoa Ramboarisata is a brown heterosexual mother, originally from Madagascar, a prior French colony,
and is currently a professor of strategy and CSR at a French-speaking
management school situated on the un-ceded land of Tiohtià:ke, also
known as Montreal, Canada. Dimbi Ramonjy is a brown heterosexual
father, originally from Madagascar, a prior French colony, and is currently professor of strategy and CSR at Excelia Business School, in La
Rochelle, France, CSR teaching coordinator, and member of a steering
committee for pedagogical innovation at his school.

Celine's Journey: Mind the Gap between the Train and ...

Five years ago, I was entrusted with the responsibility of a CSR class module, that coordinate six different courses for the Master in Sustainable Development of the Executive program of PSL-Paris-Dauphine University (France) program which was completely overhauled two years ago. The Directors suggested that I create a new syllabus for "CSR, Anthropocene and new business models" which was both inspiring and daunting since I was given carte blanche. In collaboration with my colleagues, we decided on the scientific content together, while I took charge of the theoretical framework – my expertise. As head of the module, I am responsible for evaluations.

Transformation

I begin with a historical tour of the work of Howard Bowen, including his "Social Responsibility of the Businessman." Based on the use of historical archives, this introduction to the subject destabilizes executive professionals. I continue with Bowen's conceptual underpinnings, adding additional material from environmental humanities, texts on environmental, gender and domination issues, as well as films and paintings. After becoming acquainted with these texts, I introduce them to decolonial perspectives through academic texts, press articles, poetry, and grassroots discourse – works from decolonial intellectuals presented in relation to their political and community anchorage.

Once the students begin to grasp these concepts, I revisit the concept of CSR through a decolonial lens. It is striking to see the transformation of our students and the discovery of their critical consciousness or *conscientização*. Revisiting their own careers, many in the leadership of multinational companies, the students begin to question their past decisions, they reconsider the gendered, colonizing, and extractivist way their companies interact with local affiliates in the Global South. They often begin to question the civilizing myth of CSR.

I conclude with a capstone project which may take various forms. Sometimes, I propose a team project, the creation of a musical playlist with descriptive notes where each student must link theoretical elements from the course to an appropriate musical experience. The choice of music by the team is also evaluated. Sometimes I propose the presentation of academic articles to a neophyte audience as a framework. In the past, groups have created performances, developed organizational case studies, and written prose stories.

A Look Back

For me, beginning a class in CSR on critical and decolonial approaches is where I am the most vulnerable and the most empowered. As a teacher, I have chosen a constructivist approach, and this leads me to approach each class in complete interaction with the students. Like an improvisation, I have no idea before the beginning of the class how the students will respond to the texts. As bell hooks points out, this caring pedagogy often leads to exchanges of a richness and transformative power impossible to achieve with any other pedagogical approach. Allowing negative emotions can also foster important conversations. In tense situations, I find it important to ground the discussion in the readings.

Lovasoa's Journey: (Re)generating through Decentering

Long before I became a faculty member, back in the 1970s, colleagues at our business school at the University of Québec in Montréal (Canada) had created courses in the fields of *Business & Society* and *Business Ethics*. The latter were reinforced by the creation of the department of strategy, social and environmental strategy in the 2000s. My mandates and those of other recently hired colleagues within that department were to update existing courses and to develop the curriculum with our respective expertise (critical studies, philanthropy, life-cycle analysis, ecological transition, sustainability, grand challenges). Recently I had the opportunity to transform a core course at the executive MBA program titled "Economic, socio-political, and cultural contexts of organizations."

Transformation

I started teaching this course a decade ago, using a traditional approach. Starting five years ago, however I was triggered by two events. First, a grant award allowed me to conduct research on responsible management education and my encounters with business professors around the world increased my awareness in the potential of critical pedagogy. Second, a colleague teaching "Strategy and competition" added readings in CSR from the point of view of Michael Porter. I realized that it was necessary to develop something completely different to provide our students with plural perspectives.

My course is instructed over four weekends with a fifth for presentations. I also find the most destabilizing phase at the beginning, where through deconstruction students discover the downsides of the socially responsible and sustainable business practices, they have taken for granted. I do not introduce scholarly writings, instead using press articles, radio and TV programs, and NGO or corporate documents to discover for themselves how biodiversity compensation programs, BOP (Bottom-of-the-pyramid commercial practice), and codes of conduct generally fulfill a civilizing function, and present an essentialist view about vulnerable stakeholders. Students discover how CSR is often paternalistic and disciplinarian, excluding the voices and the knowledge of the impacted communities.

On the second weekend alternative case studies are introduced to decenter the sources of knowledge. Two examples are worthy of mention: the Catherine Donnelly Foundation in Toronto shifted from a traditional, socially responsible investment approach to a new philosophy founded on Indigenous "healing-through-the-land;" and The Clinique Minowé, a health and social service provider in Val d'Or, Québec developed a decolonized business model which supports Indigenous people's cultural identity.

On the third weekend students are introduced to the Global South and Aboriginal perspectives, and other periphery viewpoints such as scholarly readings from grassroots movements and struggles, to present generative *versus* extractive alternatives. These concepts are developed through lectures and debates on the fourth and last weekend.

To enhance *conscientização*, I have developed assignments that raise awareness of the importance of understanding the underlying assumptions, and the need for a diversity of sources for inspiration. For example, students are asked to comment on Malcom Ferdinand's (a philosopher and an expert of Caribbean decolonial ecology) interpretation of *The Slaveship* (a painting by William Turner). In lieu of an article, Ferdinand's take provides a vivid depiction of how today's climate policies and practices, often founded solely on a cost-effectiveness logic, could miss the port of social justice by excluding vulnerable stakeholders. Letting a philosophy enter the business classroom may seem risky. However, as per my experience, executive MBA students appreciate being both challenged and inspired by outsiders. Inspiration and not transposition or universalization is a keyword and different assumptions generate different outcomes is a key takeaway.

A Look Back

I find it imperative to take the time at the very beginning of the term to explain that the course does not seek to generate win-win recipes and that students will be taken outside of their comfort zone. I also assure them that instead of bashing the individual manager and the individual corporation, our work will question the system and we will walk together along a path of (re)generation. A constant difficulty is in finding materials. I must do *bricolage* since alternative cases are often difficult to find.

Dimbi's Journey: Leading Transition from Undergraduate Level

My school's commitment to CSR and Sustainability goes back over 20 years and teaching these topics to all students at all levels is one of the six pillars of its educational policy. One module, on "International economy & sustainable development" has been part of the second year of the International Bachelor Business Administration program since 2011. Its main objective is to present the sustainable development model as an alternative to the dominant capitalist economic model. I was tasked with updating and coordinating it.

Transformation

This module is divided into two sections. The first refutes the taken-for-granted trickle-down-effect of capitalism using heterodox approaches to demonstrate that there is a structural asymmetry between actors which prevents an equitable development and argues that the dogma of unlimited growth is unsustainable in a world with finite resources especially where climate change questions the very existence of humanity. The dysfunction of capitalism for the periphery, either because of their economic role, social status, race, societal orientations, or otherwise is particularly highlighted.

The second section presents an alternative using the United Nations 17 Sustainable Development Goals – especially the fight against poverty, inequality and injustice, and climate change. CSR, following ISO 26000 standard,[6] is used to qualify an organization's contribution to sustainable development. We present cases from capitalist companies (VEJA,[7] Le Slip Français[8]) that have really taken the CSR turn and, those of actors in the new socio-economic movements including fair trade as well as citizen and participatory finance, and the social economy (Label Emmaüs,[9] MAIF[10]) as successful alternatives.

Conscientização is specifically addressed through encounters with oppressive situations. One example is an analysis of the Rana Plaza tragedy, a factory collapse in Bangladesh in 2013. We focus on first-hand accounts of the workers and the NGOs fighting with them for justice.

We also put the textile industry into perspective by demonstrating the harmful impacts of fast fashion which highlights each actor's responsibility in this industry, including those of consumers and citizens.

Seeing images from the collapsed building and hearing the voices of the victims may seem disturbing, but in my opinion, it is necessary for students to begin to develop the critical consciousness necessary to see diverse realities of capitalism outside what is regularly conveyed in our mainstream media. And putting this exercise at the end of the course gives them time to develop a critical approach. The students are asked to reflect on their own consumption and to propose changes, both for themselves and for those around them. Many of them experience feelings of shame and disapprove of the behavior of profit-seeking companies and of consumers on the lookout for bargains. Others, more in the minority, defend that consumers with low purchasing power need these clothes at low prices, while recognizing the misdeeds of fast fashion. In any case, most students discover this drama in depth and this exercise constitutes an electric shock for them. After this lecture we begin with tutorials focusing on alternatives and positive solutions from companies committed to sustainability and CSR.

A Look Back

Being the head of the strategy department at the time made it easier for me to implement these changes when the course was first introduced. I'm happy to report, however that the module has endured even though I am no longer a director and despite regular assessments of the curriculum.

More importantly, there has been clear interest from students for a module focused on social and ecological transition instead of a classical course. It also appears to be appealing to students because it offers them an early opportunity to integrate sustainability and CSR in their academic curriculum (dissertation, internship, specialization's choice). It also reinforces their commitment to our school's pedagogical approach, which aims to develop personal, civic, and ethical skills intelligence beyond the usual cognitive skills.

Conclusion

Management studies as a discipline has promoted capitalism as an ideal way of life without questioning its entanglement with colonialism or the climate crisis. Decolonial approaches give us the grammar to unveil the invisible dominance of the Western episteme. Using pluralism, we assist students in their learning of alternative narratives and practices, which requires a greater understanding and use of other disciplines, including history, anthropology, political science, law, geography, and philosophy. It also asks us to become aware of other realities from the periphery and to engage with what some colleagues would find as unworthy or weird organizations, people, and knowledge.

The most important tools have been action research, research partnerships and personal outreach such as being members of civic associations. Not that it is all easy – such a choice entails additional work, additional engagement, and the occasional emotional rollercoaster. Convincing the grant institutions that our work is scientific and deserves financing, that the results of this type of activity, which some would not find relevant to research in business are worthy of publication in well-established OMT outlets, and being native French speakers, each adds another layer of difficulty to our search for legitimacy alongside neoliberal business scholarship (Blanchet & Berrier-Lucas, 2021). Despite those struggles, we are still hanging in there. Tenure has helped a lot. We also feel fortunate to be in schools where ecology and humanism are not just buzzwords. We are incredibly grateful to those who we owe our knowledge, especially from the most vulnerable communities and we continue to derive inspiration and support from both inside and outside academia. Building coalitions and nurturing communities/is our way to "selfcare as warfare" (Lorde, 2017, p. 95, Epilogue).

Notes

1 The Portuguese term "conscientização" literally means conscientization. It was used by the Brazilian philosopher of education Paolo Freire to describe the development of a critical attitude toward an oppressive context.
2 Ubuntu (African philosophy) and Buen vivir (Andean indigenous traditional worldview) are just two examples of non-Western wisdoms among many others which have been overlooked by business scholars despite their potential strengths in framing and nourishing alternative models of interactions between organizations and communities and between organizations and the natural environment. As argued by Giovannini (2012), Buen vivir suggests a type of development, a use of resources, a view of cultural traditions, and a community participation which can be inspirational for the reinvention of enterprises in a way that is inclusive of local actors and not exploitative of nature. On their part, Woermann and Engelbrecht (2019) asserts that Ubuntu

ethics, founded on the primacy of solidarity, humanism, and communalism can be a viable alterna btive to mainstream stakeholder theory.
3 RIODD is a Francophone association for CSR and sustainability scholars.
4 Our translation.
5 In line with our decolonial approach we intentionally favor the term "posture", over "teaching philosophy."
6 https://www.iso.org/publication/PUB100401.html
7 https://project.veja-store.com/en
8 https://www.leslipfrancais.fr/le-vetement-local
9 https://www.label-emmaus.co/fr/
10 https://entreprise.maif.fr/accueil

References

Ahmed, W., Kader, H., Khan, A., & et al. (2019). Manifesto "Decolonising the curriculum project: Through the kaleidoscope". (https://decoloniseukc. files.wordpress.com/2019/03/decolonising-the-curriculum-manifesto-final-2.pdf, accessed February 3rd 2023).
Albert, M. (1991). *Capitalisme contre capitalisme*. Seuil.
Alvesson, M., Bridgman, T., & WillmottAmable, H. (2009). *The Oxford handbook of critical management studies*. Oxford University Press.
Amable, B. (2003). *The diversity of modern capitalism*. Oxford University Press.
Banerjee, S. B. (2003). Who sustains whose development? Sustainable development and the reinvention of nature. *Organization Studies*, *24*(1), 143–180.
Banerjee, S. B., & Arjaliès, D.-L. (2021). Celebrating the end of enlightenment: Organization theory in the age of the anthropocene and Gaia (and why neither is the solution to our ecological crisis). *Organization Theory*, *2*(4), 263178772110367. https://doi.org/10.1177/26317877211036714
Banerjee, S. B., & Berrier-Lucas, C. (2022). Foreword decolonizing the business schools: A journey on paths less traveled. *Revue de l'organisation responsable*, *17*(2), 36–41.
Blanchet, V., & Berrier-Lucas, C. (2021). Une alternative à l'hégémonie anglophone : Enjeux et propositions. *Revue de l'Organisation Responsable*, *16*(3), 3–12.
Boyer, R. (2002). Variété du capitalisme et théorie de la régulation. *L'Année de la régulation*, *6*, 125–194.
Cariño, C., Cumes, A., Curiel, O., Garzón, M. T., Mendoza, B., & Ochoa y Alejandra Londoño, K. (2013). Pensar, sentir y hacer pedagogías feministas descoloniales esDiálogos y puntadas. In C. E. Walsh (Éd.), *Pedagogías decoloniales : Prácticas insurgentes de resistir, (re)existir y (re)vivir* (1era. edición, pp. 509–536). Abya Yala.
Clegg, S., Dany, F., & Grey, C. (2012). Introduction to the special issue critical management studies and managerial education: New contexts? New agenda? *M@n@gement*, *14*(5), 272. https://doi.org/10.3917/mana.145.0272

Contu, A. (2020). Answering the crisis with intellectual activism: Making a difference as business schools scholars. *Human Relations, 73*(5), 737–757.

Currie, G. & Knights, D. (2003). Reflecting on a critical pedagogy in MBA education. *Management Learning, 34*(1), 27–49. https://doi.org/10.117 7/1350507603034001129.

Dar, S., Liu, H., Martinez Dy, A., & Brewis, D. N. (2021). The business school is racist: Act up! *Organization, 28*(4), 695–706. https://doi.org/10.1177/1350508420928521

Dei, G. (2016). Decolonizing the university: The challenges and possibilities of inclusive education. *Socialist Studies/Études Socialistes, 11*(1), 23–23. https://doi.org/10.18740/S4WW31

Ergene, S., Banerjee, S. B., & Hoffman, A. J. (2021). (Un) sustainability and organization studies: Towards a radical engagement. *Organization Studies, 42*(8), 1319–1335.

French, R. & Grey, C. (Eds). (1996). *Rethinking Management Education.* Sage.

Fotaki, M., & Prasad, A. (2015). Questioning neoliberal capitalism and economic inequality in business schools. *Academy of Management Learning & Education, 14*(4), 556–575.

Fournier, V., & Grey, C. (2000). At the critical moment: Conditions and prospects for critical management studies. *Human Relations, 53*(1), 7–32.

Freire, P. (1970). *Pedagogy of the Oppressed.* Herder & Herder.

Gilmore, S., Harding, N., Helin, J., & Pullen, A. (2019). Writing differently. *Management Learning, 50*(1), 3–10. https://doi.org/10.1177/1350507618811027

Giovannini, M. (2012). Social enterprises for development as buen vivir. *Journal of Enterprising Communities, 6*(3), 284–299.

Grove, R. H. (2010). *Green imperialism: Colonial expansion, tropical island edens and the origins of environmentalism, 1600–1860.* Cambridge University Press.

Haraway, D. (1988). Situated knowledges: The science question in feminism and the privilege of partial perspective. *Feminist Studies, 14*(3), 575. https://doi.org/10.2307/3178066

hooks, bell. (1994). *Teaching to transgress: Education as the practice of freedom.* Routledge.

Liboiron, M., & Lepawsky, J. (2022). *Discard studies: Wasting, systems, and power.* The MIT Press.

Liu, H. (2022). Teaching for freedom, caring for ourselves. *Journal of Marketing Management,* 1–9. https://doi.org/10.1080/0267257X.2022.2131268

Lorde, A. (2017). *A burst of light: And other essays* (Ixia Press). Dover Publications.

Mignolo, W. D. (2011). *The darker side of western modernity: Global futures, decolonial options.* Duke University Press.

Mignolo, W. D., & Walsh, C. E. (2020). *On decoloniality: Concepts, analytics, praxis.* Duke University Press. https://doi.org/10.1515/9780822371779

Nkomo, S. M. (2021). Reflections on the continuing denial of the centrality of "race" in management and organization studies. *Equality, Diversity and Inclusion: An International Journal, 40*(2), 212–224.

Perriton, L. & Reynolds, M. 2018. Critical management education in challenging times. *Management Learning, 49* (5), 521–536. https://doi.org/10.1177/1350507618795090.

Quijano, A. (2000). Coloniality of power and eurocentrism in Latin America. *International Sociology, 15*(2), 215–232. https://doi.org/10.1177/0268580900015002005

Ramboarisata, L. (2016). Des MBA responsables? Un éclairage institutionnel et discursif. *Cahiers du Centre OSE(3).* https://ose.esg.uqam.ca/wp-content/uploads/sites/65/Cahier-de-recherche-3-Des-MBA-responsables-Un-%C3%A9clairage-institutionnel-et-discursif.pdf.

Ramboarisata, L. (2022). Post-pandemic responsible management education : An invitation for a conceptual and practice renewal and for a narrative change. *Journal of Global Responsibility, 13*(1), 29–41. https://doi.org/10.1108/JGR-12-2020-0110.

Ramboarisata, L & C. Gendron (2019). Beyond moral righteousness: The challenges of non-utilitarian ethics, CSR, and sustainability education. *The International Journal of Management Education, 17*(3), 1–12. http://dx.doi.org/10.1016/j.ijme.2019.100321.

Sauerbronn, F. F., Lima, J. P., & Faria, A. (2022). Decolonizing-recolonizing curriculum in management and accounting with southern Praxis. *Academy of Management Proceedings, 1,* https://doi.org/10.5465/AMBPP.2022.14410abstract.

Spivak, G. C. (1988). Can the subaltern speak? In C. Nelson & L. Grossberg (Éds.), *Marxism and the interpretation of culture* (pp. 271–313). University of Illinois Press.

Teasley, C., & Butler, A. (2020). Intersecting critical pedagogies to counter coloniality. In S. R. Steinberg & B. Down (Éds.), *The SAGE Handbook of Critical Pedagogies* (Vol. 1–3, pp. 186–204). SAGE Publications Ltd. https://doi.org/10.4135/9781526486455.

Walsh, C. E. (2015). Decolonial pedagogies walking and asking. Notes to Paulo Freire from AbyaYala. *International Journal of Lifelong Education, 34*(1), 9–21. https://doi.org/10.1080/02601370.2014.991522

Woermann, M., & Engelbrecht, S.(2019). The Ubuntu challenge to business: Froam stakeholders to relationholders. *Journal of Business Ethics, 157*(1), 27–44.

Yousfi, H. (2021). Le management international, doit-on finir avec le mythe de l'hybridite culturelle? Retour sur les apports des approches postcoloniale et decoloniales. *M@n@gement, 24*(1), 80–89.

4

REGENERATIVE FINANCE AND ECONOMICS FROM START TO FINISHED (FOR NOW)

Ken Sagendorf

Abstract

Systems; Thriving versus survival; Regeneration; Stewardship. These constructs were the foundations of the vision of our new business college from the start. And they ran (perhaps even continue to run) directly into long-standing traditions and understandings of the faculty and administration. This work shares the journey of proposing a new MS degree in Regenerative Finance and Economics and ultimately being told "no" by our institution. The work shares the process of gathering an increasingly larger set of stakeholders and building excitement for offering a truly distinct business degree that could graduate changemakers into the world who would be prepared to ask the right questions and put new perspectives, philosophies, and practices in play that could change the triple bottom line conversation. And it outlines us ultimately being asked to remove the proposal in the Anderson College of Business at Regis University, a Jesuit Catholic university, in Denver, Colorado. The chapter finally reflects on what could've been done differently to have this curriculum become the anchor of our college's vision and future.

Context

The Regis University Mission is to seek "to build a more just and humane world through transformative education at the frontiers of faith,

DOI: 10.4324/9781003457763-4

reason and culture." In 2015, Regis issued a call for a dean for our new business college. It stated,

> This new College will prepare graduates to live purposeful lives bringing Jesuit values into free market and social enterprises for the betterment of society. The new College offers a real opportunity to differentiate itself by marketing the distinctive qualities of a business program based on the values inherent in Jesuit education.

The Anderson College of Business was founded on a stewardship vision – to help businesses become stewards of society with the goal of improving the quality of life on earth. I came to our college to start an Innovation Center because of this vision and the work of my center was intentionally focused on changing business education in this light.

At the beginning of starting The Innovation Center, I worked with alumni of our university and the business community to identify what "innovation" meant in this context of a Jesuit business school. We landed on a definition that included three ways of thinking that the business world needs (critical, creative, and systems thinking), four kinds of leadership that the world needs (self-awareness, ingenuity, love, and heroism), and the companionship of our alumni and the community to anchor everything. At its heart, the Innovation Center was built to bring together people to design systems and solutions for our curriculum and the complex challenges of the world.

I was fortunate to have two colleagues who simultaneously started other Centers to do this work within our college and our community. As Center directors, we were tasked with gathering faculty and staff from across the college to outline and co-create principles of stewardship that would guide our work, our curriculum, and our approaches to business and business education. We collectively defined stewardship as:

- Stewardship defines life as all living creatures and the environment.
- Stewardship calls us each to work together on solutions to society's complex problems.
- Stewardship focuses on the long-term impacts of decisions.
- Stewardship requires personal responsibility in understanding the systemic effects of one's actions.
- Stewardship is inclusive and requires us to be other-focused.

Description of Our Process

The process of changing our college and eventually proposing the Regenerative Finance and Economics degree program proceeded through several steps to integrate sustainability concepts and develop necessary resources and tools. The Innovation Center was one of three that were created at the start of our college. My partners were Dr. Beth Caniglia who started the Sustainable Economic and Enterprise Development (SEED) Institute, and Dr. Eugene Wilkerson who created the Workforce Development, Ethics, and Lifelong Learning (WELL) Center. We built these three centers at the launch of our business school to showcase to external audiences a triple bottom line approach: SEED (Planet), WELL (People), and Innovation (Profit). Together, we took a holistic and new perspective into the community and the connections between us framed our work. While academic Centers and Institutes play different roles at different places, ours were meant to expand our business education, our ecosystem, and our funding.

With the support of our Dean, our community-centered work included working with local governments and agencies, hosting public town halls, and leading design-thinking workshops across the city. Our work together in the Centers attracted interest from colleagues at Jesuit universities. Our academic conference presentations about connected stewardship led to discussions about building programs that could make a big difference in sustainability. We were drawn to the finance and economics discussions as we thought that there was the most potential for positive change if we could change the profit-primacy embedded in capitalism. Our general discussions turned to gap analyses.

Some questions we considered were: Who is included and excluded in the current ways we educate in these fields? How are wealth and power connected? When is a growth-at-all-costs warranted and what are the results when this happens? Is the role of government regulation helping over time? Will the planet survive if we continue on this path? These questions and our quest to find answers invited other connections in our community and included esteemed folks from academe and the private sector. A list of participants can be found in the Resource section at the end of this chapter.

Participants in these conversations were excitedly volunteering as we outlined potential ways to change the landscape of business education with an increasingly larger systems-focused lens. All of this conversation, coupled with the call for our college to be differentiated in the market, and examination of what some other colleges and universities were offering led to us to develop a proposal to offer a MS in Regenerative Finance and Economics (MRFE).

We invited our college faculty into this conversation and proposed this new degree at the university level. The main way our proposed MRFE would be different is its consideration of more than just financial or economic capital in these fields. Our approach was to extend the disciplines to consider multiple forms of capital, including natural, human, social, and intellectual capital. We also looked at intersectionalities between these capital sources so that impacts of financial and economics decision-making were front and center in this approach.

In our gap analysis, we determined that our current finance and economics course offerings were really preparing students to work in the legacy financial and capital markets. Our proposed degree intended to do more. Our proposal stated:

> The MRFE will not only provide students with quantitative and theoretical tools but also with a holistic systems-focused approach to wealth-building in innovative, adaptive, and responsive ways that improve the health of our people and planet, making our graduates distinctive from others. Directly aligned with our mission and vision, graduates will be prepared for successful careers in regenerative finance/economics with potential employers such as investment and commercial banks, economic and financial asset management companies, consulting firms, and policy-oriented organization. They will also be prepared to take on leadership roles in fields like impact investing, social entities, for-benefit enterprises, and micro-finance.

We believed that, while any finance or economics graduate might find their way into these organizations based on personal choice, we were specifically aiming to have our graduates be prepared to lead in those spaces. By leading, we specifically meant being prepared to push for systems-level changes. This approach to prepare students to both work in the world as it is and to serve as change agents was intentional. We believed this distinctive approach could be one of the fastest ways to transform education and business.

We worked with our networks and faculty to identify the learning outcomes for our graduates. We identified that, at the end of MRFE, our students should be able to *Reimagine capitalism, economic modeling, and finance in the context of solutions to local and global challenges.* To do that, we needed students to:

- Be able to recognize, value, and attend to multiple forms of capital and the nuanced complexity of systems as they relate to stakeholder value and improvement over time.
- Recognize alignment and misalignment of regenerative systems with *Laudato Si'* and Catholic Social Teaching.
- Be able to work across multiple sectors, translate knowledge into action, and evangelize the regenerative paradigm.

Table 4.1 shares a high-level view of the proposed curricular flow of the program moving from knowledge gathering to skill development to active application and community connection. Note that the outcomes included work on public policy, new knowledge creation, and public presentation, and specific, but broader connection-making in the finance and economic space. This was the tie to creating new change-agent leaders who would be equipped to challenge the status quo in economics and finance.

We intended to incorporate these areas of study into some of our existing courses and create new courses where needed. Along with the collection of course titles that provided similar basics such as investments and portfolio management and financial institutions management, we planned to redevelop the following new courses with a regenerative lens:

- Applied Financial Economics
- Research Methodologies/Econometrics
- Political Economics
- Monetary Theory
- Macroeconomics Theory
- Microeconomics Theory
- Sustainability Economics

It should be noted that we did not get creative with course titles in our proposal because we believed potential students and others needed to recognize familiar concepts to generate enrollment. However, we

TABLE 4.1 Year 1 and Year 2 Regenerative Finance and Economics Learning Approaches and Outcomes

Year 1	
Areas of Study	*Proposed Outcomes/Experiences*
Ecological economics/ systems science	Students will be exposed to and study economic and business contexts from the perspectives of ecological economics and science-based systems approach.
	Students will explain how dominant economic and finance frameworks have contributed to 21st century social and ecological crisis. Students will contrast the fundamental assumptions and approaches of these dominant frameworks with those of alternative economic and financial frameworks that have been practiced but largely dormant.
Accounting	Students will be exposed to emerging practices in Integrated Reporting and develop an integrated accounting report.
Finance	Students learn and apply conventional principles of corporate finance as well as multiple capitals framework, the "triple bottom line," and the stakeholder alternative to maximization of shareholder value.
Regenerative ethics	Students will draw the implications of Catholic Social Teaching and *Laudato Si'* for business ethics, public policy, business policies, economics, and finance.
Year 2	
Ecological economics/ systems science	Students distinguish between regenerative processes and sustainable processes.
Regenerative economics and finance/systems science; public policy	Students contrast regenerative, sustainable, and conventional finance practices and their implications for public policy and stability of financial markets.
Regenerative economics and finance; public policy	Students analyze the macroeconomic, financial, and public policy implications of new forms of money and of conventional investment strategies, asset pricing strategies, and banking practices.
Ecological economics/ regenerative economics and finance/systems science	Students explicitly connect the ecological/systems approach of regenerative paradigm to *Laudato Si'*.
Regenerative economics and finance/systems science	Through experiential projects with either stakeholders (e.g., Regenerative Communities Network) or individual businesses, students observe and/or develop best practices in regenerative business and finance.

would teach some of these concepts in a considerable different way than students might experience in other, more traditional finance and economics degrees.

We were simultaneously setting out to build a hugely experiential program. The opportunity for MRFE students to apply their learning was foundational to the program design. During their courses, students would be introduced to and interact with the Regenerative Communities Network here in Denver. They would have access to work being done in the other 15+ regenerative communities across the country and world. The professional network of these finance and economics professionals were built-in to support graduates of the program. We also aligned the work of our SEED Institute to support students and community.

Successes and Failures

Successes of this process were the expansive, cross-institutional, and community collaborations, and tight collaboration among three Center directors. It was also enriched by conversations among more than 20 thought leaders and volunteers in conversations that spanned 4–6 months inside and outside the university.

Developing the framework for this degree program was amongst the most meaningful work I have ever done in higher education. I assign this level of meaning because of the focus on sustainability and people.

In education, I have always felt pressure from others that business was somehow "bad" for not understanding its influence and impact or for leaving planetary and environmental concerns out of its considerations. And often I hear the quick defensiveness from my colleagues. In a walking conversation with the Dean of our Liberal Arts College, a friend and mentor, I stated that there ought to be a required business course to balance out messages from some faculty that proclaimed business was evil. He responded that the faculty did not say business was evil, but that *capitalism* was evil. I asked who made that distinction for students? It was a subtle and yet, important exchange. Understanding comes from exchange. We can do better. We can include more people in the exchange. Always. The past or even the present doesn't need to define the future.

Our work on the MRFE program was about changing the perspectives of people, broadening their lens, and driving better approaches that could lead to inclusivity, climate-consciousness, and making money. This approach was the infamous "and" we are seeking. The more people we engaged, the bigger and better the "and" got in terms of its potential as a business education. The process of creating MRFE was a success because we identified a unique concept that could potentially change the trajectory of business.

With full irony, the parts of the process that we did not do well: people and politics. We may have been slightly blinded by our excitement. No, we definitely were. Our faculty in both finance and economics were traditionalists in their disciplines. They had started or held successful careers with old paradigms, so it took a while to convince them to approach these fields differently. New curriculum concepts were certainly harder than the way they were taught or worked. The curriculum didn't come from them; it seemed external. Thus, the champion for the MRFE program proposal did not come from the disciplines. Discipline champions would have made the proposal stronger in the eyes of the institution.

In reflection, we made a grave error in not including more faculty. The excitement and passion of our college-level vision didn't match the boots-on-the-ground engagement of our own faculty in our finance and economics programs. There was great excitement about the potential of the MRFE from folks outside of our college, but our faculty did not fully participate in the six months of excited and passionate development. They may not have understood the philosophy of regeneration in their own fields. To accept the need to change economics and finance courses, faculty needed to recognize current shortcomings of their disciplines. While faculty were invited to and participated marginally in development work, the continued time commitment made it difficult for them to consistently participate. As our team began to create proposals for our university approval, faculty were invited to circular design sessions. This is where we had a major breakdown.

As commonly happens in similar faculty sessions, participants tend to share everything that we experienced in our own educational upbringing and such sharing can bog down the process. As we discussed what we should be included in the new program, we ran into disagreement about whether we should teach traditional concepts first and then teach them how to make sense of the new/different content. In writing this chapter, I reviewed meeting notes and first drafts of the degree proposal and recognized a mismatch in not having a faculty champion. Our champions were from our Centers, our dean, and from an external audience.

Our university had long offered respected business degrees. But the formation of a Business College within the university was only a year old, we were moving very fast, we needed to push multiple degree programs through the institutional approval processes, and we designed and named new faculty expectations. Colleagues who were on the university academic council at the time, recently noted that our college was putting so many new degree proposals through that they "had enough from our college." Ultimately, we received an unusual and higher-level of scrutiny from the administration.

There was a palpable feeling on campus that the business school was getting too much or doing too much too fast. We launched three new Centers which was assumed to divert resources away from faculty and students, although no operational budget was used. We garnered the largest donation in the university's history to name our school. Politically, we unintentionally exhausted social capital among other colleges in the university. Looking back, we should have done more to manage up and include administrators in the planning and excitement of the unique opportunity. Whether we needed more research, more data, more testimonies, I remain unsure. We are a centralized decision-making academic body, and we should have spent more time in conversation with the leaders of the Academic Council so they could feel and understand the potential longitudinal impact of this innovative degree.

In our development group and the Centers, we were busy designing and hosting community-based programing. However, we should have done more to include our administrative and faculty colleagues more. One tool that we often spoke about in our conversations, but did not leverage sufficiently, was the publication of *Laudato Si'*. In our Jesuit institution, our Jesuit Pope and his encyclical aligned with our efforts for MRFE to change business and our world. Overall, more patience and time spent with the gatekeepers in our institution could have led to a different outcome.

Conclusion

Ultimately, the MRFE degree proposal was rejected. One reason was the belief among some administrators that there were no potential jobs in regenerative economics and finance for our graduates. The degree was not approved. University politics ended its development (for now). Our dean moved to another university, two of the Center directors left, and much of the stewardship vision lagged as a result.

However, not all is lost. Remnants of stewardship content are integrated in activities and courses like marketing and innovation. I love how students struggle to balance value for society with traditional wealth development for a company. We now have undergraduate sustainability fellows in our SEED institute. As a result of our work, we authored a book, *Regenerative Urban Design, Climate Change, and the Common Good* (Caniglia et al., 2020). Some of our work moved forward but not through a degree program at Regis University. More importantly, the conversation about sustainable business education continues to grow through my own work with the Global Movement Initiative, and annual presentations at conferences include a growing, global conversation with thought leaders in the field. Although the work didn't happen as we thought, these conversations continue to strike a very raw nerve with many folks working to educate future leaders in these fields.

Personal Learning Outcomes and Recommendations

Despite our focus on our mission at my university, other similar higher education institutions that are slow moving, traditional, and struggling will only grow through individual efforts and passions to offer necessary education valued by society. Some universities fear investing in different projects they cannot easily see through enrollment or profit lenses. This is likely acute for smaller, private schools with limited or strained resources. Leadership and support are necessary to create a structure that connects faculty, chairs, and deans as like-minded cohorts to create innovative ideas and programs. One passionate individual can do a lot but to make systemic change we need an infrastructure to support progress.

Organic connection-making remains one of the highlights of my academic career. Collaborative work with colleagues expands my vision, increases the depth and speed of my ability to learn about brand new (to me) fields, and enriches my life through quick camaraderie. Collaboration and like-minded colleagues will help us continue to push boundaries in changing universities, business, and stewardship.

Resources

Active participants in the months of conversation leading to the development of our MFRE proposal:

- Dr. Jim Stoner, James A. F. Stoner Chair in Global Quality Leadership, Gabelli School, Fordham University; Co-author of Fundamentals of Financial Managing
- Dr. Frank Werner, Gabelli School, Fordham University; Co-author of Fundamentals of Financial Managing

- John Fullerton – Founder and President, Capital Institute
- Dr. Stuart Cowan – Co-Founder, Autopoiesis LLC; Former Chief Scientist; Smart Cities Council
- Mike Ibarra, Senior Vice President, Investment Management, Amalgamated Bank
- Hunter Lovins, Author, co-founder of the Rocky Mountain Institute; Founder, Natural Capitalism Solutions
- John Knott, Founder & CEO, Citycraft Ventures
- Dr. Mairi-Jane Fox, Ecological Economics Ph.D., Director of Carbon Planning and ESG,
  Arbor Day Carbon
- Dr. Marc Orrs, Founding Director of Sustainable Development Program, Lehigh University and current Teaching Associate Professor in Engineering, Design, and Society at Colorado School of Mines
- Dr. Elizabeth Walsh, Visiting Professor, Architecture and Urban Planning, University of Colorado Denver and current Program Coordinator for the University of Denver Grand Challenges Urban Sustainability Cohort.

Reference

Caniglia, B. S., Frank, B., Knott, J. L., Sagendorf, K. S., & Wilkerson, E. A. (2020). *Regenerative urban development, climate change and the common good*. Routledge, Taylor & Francis Group.

5

TEACHING SUSTAINABILITY MANAGEMENT AND THE CREATION OF THE MSC SUSTAINABLE SUPPLY CHAIN MANAGEMENT AT EXCELIA

Jesus Gonzalez-Feliu, Valérie Fernandes, and Morgane Fritz

Abstract

The authors of this chapter belong to Excelia Business School, a French business school based in La Rochelle, France. The authors chose to write together as they represent three different levels in Excelia Business School, which are interconnected: strategic level (with the Dean); management level (managing relations between the program directors, the Dean and the educators, and leading curriculum construction in supply chain management), and teaching level (one educator–researcher). The three authors are also members of the same department: the Supply Chain, Purchasing, and Project Management (SPP) Department. Valérie Fernandes, the Dean of the faculty, will tell you about the school's philosophy and strategic positioning regarding sustainability management. Jesus Gonzalez-Feliu, Head of the SPP Department, will tell you about the recent creation of the MSc Sustainable Supply Chain Management. Finally, Morgane Fritz, Associate Professor in (Sustainable) Supply Chain Management, will tell you about her proposition of new courses for this Master and other programs.

Onboarding Faculty in a Collective Journey – *Valérie's Story*

Excelia Business School has long been recognized as a pioneer in France regarding the teaching of sustainability management. This is part of the school's DNA. In 1999, we were the first French Business School to launch a MSc focused on environmental management. A few years later, in 2005, we launched Humacité, which is a humanitarian,

DOI: 10.4324/9781003457763-5

social, or civic service-learning initiative in France or abroad as part of students' business management studies. It is based on the shared values expressed in the school's mission to train learners to become responsible professionals, and prepare them for lifelong employability, and to contribute to the transformation of organizations and the development of its regions. Humacité has defined a precise framework to meet the set objectives and train responsible managers, as part of its manifesto of ethical and responsible business behavior. It exposes students to cultural, social, economic, political, and religious differences and thus helps to develop their humanitarian values, through their commitment to people in difficulty or who are disadvantaged or deprived of their fundamental rights. Built into the curriculum of all school programs since 2008, the school has worked with more than 2,200 not-for-profit or community-based organizations worldwide who have provided more than 6,575 Humacité projects in areas such as education, public service, citizens' rights, heritage education, and the environment. Approximately 575 projects are carried out in the school each year.

In 2020, we launched Climacité®, which is a key component in the school's approach to personal and professional development. Its key objectives are to train responsible citizens who are aware of their duty toward the planet, enable young people to face up to anxiety-provoking societal issues by discovering their individual capacity for action, contribute to training in sustainable development and social responsibility of future managers, and strengthen the employability of learners through a unique and impactful experience. Humacité and Climacité are key components in the school's approach to personal and professional development and contribute to training future citizens and managers who are aware of their duty and responsibilities to society and to the environment.

When I joined Excelia in 2010, I was very sensitive to Corporate Social Responsibility (CSR) and sustainable development through my teaching and my research areas. I was very impressed with the work of Humacité and the MSc Program. I saw the creation of our CSR research Institute (IRSI) and participated as a researcher in the CSR research axis of the school. As a dean of faculty in 2013, I had ambitions to go deeper into transforming our curricula.

I participated in defining our competency goals for our first AACSB accreditation in 2013. One of our competency goals is dedicated to

CSR: each year, we measure the level of students for each program – both in entrance and in final year, by using specific case studies developed by the faculty and an external awareness test, Sulitest. We redefined this competency goal in 2020, adding the ecological transition dimension. Next, faculty introduced a specific course on CSR and Business Ethics in each program. Later, the faculty developed disciplinary courses focused on CSR, mostly for final year's specializations (e.g., sustainable supply chain for our SCM MSc). In 2019, we incorporated our competency goals in our syllabus, to demonstrate which courses integrate CSR notions.

However, I still held a conviction that we had to go further, deeper, and more rapidly, to cope with our climate emergency. I was very active within the executive committee to define our 2020–2025 strategic plan and the CEO appointed me to be responsible for the first strategic axis, *"affirm our position in CSR and the environment."* That appointment provided internal legitimacy as I was recognized as an expert both by the governance and by the faculty to go beyond existing programs.

In 2020, during the COVID period, I realized that it was time to engage the whole faculty in the transformation from a school teaching about CSR to a school whose competencies embrace CSR and ecological transition within our external ecosystem (i.e., French ministry of higher education, new rankings, new standards, or reinforcement for accreditation). Thus, I initiated faculty training on the redesign of our curricula alongside of programs and on developing new partnerships. In 2020, I supported Morgane Fritz's involvement in Principles for Responsible Management Education (PRME) workshops and in developing a new network of business schools, the Global Movement Initiative. More recently, I supported another faculty in her interdisciplinary research in the field of CSR and its recognition by academic management journals.

In 2021–2022, we trained 40 faculty in the sustainability mindset approach (nine hours), developed by Isabel Rimanoczy, who developed the sustainability mindset concept and principals and is convener of PRME Sustainability Mindset Group. In 2022–2023, the training is focused on ecological transition and climatology, so that faculty can integrate these dimensions more deeply into their teaching. The two-day training sessions are provided by an NGO, Les Ateliers Du Future, and made up of leaders with experience in the key areas of the universal revolution we must lead: Climate Models, Risks, Politics, New Technologies by sector (Energy, Industry, Transport, Building, Agri) and Finance (https://lesateliersdufutur.org/).

The purpose of this training is to elevate the knowledge and sustainability mindset of faculty, especially those who are not specialists in these concepts. It supports faculty efforts to evolve their courses by integrating these new sustainability dimensions in core business disciplines. In parallel, I worked with heads of programs and departments to integrate curricula with ecological transition and CSR. The results are new blocks of competencies and new courses. For example, we offer *Introduction to Climate Challenges* for all our Bachelors' students, and *Entrepreneurship and New Business Models* or *Innovation and Sustainable Growth* for our Masters' students. In 2021–2022, 27% of dissertations (Master 2 thesis) are focused on CSR.

What must be done now? A mountain of things! First, we must more precisely map the degree to which each business course addresses CSR and ecological transition. Second, we must reinforce the integration of our research into teaching. Third, as a change leader and member of Sulitest SAS since 2022, we decided to certify the sustainability knowledge of all students of Excelia Business School. We will use TASK, an international certification developed by Sulitest, "designed to assess our model of sustainability knowledge and to ensure that all individuals can incorporate the dimensions into their decisions" (https://en.sulitest.org/tools/task). In 2023–2024, all final year students (Bachelor and Master level) will be required to take the test. Fourth, we must make a big shift into teaching and reflecting on the theoretical corpus that has to be taught in order to train future sustainable managers and leaders for a sustainable world. This big shift necessitates a global movement of business schools, all around the world, to build this new theoretical framework.

Onboarding Faculty and Program Directors in the Development of a New Msc Program – *Jesus' Story*

Our department level effort was focused on the evolution of an existing MSc program, MSc Sustainable Supply Chain Management. In 2022, with the annexation of another MSc in Purchasing (held in two campuses in parallel, at Tours and Orléans), the Masters' pedagogical heads and I saw the possibility of restructuring them into a single coherent program. As a director of the teaching department where supply chain management courses are deployed, it was important to me to ensure the coherence of those Masters degrees, as well as their integration with the school's strategic goals of sustainability. Moreover, we had the need to homogenize and rethink the entire set of Master of Science curricula to create economies of scale with common courses (such as the basics of advanced management, research, and data/computer use) and create revisions with a faculty-driven approach.

As a department director-in-charge of the pedagogical responsibility of the teachings in Purchasing and Supply Chain Management, I thought (and still think) that we need to be pro-active in making these changes. I organized a first meeting with the two heads of the existing Masters to discuss ways those programs could be re-thought and incorporate the sustainability mindset and our school strategic goals. I am convinced that, as Ackoff and Greenberg (2008) state, learning organizations need to be dynamic and planned in a system thinking way. In current systems, the person that learns the most is the teacher. It seemed important to me to take advantage of that knowledge and countless experiences of faculty members to construct the new Master Program. Since three campuses needed to deploy the Master, and the school had three main strategic axes (Sustainability, Internationalization, and Digitalization), we associated each campus to one of those three axes. However, all three Masters needed to address the basics of sustainability, a strong digitalization component, and teachings and experiences on an international basis. In development, each campus would focus on a specific axis but incorporate the other two.

How could we construct this architecture and include every faculty member while respecting all the constraints? I believe that a top-down deductive approach (arriving with a clear and "closed" proposal) does not give enough place to people to propose freely what they would like to do. However, if we constructed the new Masters' structure on a pure inductive approach, we would encounter a high risk of not converging into a consensual solution (Gonzalez-Feliu & Morana, 2014). An abductive, interactive way of thinking seemed to be the best option. How to proceed then? Our department was holding an internal meeting and I thought it was a good opportunity to carry out this faculty-driven proposal of change.

To prepare for that meeting, the two pedagogical heads and I analyzed existing teaching requirements of the entire Master program.

After analyzing the existing programs, it appeared that several common blocks provided basic competences:

1 Supply Chain Strategies and Processes
2 Supply Chain Performance and Cost Control
3 Industrial Management (production, inventory, and lean management)
4 Purchasing and Supplier Relationships, transport and distribution issues including incoterms and customs
5 Supply Chain Digitalization
6 Risk and Quality Management

The rest of the modules were considered as less basic. With all that information and taking only one guidance point (the vision that purchasing and supply chain need to be integrated (van Weele, 2018), a first proposal was made based on a structure where the courses are grouped in four main categories (strategic issues, tactical-operational issues, enablers, and complementary issues). The proposal considered the historical context of the territories of each campus their guiding "specialization." Specialization areas at La Rochelle were "global" (historical Master having either purchasing or supply chain mini-specializations, international and global context), "Inbound" issues at Tours (industrial and supply-based needs by local companies), and "outbound" at Orléans (presence of important distribution companies, the cosmetic valley and proximity of Paris region, a highly consumption area that justifies a Master in distribution processes). Finally, the definition of the exact content per Master and campus was left for the faculty meeting.

Before the faculty meeting, I communicated with all department members to help everyone understand the nature and the goals of the Masters' refoundation. During the meeting I presented the main ideas. When I came to Excelia in 2020, I wanted to develop a dynamic group where everyone holds strong values but collaborates to reach a common goal. This meeting was an example of that for me. People were actively debating and proposing, and the initial proposal was rethought to make it more coherent. Since sustainability is one of the pillars of our School, most colleagues were enthusiastically proposing ideas for having sustainability guide the entire Masters' structure. Finally, we agreed on the following points:

1 The Master in La Rochelle would be centered around sustainable integrated purchasing and supply chain management (sustainability

axis), that of Tours on international and multicultural purchasing and supply management (international axis) and the one in Orléans on managing new forms of distribution systems (digitalization axis).

2 The blocs on industrial management and quality, risk, and control should have the same courses in all the campuses. In both cases the three dimensions of sustainability needed to be addressed. For the other blocs, courses would be a little different in each campus since the objects were not the same, but the basis needed to be the same. The performance and strategy courses had to be oriented around the sustainable supply chain management frameworks and go beyond the classical cost-quality-lead time visions of supply chain management.

3 Different proposals were made for other modules, based on the willingness to teach of each colleague. That meant courses were proposed by potential teachers motivated to participate in its creation.

For the specific case of the Master in La Rochelle, the three remaining modules were "management and organization of sustainable transport systems," "sustainable management of suppliers and collaborators," and "ethical supply chain management." All three were proposed by colleagues who intended to teach those courses and had expertise in one of the domains based on their research. The first module focused more on the design of environmental-friendly transport systems, the other two modules were more focused on operational management with strong human, social, and ethical components.

When this proposal was submitted for approval, decision-makers were impressed by the high coordination level (in a short time) and the strong coherence of the structures. Our proposal was accepted with very minor changes. Some notions were added to existing courses to fill a lack on the Masters' competences and the course titles were adapted to comply with the school's and the Ministry's requirements. In general, the construction of the Masters' new structure showed us that we can work on a team, that faculty-driven construction is beneficial for both the school and faculty, and, if we want to change something, we need to start by proposing the change.

After the process of creating the Masters proposal, several (mainly administrative) people in the school asked why we included a course on Ethical Supply Chain Management. Some suggested removing it.

Those people were not curriculum decision-makers, and I declined their suggestions for two reasons:

1 Courses in our proposal were championed by a person who was motivated and believed in it.
2 The Ethical Supply Chain Management course (and all other courses) had been examined and validated by an entire department, then pedagogical and program heads, then the final proposal was submitted to the decision-making instance of the school, which validated it. It was a legitimate inclusive process.

I think that this experience taught me an important lesson: the only thing that is more difficult than starting something new is stopping something old (Ackoff & Addison, 2012) but if we do not even try to propose something new, we will never start the change.

Teaching the Way You Feel Is Right for You, Students, Society, and the Environment – *Morgane's Story*

I arrived at Excelia in 2018, after my PhD in Sustainability-oriented Management, which I completed at the University of Graz, Austria. During my PhD, I was working at the Institute of Environmental Systems Sciences (IESS), which gathers people from very different backgrounds (Management, Modelling, Biology, Physics, Engineering, etc.) but with one common goal: to contribute to research in sustainability management with a systems perspective. After six years in Austria, I felt it was time for me to go back to my home country, France. I wanted to find a place with a similar environment and people with a similar state of mind or passion for sustainability as I enjoyed at the IESS Institute. That is exactly what I found at Excelia, and I am very happy I chose this business school.

When I started research and teaching in 2018, my work was split between the Strategic Department (where most sustainability-related courses were given) and the Supply Chain Department (where there were few sustainability-related courses, but I was totally free to include all the sustainability topics I was working on in relation to the course). Such freedom was a blessing as I am a person who cannot teach something if it is not related to sustainability.

Sustainability is part of my everyday life, is my passion, and is part of almost all my decisions. I cannot really explain why. Maybe because when I was a kid I lived in Germany and very much enjoyed sorting the different colors of glasses and throwing them in the recycling bin! (I still like it very much). Consequently, I started my classes with examples from my PhD experience where I worked as a project employee for different European and Austrian projects, good and bad examples of company practices from the news. In the strategic department, I taught a "CSR and business ethics" course and, as I really like to master everything I need to teach about, I worked a lot on ethics literature and practice.

I quickly realized that ethics needs to be practiced and cannot be taught only. So, I designed exercises where I asked students to take actions and reflect upon their feelings related to this action. That was inspired by the PRME Working Group on the Sustainability Mindset led by Isabel Rimanoczy, and I published a book chapter giving more details on this experiment (see Fritz, 2021). This experience was incredible: I read stories of students that really moved me, and Isabel Rimanoczy told me this was a powerful exercise because I pushed students to talk about their emotions, and emotional learning is one of the most powerful ways to make people change their mindset.

That led me to think how I could do something similar in the other classes I taught? I did not take immediate action as I was very focused on research and teaching. I set the idea aside until January 19, 2023, where I almost died in a car accident. I "just" had a head trauma, but I wanted to go back to work as soon as possible. I went back to school with the course I had created a few years ago, "Sustainability and Digitalization." This is a course where I push students to exert their critical thinking skills to both the good and bad sides of digitalization in business and society. Due to my accident, I could not use my power point to teach as I used to and was worried about how I could remember each student's name to be able to give them an individual grade. It was too much for my head.

So, I prepared the content of the class hour-by-hour and shared an updated version of my power point with them, on our online platform, in addition to other material. I also thought it would be a good solution to ask them to write kind of a diary (like we use in research with the research diary) where they first write their expectations of the class during the first session and then, their day-by-day activities, and thoughts or questions until the last session of the class, including a bibliography (so that I could check what they read and could see if they looked for additional material). In this way, I could see their individual expectation for the course, the resources they read/watched/

listened to, and the impact my teaching and the exchange of ideas with their classmates had on them. Some of them really changed their mind regarding the compatibility of digitalization and sustainability. Others did not change their mind but almost all of them stated that they had learned something new and became more aware of the tensions between the two concepts.

I observed that students were much more engaged than before with this way of teaching. I also noted the power we have as teachers to help students become open-minded and able to take the best possible decisions as managers in the future. I reiterated this way of teaching *without* power point and *with* a diary in another course called "Research Project For Supply Chain Management" and "Ethical Supply Chain Management," a new course I created last year for the MSc Sustainable Supply Chain Management. I observed that students were much more open, participative, willing to share their experience and resources, eager to learn more, curious. They understand that sustainability management is not only ticking boxes, it is not black or white, but instead, it is a matter of considering choices, making decisions, being aware of their impacts on a variety of stakeholders (including the environment), and doing the less harm possible to others and the environment.

Finally, I found a way to transmit these messages effectively to the students and hope they will keep that in mind in their current and future work. I share below an example of students' reaction to this pedagogical approach: "This diary is a good exercise and allows me to realize that I face ethical dilemmas almost daily, both as an employee and as a consumer." I am thrilled I reached an important goal for me: to help student realize how important ethical dilemmas are and how important it is to identify and solve them, which is probably one of the greatest challenges for management education and practitioners.

Overall Take Aways

Our three stories, related to different levels in a business school, are aimed at showing some key points:

- It is very important to believe in what you do.
- Be proactive in bringing the change we need to the way management is taught nowadays.
- Everyone can contribute, and, as the saying goes, "alone you go faster but together you go further."

- Since a system is more than the sum of its parts, group co-construction leads to a proposal that responds better to the social system nature of the educational system.
- Interactive construction allows a higher reactiveness and flexibility.

Indeed, in the first year of this new schema, courses were adapted based on feedback that allowed us to evolve the course to meet students' and companies' needs. The sustainability dimension of the Master had a direct impact on the students' choices (the Master got 30% of double degree students that could choose another supply chain program and came for the sustainability dimension).

We encourage every faculty member who feels they want and can change "traditional" teaching of management into responsible/re-generative/positive impact management to propose these changes to different colleagues and throughout the different levels of a business school. Training of faculty on sustainability-related topics can be useful as long as they are not normative, otherwise the risk to develop top-down approaches is high. Such training should also be planned based on faculty needs. For example, a recent set of training courses were proposed by Excelia but a group of 20 faculty members asked for a slightly different training. The request was accepted by the faculty, representing a bottom-up approach.

In a context where digitalization has dramatically increased and where we receive so many e-mails (which wastes energy), we propose to go back to basic human relations and talk to each other whenever it is possible. Teachers let's rethink our job! As Nelson Mandela stated, "education is the most powerful weapon to change the world." Imagine our responsibility to contribute to future generations of managers! We should also rely on students: they can co-create the course with you, you can learn from them as much as they can learn from you. You do not need to know everything, which echoes Isabel Rimanoczy's book, "Stop Teaching" (Rimanoczy, 2016). Indeed, it is time to stop teaching and start learning, since it is at learning where faculty members are the best.

References

Ackoff, R. L., & Addison, H. J. (2012). *Ackoff's F/laws the cake.* Triarchy Press.
Ackoff, R. L., & Greenberg, D. (2008). *Turning learning right side up: Putting education back on track.* Pearson Prentice Hall.

Fritz, M. M. (2021). Students as change makers to achieve the sustainable development goals. In Isabel Rimanoczy and Ekaterina Ivanova (Eds), *Revolutionizing dustainability education* (pp. 133–141). Routledge.

Gonzalez-Feliu, J., Morana, J. (2014). Assessing urban logistics pooling sustainability via a hierarchic dashboard from a group decision perspective. In Macharis, C., Melo, S., Woxenius, J., Van Lier, T. (Eds), *Sustainable Logistics*, Emerald, Series Transport and Sustainability (N. 6, pp. 113–135). Emerald Group Publishing.

Rimanoczy, I. (2016). *Stop teaching: Principles and practices for responsible management education*. Business Expert Press.

Van Weele, A. (2018). Purchasing and supply chain management. Cengage Learning EMEA.

6

TRANSFORMING FINANCE EDUCATION IN BUSINESS SCHOOLS

A Finance Course Aligned with Sustainability

Luis Raúl Rodríguez-Reyes and Gabriel Penagos

Abstract

Environmental degradation, extreme poverty, and other ills humanity faces are unacceptable for modern society. Significant advances have been made in the last century, but there remain challenges to reaching a world where the promises of sustainable development are a reality. In this chapter, we share the story of the Finance Group, a small and diverse group of scholars from Jesuit business schools around the globe who answered the call from the International Association of Jesuit Universities to change business education. In designing a Finance course aligned with sustainability concepts, we hope to inspire future generations of business professionals to excel in finance and become the socially minded leaders the world needs.

This endeavor has been a transformative experience, a path for personal growth, and a challenge to our preconceived notions of business learned from years of education and teaching in economics and finance. We share our successes and failures while designing this course and provide well-intentioned advice for future projects. Our approach does not demand an end to individual freedom of choice or the elimination of company profits but instead hopes to strike a balance between the well-being of all stakeholders, shifting the shareholder wealth maximization paradigm as the sole operating principle of business behavior to a more comprehensive view.

DOI: 10.4324/9781003457763-6

Context

Our initiative came together to build a new course of finance based on the principles of sustainability portrayed in the encyclical *Laudato Si* (Pope Francis, 2015) and the United Nations 2030 Agenda for Sustainable Development (United Nations, 2015). It emerged from a call to change business education made in 2020 by the International Association of Jesuit Universities (IAJU) via the IAJU task force, which provides academic and operational leadership to the Jesuit business community, including the development of new models of business education.

The IAJU task force published a White Paper of the Inspirational Paradigm for Jesuit Business Education (IAJU, 2020), in which they diagnosed the current state of the world and called for a change to the way business subjects are taught in universities. They invited business schools to create opportunities for positive change, alleviating a world suffering from extreme poverty and environmental degradation, with insufficient nutrition, healthcare, decent jobs, and clean water, among other ills. Their call to universities was twofold:

- To generate new knowledge that informs and transforms the way business is conducted through their research; and
- To help raise awareness and provide a framework for reflection on the role each student plays in being part of the solution and to support students and faculty as they develop concrete strategies for becoming part of the solution to these challenging issues.[1]

The IAJU task force organized a discussion among scholars in the Jesuit business school international community and a dialog with some leading figures in the global business community to promote and foster initiatives emerging from this call. In the first international meeting in June 2020, the discussion was organized by general business subjects. Some of us attended that first international meeting, which is how we became the Finance Group.[2]

Our group found common ground early on and agreed on a core set of beliefs: mainstream finance education is, in general, centered on a profit maximization paradigm, which incentivizes individualistic behavior, with consumption as a measure of well-being and a preference for short-term wealth creation. This paradigm benefits firms owned by shareholders, with the primary objective being to maximize their wealth (Werner & Stoner, 2018). This short-term myopic behavior causes some of the worst problems we suffer as a global community – environmental destruction, the imbalance between returns to employment versus returns to capital, and other ills that contribute to our current unsustainability. To heed the call of the IAJU and contribute to a new paradigm in which people, the planet, and firms can thrive, we determined our teaching and research would need to change. We constructed our finance course to humbly contribute to a new way to teach business subjects with sustainability at its core.

Please note that we are not proposing to end or hamper individual freedom of choice or eliminate company profits. Instead, we propose a balance between the well-being of all stakeholders. We are looking for a shift from the shareholder wealth maximization paradigm as a sole guide for business behavior to a more comprehensive view of the production-distribution-consumption chain, in which sustainable development provides the guiding principles for human behavior.

Description of the Process

The first meetings of the Finance Group – or Finance Task Force as we called ourselves in those early days – were devoted to setting our goals, preparing a presentation, and creating a workshop for the 2020 IAJU/IAJBS/CJBE Virtual Global Conference held in July 2020. Our goal was to design a curriculum for a 14-week introductory finance course, and we intended to invite other Jesuit business community members to join us at the conference (Finance Task Force, 2020). Fortunately, some scholars answered the call and joined the team in the following months, increasing our group's strength and geographic representation.[3] The final list of our Finance Team is provided in Table 6.1.

TABLE 6.1 The Finance Team Members[4]

Name	University	Country
Alice Ann M. Parlan	Ateneo de Manila University	Philippines
Diego José Quijano	Universidad Centroamericana J.S.C.	El Salvador
Frank M. Werner	Fordham University	USA
Gabriel Penagos Londoño	Pontificia Universidad Javeriana de Bogotá	Colombia
Luis R. Rodríguez-Reyes/ Team leader	ITESO	México
Mauricio Tunnermann	Universidad Centroamericana	Nicaragua
Michael C. Tan	Ateneo de Manila University	Philippines
Omid Sabbaghi	University of Detroit Mercy	USA

Source: The authors.

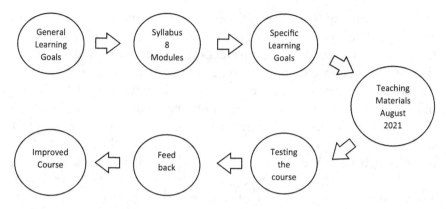

FIGURE 6.1 The process of developing the finance course.

With the added strength of new team members, the natural learning process of the team, and the support we received from the IAJU task force, we revisited our goals. In August 2020, we agreed on a new, more ambitious objective: to develop an introductory finance class to be taught asynchronously, including a syllabus and materials to cover a 14-week course. To reiterate, we went from creating a curriculum to developing a whole asynchronous finance course organically in a couple of months. Moreover, we divided the process into two stages: development and production (Finance Group, 2020).

The development stage included the construction of general learning goals, specific module learning goals, and the teaching material design for an eight-module finance course. This stage lasted from the group's inception to the end of January 2021. The production stage took seven months, ending on August 31, 2021.

Two critical elements for the production stage were the availability of funds and team members' commitment. In December 2020, the IAJU task force made its first grant call for proposals to develop teaching materials that integrate the principles of the Inspirational paradigm in the classroom. We applied and got the top spot among 31 submissions and a grant for $9,720, which we used to purchase cameras, sound equipment, editing software, and in some cases, to outsource the technical issues. In addition to IAJU's funding, some participant business schools provided help, such as software access, research assistants, and technical advice. In a personal comment, if you are starting a similar endeavor, we recommend acquiring all the help you can get; you will need it.

The second key element was the commitment and resilience of team members. During the production stage, participants of the Finance Group were involved in the production, compilation, and organization of the necessary material to teach each one of the modules. Since we had to overcome the barriers of physical distance, we each selected modules we liked and produced teaching materials individually, mainly short original videos. The team made this decision to better connect with the younger generation and to align with how they learn and receive information. We discussed the possibility of writing a textbook, a series of international lectures, and other options. Still, we finally agreed to adapt to a new way of teaching and settled on short videos for this reason. We decided to communicate the course's main content in short videos, but for most of us, these were new skills. Suddenly, we needed to write scripts, be familiar with the recording process, and learn about good-quality editing.

We produced our material in English, which was *not* the primary language for most Finance Group members. Our living rooms became recording studios and editing rooms. We shared tips about the best and the cheapest cameras, lighting solutions, green screens, and microphones and gave each other friendly feedback. Another challenge was the backdrop of the COVID-19 pandemic, which required long periods at home, and where some members faced social unrest or insecurity issues in their countries.

The complete course was delivered at the end of August 2021, uploaded to a CANVAS learning software (LMS) hosted at ITESO University in Guadalajara, Mexico, and available to be shared or exported to CANVAS or other LMS platforms at any university worldwide. Details on freely accessing the course's materials are in the outcome section. Please note that there is no charge or fee for using the material developed by the Finance Group; we only ask you for the proper citation.

Changes in Business Finance Pedagogy

As mentioned, we want to contribute to a new future where people, the planet, and firms can thrive. We look for a balance between the well-being of stakeholders and moving away from the shareholder wealth maximization paradigm as the sole guide for the behavior of firms and individuals.

Transforming our good intentions into a functioning finance course for the classroom and beyond proved to be a complex issue. The course includes modules on corporate finance, personal finance, financial markets, and social finance, each different in content and approach. Having a single approach to sustainability that fits each was almost impossible. Consequently, each team member was assigned one class module based on their professional experience, main research focus, and personal preferences.

Each member oversaw the best way to incorporate sustainability into their module's contents and materials. To guide our efforts in this task and to have a consistent framework, we used the following three questions:

1 How can United Nations Sustainable Development Goals and the encyclical letter *Laudato Si* be integrated into finance teaching?
2 How can we inspire and teach a new generation of finance professionals worldwide to be the social-minded and ethical leaders the world needs?
3 How can we combine this with the excellence in financial science that meets the challenging and changing needs of the world?

Each team member was tasked with analyzing and selecting a theoretical framework that made sense for the course's progress. Such concepts and theories also needed to include the tools and skills expected to be known by finance students. Our goal was to provide training that would allow young finance professionals to excel in their fields and inspire them.

Thankfully, changing how people conduct business and transforming it into a significant force for social progress has been a long-standing interest of many scholars, practitioners, and NGOs. There have been several theoretical and practical developments in the past decades. Concepts such as corporate social responsibility, stakeholder theory, sustainable development, and corporate sustainability have all been a part of business for many years (Chang et al., 2017). Ultimately, each module was built with a particular perspective on sustainability, sometimes a personal view, designed by each team member. We found common ground at the end of the process, which was somewhat expected since we shared our advances along the way. We meet eight times in full sessions and many other times in one-on-one meetings in which we share advances, ask and give feedback, and review specific issues.

There were two definitions of Sustainability prevalent along the course. First, Sustainable Development, in the sense of the ecological safeguard for future generations and its relationship with social inclusion and the end of poverty (United Nations, 2015), and second, the care of our common home and our responsibility in climate change and global Sustainability (Pope Francis, 2015).

In terms of theoretical framework, we mostly used the Stakeholders theory (Freeman, 1984/2010) and the triple bottom line theory (Elkington, 1997). We highlight that the firm requires to serve its stakeholders because its operation and chances of long-term survival depend on its interactions with them. We also use the three dimensions of the firm's bottom line, social, environmental, and financial, included in the triple bottom line theory, to highlight the balance a firm should have among its three dimensions, not only as a reporting tool but also as a philosophy to operate. We also use other approaches, such as ESG (Environmental, Social, and Governance), as a criterion to guide the investment selection led by sustainability objectives.

In sum, the essential concept that permeates our course is Sustainability in the form of practices and policies that can be implemented and harmonized with the firm's development and in agreement with stakeholders' objectives. Our proposal is consistent with the shift of the firm's goal from maximizing shareholder wealth to an environmental and social purpose. That is, profits for the firm are, under the new paradigm, only one of the firm's goals, not the primary outcome shareholders can expect and act to acquire.

Success and Failures

There were several instances of success in the development of this project. We highlight three of them: the achieved outcome, the course-developing process, and the creation of an international network to teach, promote, and research the place Sustainability should have in business theory and practice. Moreover, we also discuss in this section what we consider our main failures and how we propose to solve them.

The first story of success we would like to share is that we accomplished our main objective, delivering an online, asynchronous finance course on time, spending a minimum budget, and sharing it for free. This course is aligned with the sustainability principles depicted in *Laudato Si* (Pope Francis, 2015) and the United Nations 2030 Agenda for Sustainable Development (United Nations, 2015) and meets the goals set by the IAJU's White Paper and the requirements of IAJU's grant proposals. We consider all these accomplishments as a positive outcome of the process.

The course-building process was also a success for us; the decision-making process was organic, and everyone on the team had a voice and the freedom to choose participation and materials. As a result, we were able to innovate in content and in the delivery method of that content, and remarkably, after long months of volunteer work and the stress associated with an international project, we are still dear friends.

Finally, the expanding international network that has emerged from our participation in the project has proven to be of great value. These connections, fostered by IAJU and the International Association of Jesuit Business Schools (IAJBS) have allowed us to participate in teaching, meetings, research projects, publications, etc., with a growing number of partners for sustainability, both inside and outside the Jesuit business school umbrella, including the Global Movement Initiative, PRME, the IAJBS World Forum, the SMLA network, and AUSJAL.

When we were first defining the scope of our project, we had meetings with the IAJU task force and within the Finance Group. Initially, it was unclear whether an asynchronous online finance course would work as a unit or if the modules should be designed to be used independently. We questioned whether an entire course could be implemented given the natural resistance from institutional gatekeepers. Our solution was to create a course that could be used either as a complete course or just the modules. We developed a dual-purpose course that made sense as an integral eight-module class, but also had the flexibility to be understood as separate modules. For those who use the entire course, we added an introduction to present the content to faculty and students, explaining the purpose of the course, its flow, and the grading process. However, individual modules are self-contained and can be used as a part of a more extensive course designed by another teacher.

A remaining challenge is that as of April 2023, the complete course has not been taught yet at any university. After more than a year of publication and several promotions, we realized our mistake in not negotiating the implementation of the course with institutional gatekeepers in advance. As we were designing the course, we had hoped that the high-quality modules we produced would be enough to incentivize the adoption of at least a significant proportion of the course in any university. We still believe a good promotion tour with universities and teachers, inside and outside the Jesuit business community may help. In 2021 we presented the finance course at three international virtual events, in special sessions at the IAJU World Forum, the Financial Management Association, and the Academy of Business Education. We continue to reach out to institutional gatekeepers to determine how this can be accomplished. An alternative we considered is to offer the course on a university's online platform as a non-degree program.

However, not all are bad news. The developed material is currently in use, although not as initially intended. At ITESO, the Jesuit University of Guadalajara, videos from several modules have been curated into new modules and are part of the curriculum in two classes: Microeconomics and Stock-Market Investment Strategies. In the Microeconomics course, we use videos from Modules 1 and 3 to introduce the concept of sustainability, the market as a human institution, and the role of the firm and entrepreneur in the new paradigm. In the Stock-Market Investment Strategies class, we use videos from Modules 1, 3, and 4 to introduce the concept of sustainability, its relationship with financial practice, and the role of the financial manager, ESG, and green finance.

The results of this emerging strategy are promising. As of April 2023, the course accumulated 1,600 views (equivalent to 77.3 hours of viewing), all in a demographic group between 18 and 24 years of age. This statistic is significant. First, it means that we are reaching the age bracket we had initially targeted and indicates that the materials are attractive to students. Second, it suggests that distribution on social media may be warranted.

The Course

The final product is a modular, customizable, asynchronous finance course with sustainability at its core, designed to be taught in a 14 to 16-week class. It includes 56 original HD videos, as well as study guides, activities, quizzes, and tests. The course has eight content modules and an introductory module available on a CANVAS virtual learning platform. Details are available in Table 6.2. Each module starts with a student guide and an HD video and includes key concepts, reflection questions, activities, and a graded quiz or test.

TABLE 6.2 Finance Course Content

Course Modules	Developer
Introductory Remarks	Luis R. Rodríguez-Reyes
Module 1: Market Economy, Sustainability, and Finance	
Module 2: Personal Financial Management	Alice Ann M. Parlan
Module 3: Corporate Financial Management	Frank M. Werner
Module 4: Financial Markets	Gabriel Penagos Londoño
Module 5: Global Financial Management	Omid Sabbaghi
Module 6: Social Finance, Financial Inclusion, and Financial Literacy	Mauricio Tunnermann
Module 7: Public Finance	Michael C. Tan
Module 8: Towards a Post-Pandemic Financial Management Framework	Diego José Quijano

Source: The authors.

All course products are freely available to universities or individuals on the Ignited website, https://www.ignited.global/case/business-and-management/principles-financial-management-teaching-finance-aligned-sdgs-and, where you can download a complete version of the course. Alternatively, if you want access to the videos, they are available on YouTube at https://www.youtube.com/channel/UCmM_ToDd6-d02QUeDpW7uNQ.

We provide these materials to help you teach sustainability at your university or learn on your own. We only ask that you please follow the proper citation rules. We hope any student who completes the course's key elements will be inspired to use these new skills to serve teams, organizations, and society. We believe they will understand the drivers of excellence in financial science and how they are linked to evidence-based practices. They will also learn what it means to be an ethical, socially minded leader able to contribute to a flourishing, ever-changing world.

Personal Learning Outcomes and Recommendations

For us, the process was a transformative experience, a path for personal growth, and a challenge to our preconceived notions of business learned from years of education and practice in economics and finance. We recommend any student, teacher, researcher, or professional in business begin such a process of thinking and creating; it will change you and lead to a sustainable future for the good of everyone.

The first step is imagining a world in which another future is possible – where the people, the planet, and its firms can all prosper. It means working toward a world in which future generations will have better opportunities for their development, a world with less poverty and inequality, and where development is inclusive. In summary, a world in which no one is left behind.

Several practical recommendations have also emerged from our experience.

1 If you are developing teaching materials, small is better. A contained small educational product, such as a case, a small series of videos, or even a module, may have better possibilities for adoption and proportionally a more significant impact than a large product.
2 If you intend to develop a complete course, negotiate a clear path for its adoption with institutional gatekeepers in advance. Moreover,

if you are part of a funding institution, we suggest asking for institutional commitment for adoption as a part of the granting process.

3 The distribution channel is critical. Traditional distribution channels have not yet succeeded for us, but the YouTube channel, paired with newly designed smaller modules distributed among our students at ITESO, is showing some promise.

4 If you develop videos, keep them short, less than seven minutes; they are a good fit for students.

Conclusion

The Finance Group started this initiative to contribute to a better world by teaching and inspiring new generations of finance professionals. They donated their time and experience to this collective effort. The initiative's main objective was accomplished. We produced original teaching materials, including HD videos, study guides, quizzes, and tests; enough to cover a 14 to 16-week course. A small and diverse team of scholars from Jesuit business schools around the globe dedicated many months of theoretical and practical work to a task that seemed at least complex: combining sustainability, business theory, and financial practice into a course and communicating our findings in an inspiring way.

There are still significant challenges ahead for us. The developed materials still need to be exploited to their full potential. The distribution and adoption process has been slow in the traditional channels. However, there are some recent developments that at least generate a promise. Our best distribution channel is YouTube, showing the time we spend learning to communicate with the new generation of students that acquire information from the web, streaming, and other electronic means but still need to be inspired was time well spent.

In this chapter, we provided the reader with our story; we candidly shared our experience with you, the good and the bad, with not holding back. We invite you to step into the process of changing the world and be that change agent in constructing a sustainable world. So, take the step and start imagining a world in which another future is possible, where the people, the planet, and firms can all prosper. Start working for a world in which the next generations will have a better perspective of their development, a world with less poverty and inequality, in which development is inclusive, that is, a world in which no one is left behind.

Notes

1 IAJU (2020), page 2.
2 The initial members of Team Finance were Alice Ann M. Parlan, Diego Quijano, Mauricio Tunnermann and Luis Rodríguez-Reyes.
3 Gabriel Penagos, Frank Werner, Omid Sabbaghi and Michael Tan joined the group in the following months.
4 This document is written by two members of the Finance Team. To the extent the facts are available to us; based on minutes, presentations, and sometimes memory, our recollection, interpretation, and recommendations may differ from other members of the team.

References

Chang, R. D., Zuo, J., Zhao, Z. Y., Zillante, G., Gan, X. L., & Soebarto, V. (2017). Evolving theories of sustainability and firms: History, future directions and implications for renewable energy research. *Renewable and Sustainable Energy Reviews, 72*, 48–56.

Elkington, J. (1997). *Cannibals with forks: The triple bottom line of 21st-century business.* Capstone.

Finance Group. (2020). Key takeaways – minutes of the meeting of the Finance Group on 6 August 2020.

Finance Task Force. (2020). Rethinking core business courses for the new normal. Presented on 15 July 2020 at the IAJU/IAJBS/CJBE Virtual Global Conference.

Freeman, R. E. (2010). *Strategic management: A stakeholder approach.* Cambridge University Press.

International Association of Jesuit Universities - IAJU (2020). An inspirational paradigm for jesuit business education (the white paper). Retrieved from: https://iaju.org/working-groups/newparadigm-jesuit-business-education.

Pope Francis. (2015). *Encyclical Letter Laudato Si of the Holy Father Francis.* Dicastero per la Comunicazione-Libreria Editrice Vaticana. Retrieved from: https://www.vatican.va/content/francesco/en/encyclicals/documents/papa-francesco_20150524_enciclica-laudato-si.html

United Nations. (2015). *Transforming our World: The 2030 agenda for sustainable development.* U.N. Publishing. Retrieved on 26 January 2023 from https://sdgs.un.org/2030agenda.

Werner, F., & Stoner, J. (2018). Sustainability and the evolution of the shareholder wealth maximization paradigm. In *Research Handbook of Finance and Sustainability.* Edward Elgar Publishing. https://doi.org/10.4337/9781786432636.00018.

7

STUDENTS INITIATE CHANGE

Design Thinking Challenges at the University of Graz

Magdalena Rusch

Abstract

The sustainability challenges that we, as a society, face are complex and multifaceted, requiring holistic and interdisciplinary approaches. Universities and business schools are uniquely positioned to provide this kind of expertise and leadership, and it is, therefore, crucial that they play a central role in addressing these problems.

This chapter tells the story of a course that was brought to life by students who felt the need for (curriculum) change and were driven by their passion for incorporating elements they felt were missing. The course aims to provide a platform for discussing a more sustainable world and gaining knowledge about sustainable businesses and encourages a hands-on approach to turning that knowledge into action. This resulted in implementing "Design Thinking Challenges," which helped students acquire the skills needed to identify and articulate problems and fostered a collaborative learning environment to explore complex issues, question assumptions, and develop solutions for real-world sustainability problems. The aim was to empower students to take meaningful action toward a sustainable future. This chapter provides my personal perspective of what it was like for students to introduce a new course and what lessons and recommendations can be learned from this experience.

DOI: 10.4324/9781003457763-7

Context

Humanity looks toward a future shaped by pressing issues of sustainability, such as the climate crisis, biodiversity loss, overconsumption, or social inequality and therefore needs new problem-solving approaches. Universities and business schools play a special role in this endeavor because they are expected to equip students with the knowledge and skills to navigate these challenges. Therefore, I would like to ask you a question

Are universities and business schools currently adequately equipping students with the knowledge and skills needed to address sustainability challenges?

During the first years of my studies, I did not feel this was the case. I was frustrated that only one type of economic model was taught; the management theories we talked about focused on shareholder values instead of integrating a wider group of stakeholders. It seemed that managers were only there to maximize the profits of businesses, no matter at what environmental and social costs. What I learned in management and business classes was often characterized by short-term thinking, and the word "profit maximization." Socially and environmentally relevant issues were missing, or they were approached from a rather traditional or shallow sustainability perspective.

At the time, however, it was hard to see that this was a very narrow view, but I thought that this was simply the way business and business education worked. During my Master's studies, I was fortunate to learn that there are other theories (e.g., stakeholder theory, the triple bottom line, ecological economics, etc.) where, for example, nature also counts as a stakeholder or its intrinsic value is appreciated, more dimensions than just the economic one are crucial, and that there are business models with a sustainable core. Such businesses regard social, environmental, and economic sustainability as core values. For example, some aim to address social or environmental problems while generating revenue but prioritize impact over profits, adopt circular business models and design products for durability, or promote closed-loop systems to minimize waste.

The opportunities for sustainable businesses are manifold, and the exact design can take many forms. But why do I need a specialization in sustainability management to learn all this? Should not this be at the very core of economics and business curriculum? My answer to this question is, absolutely. If we take higher education seriously, we must prepare students for big societal challenges like the climate or biodiversity crisis shaping our future. Sustainability topics should be integrated into many more compulsory and not only elective courses at universities and business schools to be able to tackle such complex issues together. We need to be exposed to different perspectives as soon as possible and learn to think critically about how we can make a positive impact on the world. That's why I've been advocating for more sustainability courses to be incorporated into the curriculum and for the existing curriculum to be more interdisciplinary.

To connect with other motivated students, and because I personally believe in the need for change in the higher education system, I joined a student organization called oikos. Oikos is an international student-led organization with the mission to transform economics and management education by empowering student change agents, raising awareness for sustainability opportunities and challenges, and building institutional support for curriculum reform. The oikos chapter in Graz provided the environment for students to inspire each other, discuss bold ideas, and implement projects with like-minded people. Soon this created the desire to contribute to a more sustainable campus and university actively. This was the reason why I joined the organizing team of the Sustainability Days of the University of Graz together with three other people from oikos Graz in 2018.

The Sustainability Days at the University of Graz[1] have taken place every year since 2016. Over time, they have become one of the most important sustainability events of the year at the University of Graz. The Sustainability Days started as a bottom-up initiative by students in 2016 and have been organized by a team of motivated students every year since. From 2017 onwards, the rector, vice-rectors, and other faculty members supported the organization of the Sustainability Days. The initiative is intended to serve as a role model and stimulus for a vibrant and sustainable campus that students and employees can actively shape. The focus is on raising awareness for sustainability issues at various levels, such as in teaching and research, and sensitizing students and employees to climate protection measures and more sustainable behaviors on and off campus. Additionally, it serves as a platform where individuals from the University come together to ignite inspiration, stimulate exchange, and spark the creation of innovative projects. Every year the main themes of these Days change and new formats can be organized. For example, one time the focus was on a sustainable campus where an idea competition was started, and the winning idea was implemented afterwards. Or in another year, a panel discussion was organized that dealt with the questions of which transformations are needed in teaching to make them fit for the future.

As a member of the organizing team, I had the opportunity to propose any format for the Sustainability Days. I was particularly inspired by my experience at the "Clean Energy Design Thinking Challenge," a three-day innovation marathon for students held at the University of Klagenfurt in 2018. This event effectively brought together various essential elements that I felt were missing during my time as a student in most classes.

These elements included

- Tackling sustainability issues requires a multifaceted and cross-disciplinary approach, and this can be particularly challenging in homogeneous teams with only students of one Master's or Bachelor's program. However, this event provided an opportunity to meet with people from diverse backgrounds to address these issues head-on. It brought together students from various disciplines and fields such as economics, physics, management, sustainability science, or psychology with stakeholders from NGOs, small and large companies, and other organizations.
- I aimed to expand my knowledge of innovative methods and structured problem-solving approaches for addressing complex (sustainability) challenges. One such technique is Design Thinking (e.g., see online resources such as the HPI Academy website[2] or Stanford's school website[3] or Brown (2008)), which emphasizes setting aside personal biases and assumptions and thoroughly understanding the problem before proposing solutions. This process involves a structured approach and multiple rounds of iteration before sustainable ideas are developed and was applied during this event.
- This event provided a chance to put theoretical knowledge into action and witness how it can be transformed into practical solutions. Corporate partners and other organizations were invited to present their (real-world) sustainability challenges, and the teams developed ideas and solutions with them.
- Team-building elements and guidance from professional coaches regarding the process, as well as reflection on individual and group

learnings experiences, were particularly helpful in fostering a sense of community and collaboration among individuals who may have previously been strangers to each other and were all united by the common goal of finding sustainable solutions. In other courses, team exercises can often be frustrating without clear guidance.

After it became clear that there was no such course at the University in Graz, I decided I wanted to implement this course in Graz to provide such an inspiring experience for other students.

Description of the Process of Changing the Course

When I first set out to implement the Design Thinking Challenge at the University of Graz, it seemed daunting and felt like an impossible dream. There were so many questions to consider: where to start, who to reach out to, and what timeline is realistic to implement it?! But I was determined to make it happen.

During the Sustainability Days of 2019, I initiated and organized a sustainability co-innovation competition for students at the University of Graz. I learned that the key to making it happen was finding people who shared my vision and were open to new ideas. With the support of a handful of motivated individuals, I was able to turn this idea into reality. It was a challenging but incredibly rewarding experience, and I am very proud of what we accomplished.

I consider the following three parts essential for starting a new course as a student:

– One essential element of the whole process was to **have a team and connect to people who supported the idea**. I was fortunate to have my Sustainability Days colleagues by my side. The other students from the team, Tatiana Soto Bermudez, Hannah Muther, and Annemarie Sindler, were vital in discussing, planning, and executing the new course. Without their help, it would not have been possible to deal with all the uncertainties, navigate the ambiguities that the project brought but implement a new university course in the end. I am incredibly grateful for their support and contributions. For example, one big advantage was that we were part of the target audience for the course. We often discussed the needs and wishes of students and used that to our advantage. We constantly asked ourselves what kind of change we wanted to see and bring with this new course, what we wanted to learn but missed in (business) classes, under what conditions we learn new things best, and what would be needed for good teamwork within the course. This helped us to create a highly student-friendly course, and the feedback we received confirmed that our strategy was on the right track. We also used our student networks to spread the word about the new course and to get feedback from other students, which was an effective way of word-of-mouth marketing. The result was that many students heard about the new course and were excited to participate. However, other marketing channels were also vital to spreading the word about the new course, such as the official university channels, social media, or mailing lists. We also presented the new course in other classes, distributed leaflets, and installed posters on the campuses of the different universities in Graz.

– To have someone on board from within the University who was open to new ideas was a crucial component of our success. In this case, that person was Ralph Zettl, the team leader of the Sustainability Days. For example, he provided parts of the budget for the implementation of the course, and we could always ask him and his team for help, for example, for managing administrative tasks. He also often assisted us to find the right people to talk to. And also, other people like the rector, Peter Riedler, and the dean of studies at the faculty of environmental, regional, and educational sciences, Alfred Posch, supported the project and helped to make it possible. Initially, I did not know many people on the higher "leadership level" of the University, but that soon changed. **My advice to anyone looking to create change is not to be afraid to connect with people at all levels and to have conversations about your ideas.** The most crucial step is building relationships with people from different departments and not being afraid to ask for help and support. As I worked toward implementing the course, I often described my vision and shared my motivation for the project, which was like a "pitch" used in the start-up scene. I also asked for advice, resources, and contacts multiple times.

– A third critical factor in successfully implementing this new course was the support of a team of experienced Design Thinking coaches from the company SAP SE. They brought a wealth of knowledge and experience in running Design Thinking Challenges, empowering students, and providing valuable guidance and support, such as managing team processes or collaborating effectively. Together, as a team of students from oikos Graz (responsible for organizing the Sustainability Days where the course was part of), with employees from the University of Graz (providing resources and support) and people from the company SAP (responsible for the methodical guidance and brought in additional resources), we created and implemented a new course called the "Green Mobility Design Thinking Challenge" (GMDTC). This collaborative effort brought together the expertise of multiple parties and resulted in a truly innovative and impactful course.

The GMDTC brought together students from various disciplines, levels, and fields of study to develop sustainable and future-oriented concepts. This course was designed to go beyond traditional teaching formats and apply innovative teaching methods, such as the problem-solving and human-centered approach of Design Thinking, which encourages empathy, collaboration, experimentation, and iteration. The participating (corporate) partners were not only involved but partnered with the teams and were open to developing and learning themselves. For example, company representatives presented a sustainability challenge, and formulated a question around the topic (e.g., "What is the ideal mobility service for citizens in Graz and Styria in 2025 and beyond?") and worked together with the students to find desirable, feasible, viable, and sustainable solutions. As a result, we created a unique, hybrid, and transdisciplinary learning environment for students that encouraged them to break down entrenched thought patterns and pursue bold ideas.

Within two days, interdisciplinary teams of 30 students from 21 disciplines worked together with stakeholders from outside academia and the Design Thinking coaches to develop innovative solutions. Sustainability and the 17 SDGs were integral components of the course, promoting awareness and critical thinking about existing systems and the effects of entrepreneurial decisions. In the first year, students did not receive European Credit Transfer System (ECTS) credits for participation but a certificate of attendance. However, this changed after the first pilot phase. The second time we offered the course, students could earn ECTS points for their participation, which could have been recognized as a free elective in their study plans. In both cases, students never paid fees to participate.

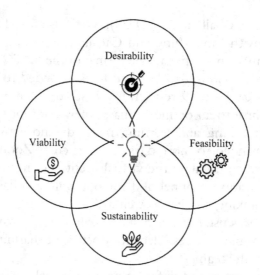

FIGURE 7.1 Four lenses of sustainable innovation in Design Thinking (author representation inspired by Santa-Maria, Vermeulen, and Baumgartner (2022).

An Integral part of Design Thinking approaches is the combination of different "lenses" for finding new solutions. Figure 7.1 shows these lenses that need to be combined for sustainable innovation: desirability, feasibility, viability, and sustainability.

Developing and implementing the course was made easier by utilizing models, frameworks, or approaches like Design Thinking as guidance and inspiration (Santa-Maria, Vermeulen, & Baumgartner (2022)). Drawing inspiration from other teaching and learning methods, such as service learning, student-centered approaches, or project-based and cooperative learning, was also beneficial. For instance, service-learning (e.g., see Resch & Knapp (2020) or Phillips (2021)) provided valuable elements related to crucial competencies such as course content, meaningful service, and critical reflection. Using these different methods and frameworks helped to create a well-rounded and effective learning experience for the students.

Successes and Failures

The success and high student demand (e.g., around 50 students applied for the course, but only up to 30 students could participate, and, after the course students asked for further courses) led to the decision to organize a second challenge in 2020, the "Sustainability

Design Thinking Challenge" (SDTC). The Sustainability Days team also changed, with Emily Jung and Carolina Rovira joining the team instead of Hannah and Tatiana. The format of the SDTC was similar to that of the GMDTC in 2019 but had to be changed to a fully online format due to COVID-19 restrictions. Instead of simply transferring the on-site course to an online format, a new concept was developed to adapt the teaching and learning methods and activities and the SDTC was expanded to more days. Tools such as Zoom, Mural, and Slack were used to facilitate the virtual event. Zoom was used as the main communication channel and for our online collaboration with the Design Thinking coaches as well as for working together in small groups. Mural was used as a virtual and collaborative whiteboard, and the teams were able to access Slack for document sharing and communication within the teams.

Both formats presented different organizational challenges but developing an entirely new course in the first year was particularly challenging. One of the biggest obstacles was dealing with the many uncertainties that arose during the planning and implementation phases and dealing with the requests from faculty or administration, as well as external stakeholders. Most notably, because there were no best practices or procedures for some planned elements, as this was the first time anyone had asked about them (e.g., special legal issues about working with company representatives or lunch delivery for students). However, we were able to convince many people to support the idea, which at the time existed only in the minds of four motivated students who were driven by their intrinsic motivation to bring change to campus.

Another challenge was that I had expected more interest from various people at the University and from outside. Initially that was not the case, and this was disappointing. For instance, getting the word out about the new course was not easy, and we had to persist in convincing people from other departments (e.g., by highlighting the benefits of the course to them or their students) to promote the course to students from other departments.

A big takeaway from the course was feedback we received when we asked students about their experience with the overall process and what motivated them to participate (translated from German):

- *I was very impressed by how much you can work out and create in a group."* – Participant 2019

- *"A little longer break. Otherwise, it was the best online event I've experienced so far."* – Participant 2020
- *"... that there are really a lot of young people who want to make a difference and that there is also hope that this will change things."* – Participant 2020

The course began to become institutionalized by the second year. In 2020, we were able to integrate the SDTC as an official University course, where students could earn credits for participating. With that, we also needed a grading system for the course. Instead of using traditional grades, the requirements for successful completion were participation and submitting a reflection paper on time. We felt that the numerical scale from 1 (very good) to 5 (insufficient/not passed) that is normally used at the University was not appropriate for this course, as the main focus was on cooperation within a team, personal development, and learning new methods and techniques to apply them to find sustainable solutions. Instead, we expected an active participation of each team member, the coaches observed their level of involvement and how they applied the content that was presented and after the course, students reflected on their learnings and challenges in a written paper which also enabled us to identify areas for potential improvement.

While the future of this course is still uncertain, it is essential to note that organizing new and innovative courses often requires more effort than organizing traditional courses and, in many cases, relies on the dedication and motivation of individuals to do the extra work. When people driving the course leave the organization, it can be challenging to continue the course and requires a good handover strategy or early consideration of potential new people taking over.

Another challenge in transforming (business) education is to go a step further than adding sustainability topics and initiate a discussion about how business and management are thought. It is necessary to shift from a profit-maximization–driven mentality for shareholders to one that prioritizes the well-being of all stakeholders, including people, the planet, and profit, to ensure a sustainable future. Implementing courses like the GMDTC and the SDTC can only be the start of or a small contribution to changing how universities and business schools approach sustainability and prepare students for the environmental and social challenges of the 21st century.

Overall Results and Low Hanging Fruits

The project was characterized by its holistic approach, bringing together a diverse range of stakeholders from within and outside higher education institutions. Collaborating with external stakeholders can provide a wealth of opportunities for other activities at universities and business schools. For instance, the partnership between universities and external stakeholders, such as corporate partners and NGOs that began with participating in the Challenge could serve as a foundation for other forms of collaboration. Initially, partners can participate in a semester project, and if the partnership proves successful for both sides, it could evolve into more intensive forms of collaboration, such as joint research projects or grant applications. Also, students benefited from the new contacts, as internships were organized afterwards and topics for Bachelor's and Master's theses were found.

Course results showed that it is possible to find business solutions that are desirable, feasible and viable, and sustainable (see Figure 7.1). Our Design Thinking Challenges successfully integrated the sustainability dimension into more traditional idea-finding methods. I highly recommend the further use of such approaches, particularly in business education, as it allows students to explore a more diverse range of options for finding and developing sustainable ideas rather than just the traditional (capitalist or business as usual) approaches. It empowers students to think outside the box and develop innovative solutions. During the course, students gained hands-on experience in effectively communicating sustainability solutions to a wide range of stakeholders, such as company representatives. They also learned how to apply their academic knowledge to create practical, sustainable innovations and how to work across organizational and disciplinary boundaries.

I hope that the implementation of the GMDTC and SDTC serves as a best practice example and a reminder of how important it is for students to have their voices heard and their ability to take ownership of their education. Often, students are highly motivated to bring change, and with the right support and resources, they can bring tremendous opportunities for universities and business schools, for example, to improve their curricula. Sometimes, all it takes is a little advice on who to contact or some encouraging words to tap into this wealth of ideas and innovation. But unfortunately, this valuable source of ideas often goes untapped. Therefore, I encourage universities and business schools to involve and empower students more often in shaping their education and actively co-create the content together with the lecturers. I believe this will contribute to developing a more meaningful and impactful education for the students.

Our story shows that committed students have the power to drive change and make a real impact in shaping their education. By taking the initiative and creating change from the bottom up, we were able to establish a new university course. Additionally, the Design Thinking Challenges format can serve as a model for other higher education institutions to implement and adapt.

Conclusion

As we look to a future shaped by pressing issues of sustainability, it is critical that universities and business schools equip students with the knowledge and skills to meet these challenges. While my own experience in higher education often left me feeling uninspired and limited by narrow-minded perspectives, I have since realized the vast potential for positive change through alternative economic models and a focus on the well-being of all stakeholders, including nature. I believe sustainability must be integrated as a core component of many educational programs to prepare for the societal challenges ahead. It is not just a specialized field but a crucial perspective that should be considered in every field or area.

By introducing the GMDTC and SDTC courses, we aimed to empower students to put their knowledge into action and to feel or experience a sense of community as well as self-efficacy in the pursuit of finding sustainable solutions for real-world problems. Through this course, students gained a comprehensive understanding of various sustainability issues and the Design Thinking approach. They also had the opportunity to sharpen their skills in areas such as project management, presentations, conducting and evaluating interviews, and working with different stakeholders. By working with professional coaches from SAP, the student teams were guided through the different Design Thinking steps that helped to develop innovative and sustainable ideas with and for the participating partners.

Working together in inter- and transdisciplinary teams was crucial for generating sustainable solutions. By setting aside their own preconceptions, students learned to collaborate and develop a shared understanding of the problem at hand. In this diverse group setting, students were exposed to different perspectives, allowing them to learn from each other and understand each other's "language" or jargon. They learned about other disciplines and values or paradigms behind them. We also tried to ensure that the differences between them were enriching rather than divisive. This is especially important when students from different fields, such as physics, business management, and/or psychology, come together. Higher education should foster formats allowing students to learn each other's "languages" and collaborate to find sustainable solutions. Let's work together to create a future where our higher education system is one of progress, innovation, and sustainability.

Personal Learning Outcome and Recommendations

One of the most valuable lessons learned is that the first step toward change is to start acting. It doesn't matter how small or insignificant it may seem, as you never know where it may lead. However, bringing change might take time, perseverance, and determination. One effective strategy for me was to seek out allies. Together with these allies (e.g., student organizations, partners from the university, or other partners like the coaches from SAP), I, a motivated Master's student, could implement a new course from the bottom up. The hard work and commitment to change were truly rewarding as I saw the progress made during the course and read the feedback and reflection papers of the students later.

To truly equip students to tackle societal challenges and develop critical thinking skills, implementing inclusive and innovative teaching, and learning concepts is essential. The key takeaway is that every step, no matter how small, counts and can lead to something bigger and more impactful. It can be frightening to take responsibility for your own education, but surrounding yourself with like-minded people who are also passionate about making a difference is very helpful and can help you find the courage to act. For me, it was crucial to be surrounded by people who shared my vision of creating a more sustainable, thriving, and regenerative world, which can start in the classroom. Organizations like oikos provide an ideal "breeding ground" where students can come together to support each other and develop a sense of community. Both aspects are crucial for the courage to start something and the perseverance not to give up too soon.

Other networks, within or outside of the university or business school, can also be a valuable source of inspiration for new methods, tools, and teaching approaches. Exchanging ideas with others can help you learn from each other and share ideas or join forces to implement innovative ideas together. For example, the exchange of experience and knowledge also took place at the meetings of the network "Alliance of Sustainable Universities"[4] – an association of universities in Austria founded in 2012 to promote sustainability at universities. If such networks are unavailable in your country, a starting point could be to initiate one.

For lecturers, involving students more often can be a source of inspiration. For example, new ideas can be developed by inviting students to take ownership of their education, including them more in class, and understanding the topics and questions that are important to them. Additionally, exploring online resources such as case studies on various topics can provide valuable insights. For example, free case studies on sustainability in business education (e.g., oikos case studies)[5] can be found online and provide a wealth of information and inspiration for educators.

Today's students are the creators of tomorrow's world, and what they learn in universities and business schools will shape their ability to contribute to a more sustainable future. We cannot build a truly sustainable world without higher education for sustainable development where students are feeling true ownership of their education.

Notes

1 *Organisationsteam Nachhaltigkeitstage Universität Graz.* Der Nachhaltigkeitstag der Uni Graz. (n.d.). https://nachhaltigkeitstag.uni-graz.at/de/
2 *What is design thinking.* HPI Academy. (2021, December 9). https://hpi-academy.de/en/design-thinking/what-is-design-thinking/
3 Stanford d.school. (n.d.). https://dschool.stanford.edu/
4 *Alliance of Sustainable Universities.* nachhaltigeuniversitaeten.at. (2022, August 2). https://nachhaltigeuniversitaeten.at/
5 Oikos Case Studies. Oikos International. (2021, November 30). https://oikos-international.org/

References

Brown, T. (2008). Design thinking. *Harvard Business Review, 86*(6), 84.
Phillips, B. (2021). Reciprocal empowerment through remote service learning: How to create learning opportunities that embrace difference and foster social justice. In Padilla Rodriguez, B. C. & Armellini, A. (Eds.). *Cases on*

Active Blended Learning in Higher Education. IGI Global. 10.4018/978-1-7998-7856-8.ch004, pp. 65–85.

Resch, K., Knapp, M. (Eds.) (2020). Service learning – A workbook for higher education. An output of the ENGAGE STUDENTS project. Download via: https://www.engagestudents.eu/wp-content/uploads/2021/03/Service-Learning.-A-Workbook-for-Higher-Education.pdf

Santa-Maria, T., Vermeulen, W. J. V., & Baumgartner, R. J. (2022). The circular sprint: Circular business model innovation through design thinking. *Journal of Cleaner Production, 362.* https://doi.org/10.1016/j.jclepro.2022.132323

Additional

Please also find the after-videos of the courses here:
– Green Mobility Design Thinking Challenge (GMDTC) 2019: https://www.youtube.com/watch?v=ffxg0_Dsed0
– Sustainability Design Thinking Challenge (SDTC) 2020: https://www.youtube.com/watch?v=ankQtd8DI8Q

And some pictures of the courses here:
– GMDTC 2019: https://www.facebook.com/media/set/?set=a.864606343893769&type=3
– SDTC 2020: https://www.facebook.com/media/set/?set=a.1310885559265843&type=3

8

EDUCATING STUDENTS AS FUTURE TRANSITION INTERMEDIARIES FOR CIRCULAR ECOSYSTEMS

Jean-Claude Boldrini and Donatienne Delorme

Abstract

Higher education institutions (HEIs) have a fundamental role to play in the education of students who will soon be responsible for meeting the socio-environmental challenges of the 21st century. In this chapter, we report on a 10-year experiment to design, test, disseminate, and evaluate a circular business model called BM^3C^2. We present the pedagogical uses we made of this model during workshops and graduation projects. Our goal is to prepare students to become sustainability transition intermediaries as well as reflective and committed citizens. To this end, we believe that graduation projects are an opportunity for students to gain initial hands-on experience with sustainability issues. We also think that such projects can be improved with more interdisciplinarity and with "complex thinking." We share what we have learned during the experiment about the benefits and limitations of both the BM^3C^2 tool and the graduation projects. We also provide recommendations to colleagues or HEIs who would like to adopt these approaches.

Introduction

Faced with the challenges of the 21st century (climate change, depletion of natural resources, collapse of biodiversity, societal upheavals, etc.), higher education institutions (HEIs) have a central role to play in producing and disseminating new knowledge, in creating new visions

DOI: 10.4324/9781003457763-8

for societies, and in educating future generations about the complexity of these challenges (Figueiró et al., 2022; Kopnina, 2020; Marouli, 2021; Serrano-Bedia & Perez-Perez, 2022). We conducted a 10-year experiment to design management tools and training modules to prepare students to become, in their near professional lives, possible intermediaries in sustainability transitions (Kivimaa et al., 2019) as well as responsible leaders and committed citizens (Figueiró & Raufflet, 2015; Gröschl & Gabaldon, 2018). To effectively implement sustainability in education, the most relevant concepts, methods, and tools should be identified and selected, or sometimes created. During this process we also observed that there is a skills gap among faculty, as expectations are shifting from classical disciplinary teaching toward interdisciplinary education that integrates sustainability factors (Mokski et al., 2023; Zacchia et al., 2022).

Our research and pedagogical efforts focused on incorporating research, teaching and learning techniques to the transition toward a Circular Economy (CE) by reinforcing the links between CE and strong sustainability (Schröder et al., 2019; Serrano-Bedia & Perez-Perez, 2022). Many authors have emphasized their importance for the CE transition (Mendoza et al., 2019; Nußholz, 2017) or for sustainability transitions (Hernández-Chea et al., 2021) due to their powerful potential leverage to supporting a systemic change. Among the major CE concepts (nRs principles, closed loops, value retention …), we focused our attention on innovative business models (BMs). We see our work extending that of pioneering authors who have developed pedagogical approaches for teaching sustainability (Carew & Mitchell, 2008; Stubbs & Cocklin, 2008) or CE (Kirchherr & Piscicelli, 2019; Mendoza et al., 2019; Serrano-Bedia & Perez-Perez, 2022).

The collective experiment we carried out in Nantes Université (France) combined several activities. Table 8.1 summarizes its different phases to show "who did what and when." Beginning in 2013, after generating awareness through research and students' projects, we started, in 2015, to build and test a BM tool named BM^3C^2 through research and pedagogical experiment. It was conducted with master's level students in innovation management, environmental economics, business administration, and engineering. The experiment was linked with courses in "Ecodesign, life cycle assessment & circular economy" or "Business models in circular economy." Their duration ranged from 14 to 30 hours.

TABLE 8.1 Experiments and Research Phases to Build the BM3C2 Tool

Phase	1. Design		2. Field-test and didactization	3. Disseminate	4. Assess
	Awareness	Design			
Period	2013–2017	2018–2020	2018–2021	2019–2022	2021–2023
Main activities	Guidance of CE projects for SMEs and NGOs through research and Master students' graduation projects or workshops.	Design of a new sustainable/circular BM tool, BM^3C^2, to support the transition toward the CE.	Field-testing and didactizing the BM^3C^2 tool in workshops and in new graduation projects.	Use of the BM^3C^2 tool with various students and professionals. Presentation of the BM^3C^2 in ± 40 conferences, research seminars, and publications. Design and putting online a website presenting the BM^3C^2 tool.	Assess former practices to further improve the supervision of graduation projects.
Main actors	Boldrini J.-C., Antheaume N.	Boldrini J.-C., Antheaume N.	Boldrini J.-C., Elie M., Kengmogne H., Antheaume N., Brayer G.	Boldrini J.-C, Elie M., Kengmogne H., Antheaume N., Brayer G.	Boldrini J.-C.,Delorme D.
Main reference literature (inputs)	CE, BM innovation	Sustainable and circular BMs, circular ecosystems	Education for sustainability, environment, sustainable development, and CE		Inter/transdisciplinarity, complexity, graduation projects
Publications and resources (outputs)	Boldrini (2016a, 2016b)	Boldrini and Antheaume (2019, 2021)	Boldrini (2020)	Boldrini and Elie (2021) Website: http://www.bm3c2.fr/	Boldrini and Delorme (2022)

The following information details the four stages of design, field testing/didactization, dissemination, and assessment of the BM³C² framework. We also share what we have learned about this business tool, what we think about its dissemination in HEIs and businesses, and we provide some recommendations to colleagues who would like to use it.

Designing a Theoretical Circular BM Tool to Better Implement and Teach the CE

As presented in Table 8.1, from 2013 to 2017, we started with a phase of generating awareness and exploration of CE concepts. Initially, we found our business partners had only a partial understanding of what the CE was. Significantly, we observed that business' heterogeneity, in terms of values, needs, and expectations, could lead to misunderstandings or conflicts in changing their business practices. At that time, there were no tools or frameworks to deal with the topic of transition to CE.

Our first research work was developed to demonstrate the interest of the "value management" approach (EN 1325 and EN 12973 European standards) to conduct CE transition projects (Boldrini, 2016a) and to design sustainable product-service systems (Boldrini, 2016b). We wanted to show how to put these concepts into practice effectively. Fortunately, a growing body of literature highlighted the importance of BM innovation in advancing the CE transition (Nußholz, 2017; Planing, 2015). By working on CE projects, we were increasingly aware that the CE transition would lead to tensions in changing BMs (Boldrini, 2020). Gradually, sustainable BM frameworks (Bocken et al., 2015; Elkington & Upward, 2016; Joyce & Paquin, 2016) as well as circular BM frameworks (Antikainen & Valkokari, 2016; Lewandowski, 2016) were published.

Unfortunately, as we tried to apply these resources in our research activity or for the projects with the students, we found several limitations. First, no circular BM visually showed the flows (material, energy, etc.) and interconnections among several organizations. As it is impossible for any organization to make a transition toward the CE on its own and without representation of the necessary interconnections between BMs, stakeholders could not clearly understand where or how to coordinate actions for a shared value proposition. Second and consequently, closed loops are one of the main CE principles, but no published circular BM clearly represented the direct and reverse logistic flows between organizations. Third, the sustainable or circular value propositions did not always adopt a 3P approach (People, Planet, Prosperity). This under-represented the complexity of social and environmental systems. Fourth, neither guidelines, nor operational principles were provided to practically guide implementation. Essentially, the research we conducted revealed that existing BMs did not offer integration to CE we hoped for.

Consequently, in 2018 we began to develop our own framework, called BM³C², standing for "Business Model Multi-actor, Multi-level, Circular and Collaborative" (Boldrini & Antheaume, 2019, 2021). In our design, we put particular emphasis on (i) defining a clear and common sustainable value proposition (Kristensen & Remmen, 2019; Yang et al., 2017), (ii) identifying junk resources (typically referred to as waste) (Warnier et al., 2013) that could be valued, (iii) capturing formerly uncaptured values for sustainable innovation (Yang et al., 2017; Zacho et al., 2018), and (iv) visually representing the forward and reverse flows of material, energy, money, and information between multiple organizations (Täuscher & Abdelkafi, 2017).

Since CE requires thinking beyond a single organization level, the BM³C² framework adopts an assessment of project results at three levels: the micro level of each organization, the meso level of their network, ecosystem or sector, and the macro level (cities, regions, countries, or even the entire planet). The main contribution of the BM³C² framework is that it diagrams connections among multiple BMs. Figure 8.1 illustrates the framework with two organizations A and B.

The multilevel model thus encourages more systemic thinking about the interdependence of organizations and the proactive management of the multiple stakeholders to collaboratively connect and align their respective BMs according to CE principles.

Field-Testing and Improving the BM3C2 Tool in Classes and Real Business Cases

During a second phase (2018–2021), we tested and improved the BM³C² framework using real business cases to develop a pedagogical dimension of the model (Boldrini & Elie, 2021). Over a three-year period we organized 15 workshops lasting from three hours to one day, five- to six-month graduation projects, and five vocational workshops involving more than 450 people (students, partner consultants, and business professionals) from multiple organizations. The workshops

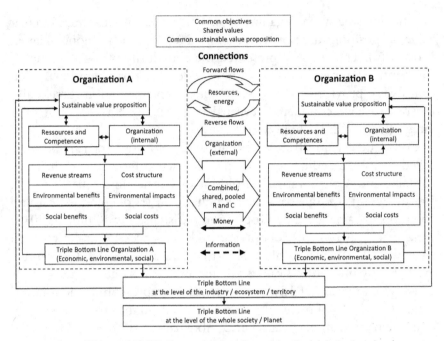

FIGURE 8.1.   The BM³C² framework. Source: Boldrini & Antheaume (2021, p. 6.

were based on real business cases that we had worked on in previous years.

During the workshops, participants were given a brief presentation of the case and the organizations involved. If they did not have prerequisites in CE or in sustainable/circular BMs, they received a brief training before the BM³C² framework was presented to them. Each participant was asked to adopt the role of one of the parties involved and to apply the BM³C² framework to the business case. Together, teams designed a sustainable value proposition that connected and aligned the BMs of each organization involved. Role-plays, creativity, and ideation sessions were experimented to both contribute to our objectives of greater circularity/sustainability and strengthen the engagement of participants. Participants could play the role of key stakeholders based on psychological profiles provided to them. Sometimes the leader of the business attended workshops and interacted with participants. Other times, student-consulting teams wrote reports for the organization with recommendations for the CE transition.

To improve the BM³C² framework we analyzed how participants used it in their graduation project reports and during workshops. At the end of the workshops, the participants were invited to complete an assessment and we analyzed 208 results. Thanks to many iterations between academic literature, experiments in various contexts (academic, professional) and assessments with hundreds of people, we became confident that the BM^{3}C^2 framework had not only strong theoretical foundations vis-à-vis the literature on CE and circular BMs but had also the same pedagogical robustness. In other words, it was teachable to students and useful for practitioners. Some of the partner–consultants involved in the experiments have adopted the framework for their customers. The experiment has also been conducted in a Cameroonian and a Vietnamese university, respectively with 114 and 16 students.

We regularly compared our practices to literature on sustainability, sustainable development, and CE education. This literature agrees on two main practices to "renew" pedagogy in HEIs. First, it favors a learner-centered pedagogy over a content-centered pedagogy, that is, a pedagogy where the learner is a cognitively active participant in the construction of his or her knowledge. This allows him or her to develop problem-solving and critical thinking skills, which are important in the education of responsible citizens (Figueiró & Raufflet, 2015). Secondly, sustainability pedagogies incorporate action-based, problem-based, peer-to-peer learning as well as experiential and collaborative approaches within small multi or interdisciplinary work groups (Kirchherr & Piscicelli, 2019; Leal Filho et al., 2018). Learning outcomes in these cases are not only cognitive but also relational and affective (Gatti et al., 2019). Furthermore, the meaning that students find in these activities increases their engagement and motivation (Figueiró & Raufflet, 2015; Stubbs & Cocklin, 2008). We concluded that our workshops where students used role-play and team effort to design a sustainable value proposition met criteria for transforming business education.

A kind of ideal pedagogical practice seems to be achieved with project-based learning, especially if it takes place in multidisciplinary teams and involves real and complex projects with high social and environmental relevance, carried out in partnership with companies, public authorities, NGOs, or other stakeholders (Gatti et al., 2019; Leal Filho et al., 2018). The graduation projects and workshops we conducted engaged students in situations where they faced many uncertainties without simple answers. Even without substantial expertise in CE, students could readily use the BM^{3}C^2 framework, and they appreciated the dimension of learning better by doing. They also recognized that project work prepares them for future problem-solving and decision-making.

The main difficulties students reported concerned limited time in the workshops and too much information but not enough quantitative data about the cases. Verbatim comments reveal other difficulties typical of the reality of innovation business projects: need for action in situations of uncertainty, systemic dimension of ecological transition issues, tensions between the factual and axiological dimensions of sustainability. Reviewing the range of workshops and graduation projects we conducted, we found that the graduation projects came closer to ideal characteristics defined in literature (van der Marel et al., 2022).

Disseminating the BM3C2 Tool and Associated Teaching Resources

The BM^3C^2 tool has now been presented in over 40 conferences, research seminars, and publications. We were gratified that Nantes Université (France) provided financial support to share what we learned in developing and teaching the BM^3C^2 framework through the website http://www.bm3c2.fr/. The website is designed to be an open educational resource and any organization or HEI that wishes to do so can easily and freely appropriate these resources. Some materials included on the site are explanations of CE and its BMs, the BM^3C^2 framework presented through two videos and an interactive matrix, and its theoretical construction. A library offers six pedagogical business cases and additional resources such as tutorials, a teacher's guide, a downloadable blank template to support collaborative work, and a bibliography. The website is currently only in French, except for one business case which is also in English. Academic colleagues and professionals have expressed their satisfaction with the free sharing of educational resources and for their quality and have indicated that they use them in their professional activities.

Unlike lectures where the teacher often provides answers to questions that the students may not yet be aware of, in our workshops and graduation projects learning becomes meaningful due to experiential learning. Students are more cognitively active, more motivated, and more socially and emotionally engaged through collaborative work with their peers. Graduation projects allowed students to experiment in the role of consultants with a real assignment defined by a business client. The use of the BM^3C^2 framework, allowed them to gain a first "hands-on" experience into a real business case. However, the most important outcome is perhaps not the acquisition of instrumental knowledge on CE and CBMs, but rather an awareness of the key role that they could play in the future as professionals as well as citizens.

Recommendations

Based on our experience, we can make a few recommendations to any HEI seeking to conduct an interdisciplinary program using the BM^3C^2 framework to implement CE. We suggest starting with one to two half-day workshops that bring together students from at least two disciplines. While multidisciplinary teams would be the best structure, we realize this often requires complex institutional support.

Once teachers are familiar with the concepts of CE and sustainability and with the BM^3C^2 framework, our second recommendation is to give priority to graduation projects, which we believe to be the best option for students to gain hands-on experience with sustainability issues and to prepare them to be future transition intermediaries (Kivimaa et al., 2019) and promote circular ecosystems innovation (Konietzko et al., 2020). HEIs that have the ambition to become key players in the sustainability transitions could utilize the BM^3C^2 framework not only to evolve toward a sustainable campus but also to align with institutional partners to implement sustainable/circular ecosystems in their territory. They might also incorporate these processes in core curriculum programs and compulsory courses.

During our journey, we learned how important it is to pay attention to the many stakeholders of these projects to ensure mutual understanding among participants, to build trust, and to develop a common language. Aligning schedules with multiple participants remains a challenge, as each actor may have other priorities to deal with. For graduation projects, it is important that the teacher has a multidisciplinary profile, and it would be even better to use an interdisciplinary supervisory team. While graduation projects are pedagogically rich, they are time-consuming, and teachers must be motivated. However, they provide valuable material for developing case studies that can be used in subsequent years to illustrate the theoretical concepts of the courses. Through this experiment, we had the great opportunity to connect our three main missions: teaching, research, and knowledge dissemination.

We think that the teams that use the BM^3C^2 tool should be truly multidisciplinary. It is why we consider that the highly interdisciplinary concepts of Edgar Morin's "complex thinking" a particularly strong common language for collectively addressing sustainability issues.

Taking a Step Back through Interdisciplinarity and Complex Thinking

Addressing sustainability problems in graduation projects challenges students with complex issues, difficulties in problem formulation, competing objectives, multiple dimensions to apprehend, and multiple but incompatible solutions (Weber et al., 2021). While graduation projects conducted for real organizations are particularly formative and well suited to sustainability education, a persistent challenge is project complexity, uncertainty, and the necessity of diverse knowledge. To enable students to have a comprehensive understanding of these wicked problems and to teach it appropriately requires HEIs to make a paradigm shift toward a systemic perspective emphasizing interdisciplinary understanding, collaboration, and cooperation (Zacchia et al., 2022). This is a direct challenge to the single discipline-centered silos constructed by most HEI's.

The most multidisciplinary teams that we were able to gather were only bi-disciplinary ones, bringing together students in a master's degree in environmental economics and student-engineers. Despite this limitation, students benefited from the virtues of multistakeholder collaboration. We believe that the pedagogical benefits of graduation projects could be even greater with more interdisciplinary teams. In this case, institutional support would be needed to make it possible for heterogeneous teams to come together periodically over many months.

To better train students to face the complexity of sustainability problems, we think that Edgar Morin's work on "complex thinking" (Morin, 2008) and education for the future (Morin, 1999) fits very well with our work. In research started in 2021, we combined a review of the literature dedicated to the sustainability education with Morin's "complex thinking." Among Morin's tremendous work, we note that he wrote a transdisciplinary *Method*, in six volumes, for thinking about complexity, and he derived seven guiding principles from it. In four books he showed how education could contribute to linking knowledge and reform thinking to preparing human beings to tackle the challenges of the 21st century (for a clear summary in English of Morin's complex thinking and transdisciplinarity, see Cruz et al., 2006 and Gröschl & Gabaldon, 2018). Morin believes that genuine understanding and effective action result from inquiry needs and confrontation with uncertainties and contradictions. This is exactly the situation of the graduation projects. His concepts for "complex thinking" such as interactions, order/disorder, distinction/conjunction, systemic, dialogic and hologrammic principles, retroactive and recursive loops, self-eco-organization can help better understanding sustainability challenges.

Morin's ambition is also to reconnect scientific knowledge with philosophical reflection and ethics. By making this ambition our own, we could help students develop critical thinking, sense of responsibility, and ethical values needed to face today's global challenges. By confronting our feedback on previous projects and the literature on sustainability education, interdisciplinarity, and complex thinking, we developed proposals to improve the supervision of graduation projects to better think, know, and act in the Anthropocene era (Boldrini & Delorme, 2022).

Conclusion

This chapter has reported on the path we followed to design, test, teach, disseminate, and assess a sustainability training tool, BM^3C^2, and on our pedagogical approach to train students to tackle sustainability issues. We believe that skills acquired, particularly during graduation projects, enable them to:

- problematize and develop strategic skills to navigate the unknown and deal with uncertainties,
- hear and understand the points of view of other actors and seek consensus to enrich collective action,
- reason on several levels, from the individual to society, and understand the links between levels in the perspective of building resilient and equitable societies while respecting planetary boundaries,
- navigate between critical thinking and collective creativity to overcome the tensions of collective action from above,
- progress in terms of reflexivity, autonomy, commitment, responsibility, trust, and awareness of our interdependencies.

To colleagues who would seek to transform management education toward greater sustainability, we recommend drawing on proposals in the academic literature: confront students with the complex problems of real projects that have high social and environmental relevance, carried out in small multidisciplinary teams and in partnership with external stakeholders.

Beyond the students, the supervisory team should be multidisciplinary. The transformation of teaching and education can be gradual. It can start with short workshops of one or two half-days, for example, to raise students' awareness of sustainability issues (Gröschl & Gabaldon, 2018; Mokski et al., 2023). It can later be deepened during graduation projects lasting several months at the master's level. Subsequently, the entire curriculum can be revised so that the principles of interdisciplinarity, complexity, and sustainability permeate each module. Gradually, the principles of the CE and sustainability can be disseminated through all training courses and components so that HEIs can become sustainable campuses (Mendoza et al., 2019) within ecosystems, with their main partners, that are themselves circular (Konietzko et al., 2020).

References

Antikainen, M., & Valkokari, K. (2016). A framework for sustainable circular business model innovation. *Technology Innovation Management Review*, *6*(7), 1–12.

Bocken, N. M. P., Rana, P., & Short, S. W. (2015). Value mapping for sustainable business thinking. *Journal of Industrial and Production Engineering*, *32*(1), 67–81.

Boldrini, J.-C. (2016a). Conduire la transition vers l'économie circulaire avec le management par la valeur. Les mutations de la filière de recyclage des films plastiques maraîchers usagés. *1ère Journée de l'innovation Abbé Grégoire*, Conservatoire National des Arts et Métiers, Paris, 31 mars.

Boldrini, J.-C. (2016b). Le management par la valeur: une méthode pour concevoir les systèmes produit – service de l'économie circulaire? *Colloque ACFAS – Science du design et recherche-action en organisation et projet complexe*, Montréal (Québec), 9–10 mai.

Boldrini, J.-C. (2020). La transition vers l'économie circulaire et ses tensions dans la mutation des modèles d'affaires. *Management International, 25*(4), 37–48.

Boldrini, J.-C., & Antheaume, N. (2019). Visualizing the connection and the alignment between business models in a circular economy. A circular framework based on the RCOV model. *XXVIIIe Conférence de l'Association Internationale de Management Stratégique*, Dakar, 11–14 juin.

Boldrini, J.-C., & Antheaume, N. (2021). Designing and testing a new sustainable business model tool for multi-actor, multi-level, circular, and collaborative contexts. *Journal of Cleaner Production, 309*, 127209.

Boldrini, J.-C., & Delorme, D. (2022). Former les acteurs des transitions en Anthropocène. L'apport des projets tuteurés dans l'enseignement supérieur. *XXXIème Conférence de l'Association Internationale de Management Stratégique*, Annecy, 31 mai – 3 juin.

Boldrini, J.-C., & Elie, M. (2021). Former à la transition écologique dans l'enseignement supérieur. L'exemple d'une pédagogie active d'apprentissage des modèles d'affaires circulaires. *XXXᵉᵐᵉ Conférence de l'Association Internationale de Management Stratégique*, en ligne, 1–4 juin.

Carew, A. L., & Mitchell, C. A. (2008). Teaching sustainability as a contested concept: Capitalizing on variation in engineering educators' conceptions of environmental, social and economic sustainability. *Journal of Cleaner Production, 16*(1), 105–115.

Cruz, L. B., Pedrozo, E. Á., & Estivalete, V. D. F. B. (2006). Towards sustainable development strategies: A complex view following the contribution of Edgar Morin. *Management Decision, 44*(7), 871–891.

Elkington, R., & Upward, A. (2016). Leadership as enabling function for flourishing by design. *Journal of Global Responsibility, 7*(1), 126–144.

Figueiró, P. S., & Raufflet, E. (2015). Sustainability in higher education: a systematic review with focus on management education. *Journal of Cleaner Production, 106*, 22–33.

Figueiró, P. S., Neutzling, D. M., & Lessa, B. (2022). Education for sustainability in higher education institutions: A multi-perspective proposal with a focus on management education. *Journal of Cleaner Production, 339*, 130539.

Gatti, L., Ulrich, M., & Seele, P. (2019). Education for sustainable development through business simulation games: An exploratory study of sustainability gamification and its effects on students' learning outcomes. *Journal of Cleaner Production, 207*, 667–678.

Gröschl, S., & Gabaldon, P. (2018). Business schools and the development of responsible leaders: A proposition of Edgar Morin's transdisciplinarity. *Journal of Business Ethics, 153*(1), 185–195.

Hernández-Chea, R., Jain, A., Bocken, N. M., & Gurtoo, A. (2021). The business model in sustainability transitions: A conceptualization. *Sustainability, 13*(11), 5763.

Joyce, A., & Paquin, R. L. (2016). The triple layered business model canvas: A tool to design more sustainable business models. *Journal of Cleaner Production, 135*, 1474–1486.

Kirchherr, J., & Piscicelli, L. (2019). Towards an education for the circular economy (ECE): Five teaching principles and a case study. *Resources, Conservation and Recycling, 150*, 104406.

Kivimaa, P., Boon, W., Hyysalo, S., & Klerkx, L. (2019). Towards a typology of intermediaries in sustainability transitions: A systematic review and a research agenda. *Research Policy, 48*(4), 1062–1075.

Konietzko, J., Bocken, N., & Hultink, E. J. (2020). Circular ecosystem innovation: An initial set of principles. *Journal of Cleanear Production, 253*, 119942.

Kopnina, H. (2020). Education for the future? Critical evaluation of education for sustainable development goals. *The Journal of Environmental Education, 51*(4), 280–291.

Kristensen, H. S., & Remmen, A. (2019). A framework for sustainable value propositions in product-service systems. *Journal of Cleaner Production, 223*, 25–35.

Leal Filho, W., Raath, S., Lazzarini, B., Vargas, V. R., De Souza, L., Anholon, R., ... Orlovic, V. L. (2018). The role of transformation in learning and education for sustainability. *Journal of Cleaner Production, 199*, 286–295.

Lewandowski, M. (2016). Designing the business models for circular economy—Towards the conceptual framework. *Sustainability, 8*(1), 43.

Marouli, C. (2021). Sustainability education for the future? Challenges and implications for education and pedagogy in the 21st century. *Sustainability, 13*(5), 2901.

Mendoza, J. M. F., Gallego-Schmid, A., & Azapagic, A. (2019). Building a business case for implementation of a circular economy in higher education institutions. *Journal of Cleaner Production, 220*, 553–567.

Mokski, E., Leal Filho, W., Sehnem, S., & de Andrade, J. B. S. O. (2023). Education for sustainable development in higher education institutions: An approach for effective interdisciplinarity. *International Journal of Sustainability in Higher Education, 24*(1), 96–117.

Morin, E. (1999). *Seven complex lessons in education for the future.* United Nations Educational, Scientific and Cultural Organization, Paris.

Morin, E. (2008). *On complexity.* Hampton Press.

Nußholz, J. L. (2017). Circular business models: Defining a concept and framing an emerging research field. *Sustainability, 9*(10), 1810.

Planing, P. (2015). Business model innovation in a circular economy reasons for non-acceptance of circular business models. *Open journal of business model innovation, 1*(11), 1–11.

Schröder, P., Bengtsson, M., Cohen, M., Dewick, P., Hofstetter, J., & Sarkis, J. (2019). Degrowth within–Aligning circular economy and strong sustainability narratives. *Resources, Conservation and Recycling, 146*, 190–191.

Serrano-Bedia, A.-M., & Perez-Perez, M. (2022). Transition towards a circular economy: A review of the role of higher education as a key supporting stakeholder in web of science. *Sustainable Production and Consumption, 31*, 82–96.

Stubbs, W., & Cocklin, C. (2008). Teaching sustainability to business students: Shifting mindsets. *International Journal of Sustainability in Higher Education, 9*(3), 206–221.

Täuscher, K., & Abdelkafi, N. (2017). Visual tools for business model innovation: Recommendations from a cognitive perspective. *Creativity and Innovation Management, 26*(2), 160–174.

van der Marel, I., Munneke, L., & de Bruijn, E. (2022). Supervising graduation projects in higher professional education–A literature review. *Educational Research Review, 37*, 100462.

Warnier, V., Weppe, X., & Lecocq, X. (2013). Extending resource-based theory: Considering strategic, ordinary and junk resources. *Management Decision, 51*(7), 1359–1379.

Weber, J. M., Lindenmeyer, C. P., Liò, P., & Lapkin, A. A. (2021). Teaching sustainability as complex systems approach: A sustainable development goals workshop. *International Journal of Sustainability in Higher Education, 22*(8), 25–41.

Yang, M., Evans, S., Vladimirova, D., & Rana, P. (2017). Value uncaptured perspective for sustainable business model innovation. *Journal of Cleaner Production,* 140, 1794–1804.

Zacchia, G., Cipri, K., Cucuzzella, C., & Calderari, G. (2022). Higher education interdisciplinarity: Addressing the complexity of sustainable energies and the green economy. *Sustainability, 14*(4), 1998.

Zacho, K. O., Mosgaard, M., & Riisgaard, H. (2018). Capturing uncaptured values—A Danish case study on municipal preparation for reuse and recycling of waste. *Resources, Conservation and Recycling, 136,* 297–305.

9

TEACHING SUSTAINABILITY FROM BENEATH THE SURFACE

The Permeable Membrane between Business and Nature

Miguel Cordova and Marina A. Schmitz

Abstract

Business and nature have more in common than we might think. Nature is engaged in synergies, ambidexterity, prioritizing resources, mergers and acquisitions, networking, strategic planning, and many other processes which we consider unique to the business world. Hence, merging these two apparently different worlds could feel awkward. However, we realized that discussing how theories, models, and perspectives we usually teach in business and management education relate to how natural ecosystems perform and survive could be truly eye-opening for students. This chapter provides insights into our motivation to dive further into the idea of bridging nature and business through sharing some marine ecosystem examples. We hope that this will encourage educators to explore the fascinating interconnected worlds between humans, nature, and business that could foster sustainable development.

Introduction and Context

The frequency of global climate challenges and their respective impact, as well as their complex interconnectedness, expose people and the planet to increased levels of harm (World Economic Forum, 2023). Leaving future generations with the same (or more) opportunities, as suggested by the definition of "sustainable development" (The World Commission on Environment and Development, 1987), seems almost

DOI: 10.4324/9781003457763-9

impossible. Even though many different approaches, perspectives, and theories acknowledge the complexity of socioeconomic systems, there is still a lack of comprehensive understanding of how these systems operate. To practice responsible management of business development, it is important to understand how these systems function and how they relate to important social needs.

We experienced the difficulties and constraints that both of our higher education institutions (HEIs) have faced in incorporating sustainability perspectives in their business and management curricula. Observing colleagues and their respective institutions around the globe, we feel that "trendy" sustainability themes are inserted haphazardly in the curricula, projects, and HEI infrastructure and processes. However, it bothers us that most seem to be unsuccessful in a way that they are not creating any impact, that is, do not challenge or change our view of business and management education. The danger of using sustainability as an "add-on," creating more "win-win" situations instead of understanding it as a possibility to establish a new business paradigm and engage in "unlearning" is clearly visible in the field. These clashes of systems and their interpretation (sometimes within the same institution) create unease and contradictions, leaving students puzzled without discussing the complexity they are exposed to. Thus, we believe there is a missing but essential piece that can help reposition "strong" or embedded sustainability teaching for those who choose to read sustainability as a lever for system change. That piece is ubiquitous and often taken for granted: the simplicity and greatness of natural ecosystems which has more in common with humans (and thus business) than the "mechanistic" interpretation from the Industrial Age we still abide by. To illustrate how we introduced this missing puzzle piece into our teaching, we highlight selected examples from marine ecosystems in this chapter that helped our students to learn sustainable business in a different way.

Business and nature have more in common than often thought. Business needs to integrate with nature to change and evolve at different levels (Gunderson & Holling, 2002). For centuries nature formed synergies, prioritized resources, engaged in "mergers and acquisitions" symbiotic relationships, and engaged in strategic networking. Human beings may not need to innovate for sustainability but engage in biomimicry. We asked ourselves: could nature provide lessons for business if we just learn from it? Since complex systems are already working well in nature, can we effectively replicate them for business to reinforce our sustainability?

We believe it is possible to explain how theories, models, and attitudes that instructors usually teach in business and management programs within HEIs are strongly related to natural ecosystems' performance and evolution. For us, embracing these theories is a viable way to integrate sustainable development with managerial concepts in classroom discussions with students (see also Ives et al., 2017, 2018; Barragan-Jason et al., 2022). We have anecdotal evidence that participation and engagement in the classroom increased by using this disrupting method to approach traditional business topics. Such discussions can certainly open new paths for reasoning and critical thinking toward sustainability as students find positive connections between business and nature and think outside the box by questioning and challenging what they have learned.

Business and Nature

As course instructors on topics such as sustainable development, business and society, sustainable supply chain management, and sea ecosystems, we found constraints in aligning sustainability topics and the impact of business. Our decision to create a new parallel between business and nature comes from long hours of observing natural ecosystems, in aquariums, the beach, and the ocean – or simple walks in local forests, immersing ourselves in deep reflections outside of the busyness of "hustle culture." Specifically, our first ideas came from the Frost Science Museum and Aquarium in Miami, the Aquarium of the Pacific in Long Beach, the Lake Bled in Slovenia, and Chocaya Beach in Peru.

Then we began to find common patterns between the behavior of marine species and organizations. After that, we delved deeply into attempts of merging business and nature and have informally discussed ecosystem topics with colleagues in coastal cities and researched natural phenomena related to marine (and woodland) ecosystems. From these discussions with colleagues about the specific marine (and sylvan) examples we collected, we obtained valuable feedback about how understandable our perspective was toward business education.

Finally, we decided to incorporate this into core courses such as supply chain management (sustainability section), sustainable development, and business and society courses to provide a new perspective on management education and transform previous versions of these already existing courses. The literature we cite throughout this chapter provided initial starting points of diving further into this topic. Additionally, we suggest that fellow educators seek the exchange with colleagues from the natural sciences or add literature from that respective field to further challenge business students.

The long-standing process of observing and reflecting on natural phenomena and multiple and simultaneous systems provide us with deeper insights. It allows us to identify special situations in nature that are particularly like those that we aim to recreate in business, as readers will find out below. We identified the following four specific cases from ocean ecosystems that are strongly related to some of the organizational fields that students learn from business and management literature.

The following details show how these cases work in nature and how they align with similar business and management perspectives we usually teach.

1 *Fish social networks.* According to Gil (2017), fish share vital information regarding predators' incursions and feeding safety spots in the ocean through their sea social networks. Even different species of fish connect within an extended social network in the ocean that promotes feeding and fleeing behaviors. Removing any individual agent would create a network disruption that would result in losing critical information for the remaining participants, which become disoriented and less informed (Gil, 2017). The social network among fish could be considered while discussing how overfishing or the conservation of species would have an impact on the entire marine ecosystem.

We also see some parallels to Social Networks Theory. Following Travers and Milgram (1969), social networks exhibit patterns of cohesion among their members and different roles regarding the connectivity they promote. Firms in a social structure tend to imitate their managerial practices (Chiu et al., 2013), and social networks change over time when their participants are removed, or they adjust their roles (Davis & Mizruchi, 1999). Hence, we have incorporated this example into our supply chain management course to teach how important the cohesion and coordination of supply chains' participants are and how past and upcoming crises have had consequences by removing strategic partners from the network. Also, we have reinforced our approach to multistakeholder collaborative topics within our sustainable development course, emphasizing the diversity and own advantages of each of the business ecosystem's actors.

2 *Ghost crabs.* "Ghost crabs" can camouflage themselves on a sand beach and quickly pop in and out as they disappear into their holes

(Explore the Shore, 2022). They rapidly flee to protect themselves from what they consider any source of threat and seal their own holes from the inside in the face of risk. Living unnoticed seems to be a relevant strategic goal for them. They use one of their claws to dig the hole that will protect them from predators in nature (seagulls, bigger crabs, etc.) and use the other claw to push the dirt out and flatten the terrain simultaneously. This simultaneous work has not only been an efficient process for building a home, but it denotes harmony with the environment by leaving the terrain flat as it was at the beginning of the digging.

We see some parallels between this behavior and the organizational ambidexterity perspective. According to Hill and Birkinshaw (2012), capitalizing on existing resources and exploring new resources for future scenarios lead to organizational ambidexterity. Also, this ambidexterity ability would allow firms to protect themselves for long-term survival (O'Reilly & Tushman, 2008) as well as leverage their resilience under times of crisis and uncertainty (Gayed & El Ebrashi, 2023). Thus, this example serves us to explain to our students how firms are constantly looking for internal as well as external resources, through their supply chains' partners, overcoming contextual constraints, and achieving organizational goals as well as global challenges such as sustainability.

3 *The tragedy of the sole.* The sole, also known as flounder or flatfish, is a predator fish that lives on the shores and hides under the sand below water, waiting to emerge from the ground to catch its prey by surprise (usually small fish or some crustaceans). One of the particularities of the adult flounder is that it is the only fish with two eyes on the same side of its head. However, it is born with eyes on both sides. During its first weeks of growth, it dramatically changes its body, becoming flat, its upside color turns dark, and its downside color turns bright. The eye situated below migrates inside, from the bottom to the upside of the flounder, providing it with two eyes on the same side. Every flatfish is born with enough internal resources and capabilities to go through this transformation at a specific stage in its life.

This behavior could be compared to Mergers and Acquisitions (M&A), as merged organizations undergo an adaptation phase, dealing with the impacts of the new environment (Mitchell & Mulherin, 1996). Implementation of M&A processes demands expert staff and qualified professionals capable of dealing with agency conflicts in organizations (Gokkaya et al., 2023), that provide specialized assistance during the transformational periods of transition of the firms. According to Grant et al. (2022), these organizational transformations would need the pre-existence of some strategic elements, such as expertise and routines in firms, to ensure a proper M&A process. Therefore, this case allows us to explain to our students how upside and downside business integration work within supply chains, and how firms would need to consider all possible effects from transformational processes toward strategic goals, such as sustainable development achievement.

4 *Sharks and their "cleaners".* Even though sharks are recognized predators, they maintain collaborative relationships with other fish species. For instance, remoras attach to the sharks to obtain food and protection while they clean sharks' skin during the ride, creating a symbiotic relationship between them. We see the same symbiotic relationships between crocodiles and the Egyptian Plover bird, for example, picking out tiny bits of food stuck between the crocodile's teeth and ensuring that the crocodile's mouth is kept free from infections. Symbiosis in nature is not only a collaborative instinct but also a mutually positive strategy to ensure survival by working together and leveraging the strengths of many actors within the ecosystem.

This behavior is very similar to the statements of the Resource Based View (RBV) of the firm that explains why synergies are sometimes so significant to implement (Barney, 1991). Wernerfelt (1995) emphasizes the importance of considering firms' heterogeneity for RBV because each actor in the business community utilizes their own resources and could be competitors, allies, customers, and suppliers at the same time. Hence, this example was helpful for us to teach how collaboration among companies within supply chains would create new sources of strategic and valuable resources for them. Also, it highlights how the accomplishment of the SDG 17 (partnership for the goals) of the United Nations sustainable development agenda would set strong capabilities for social as well as business actors to build positive alliances and strategic partnerships.

Ideation Process and Motivation

We began working together when both agreed to collaboratively conduct a Teaching Café session at the Academy of International

Business conference in the beginning of 2021. This session was about how to incorporate sustainability within business education, and we found that we share some common perspectives and have others that are supplementary to each other. Also, we discovered that, among other things, we share the same love for nature and even more, for the ocean.

These four cases emerged directly from the observation and literature review of marine ecosystems and have inspired us to reframe how we approach the business and management topics we teach. Many of us do not consider the option to incorporate environmental "cases" to illustrate business concepts. We believe that bringing such cases into business discussions will motivate and inspire our colleagues around the world, and it will help us become more aware of and benefit from lessons from natural world systems.

Here are some steps faculty could take in implementing these ideas.

1   Gather nature-inspired examples or cases. Living beings in the natural ecosystem are constantly evolving their activities to live and interact with others. Understanding the role each has toward others would help us demonstrate system complexity.
2   Acknowledge the disconnect between business and nature (described by the three divides in theory U, self-self, self-others, and self-nature) (Scharmer, 2018). Nature has plenty of similarities to our social and economic systems. Its systems are operating with efficiency and effectiveness, so nature can be an excellent point of reference.
3   Develop an interdisciplinary perspective and collective spirit. Collaboration with biologists, environmental engineers, and other related fields is strongly recommended. They would help to bridge business topics to natural phenomena.
4   Feel the presence of nature's processes within our daily lives. People are often so busy trying to understand their own complexities that they forget to look deeply inside the systems around them that they usually take for granted.

Description of the Process

Based on rich discussions and positive feedback from peers during academic conferences such as the Academy of Management (AOM), Academy of International Business Global, and Academy of International Business (AIB) Latin American and the Caribbean chapter, we decided to incorporate nature cases into our course design from the first semester of 2023 onwards. The examples that we outlined motivated us to rethink our pedagogical methods and learning content for business and management education toward sustainable development. We expect to maintain and extend this transformation over time, as we develop more cases from nature and continue dialog with colleagues and students.

These four examples were tested as a pilot with some student groups, using an inductive teaching approach, which means showing the examples from nature and their details first and then get into the discussions and feedback from the managerial or business perspectives.

In the second phase, we are organizing formal sessions during the AIB academic conferences and/or with groups of instructors of specific HEIs in 2023. We will use Teaching Cafés, Roundtable Discussions, and Professional Development Workshops to showcase our examples and gather feedback. We plan to start with educators and then collect additional insights and new cases from the scholarly community. Then, we will be ready to conduct sessions with larger groups of students in 2024 in a formal way in Peru and Slovenia (preferably in parallel), by preparing specific examples from marine ecosystems and incorporating them within the course syllabi. Also, we plan to incorporate nature-based outside-of-classroom learning experiences to extend and test our approach by elevating it to the next level. Some pilot attempts were conducted in November 2022.

Expected Results, Learning Outcomes, and Recommendations

Drawing on our initial piloting attempts, several courses in the business and management curriculum would be impacted in two ways: (1) sustainability-oriented courses would incorporate examples from the natural ecosystem, emphasizing related systems in natural environments, and (2) traditional business such as Marketing, Finance, Logistics, Entrepreneurship, International Business, and so on, could develop business applications or practices from nature. We aim to add examples from natural ecosystems to learning experiences of business perspectives in the classroom, developing sustainability-oriented skills in students, such as nature-connectedness, regenerative perspectives, and diversity and inclusion. From an educator's perspective, we want to curate several resources that allow them to use our examples and integrate them into their courses.

One of the main constraints of our idea is that it would demand knowledge of sustainability and other fields besides business and management to scale and expand. We recommend collaborating with colleagues from other disciplines such as biology, natural sciences, sociology, medicine, environmental engineering, and natural environment, among others. Another constraint would be the educators' willingness to find, relate, and incorporate cases from nature into their current business and management courses. For the project to succeed, we may need to provide special training for instructors that will use this methodology.

Moving Beyond Cases and Examples

To reconnect to nature in general, we want to provide a counter-narrative to examples from the business world that defines humans as "inputs" or "resources" that must be managed for efficiency. These concepts date back to the Industrial Age. We need to move away from "managing human resources" toward a living-systems worldview (Nature of Business, 2022). We have also experimented with exercises and experiences outside of the classroom to not only cognitively understand nature's operating mechanisms but also experience nature from an emotional standpoint.

Together with *Walkaboutyou*, we co-facilitated a session on nature-based immersion, outlining several exercises and steps. *Walkaboutyou* is an organization based in Cologne, Germany, that provides spaces of tangible connection to nature, community, and us. This creates trust and courage for authentic paths with meaning for ourselves and the world. In the language of the Australian Aborigines, a *walkabout* refers to wandering along traditional paths. *Walkaboutyou* goes back to these original principles and makes the power that has been in our genes for millions of years accessible again – by walking in small groups in nature. In this sense, *walkabouts* are workshops, seminars, and retreats that, in combination with movement in nature, are the key to more focus, resilience, and a reconnection to us – and nature.

Nature-based immersion is not only healthy (Berman et al., 2012; Capaldi et al., 2015; Nisbet et al., 2011; Park et al., 2010) but can also boost creativity (e.g., Atchley et al., 2012; Oppezzo & Schwartz, 2014; Palanica et al., 2019; Yu & Hsieh, 2020), improve focus (Berman et al., 2008), increase team spirit, cooperation and care (Pasanen et al., 2018; Weinstein et al., 2009; Wiltermuth & Heath, 2009; Zhang et al., 2014), and enable to deal with complexity and uncertainty (Ingulli & Lindbloom, 2013; Marselle et al., 2019).

Implications, Ways Forward, and Conclusions

We believe that incorporating nature cases in our business and management courses would inspire fellow instructors to find out more about the very same theories and models they teach. We also believe that this would motivate their students when discovering a new comprehensive way to understand socioeconomic phenomena. We hope it will also foster sustainability-related behavior and increase awareness and care for the planet, particularly in the business world (Nisbet et al., 2009). Using nature-based cases helps implement many recent attempts to connect nature-based principles to leadership. For example, bio-leadership (The Bio-Leadership Project, 2023) or regenerative leadership draw inspiration from pioneering thinking within biomimicry, biophilia, circular economy, anthropology, sociology, and complexity theory (Allen, 2019; Hutchins, 2022; Hutchins & Storm, 2019).

Business education has not strongly focused on interdisciplinary approaches, but by drawing parallels to systems in nature we can move away from the mechanistic mindset. Treating humans as if they were mechanical robots encouraged the emergence of a system that violates the very biological nature of human beings and how we live, function, and interact. By incorporating a nature-based perspective, we would upgrade traditional business management courses and practices into a more systemic, organic, and transformative experience. It would drive instructors to collaborate and use interdisciplinary process for their courses. It could also encourage and empower students to connect their decisions and actions with the living world. Building on analysis of systems in the natural world, business may gain a better understanding of and value for life on land, water, and air (Ferns, 2022).

To update the connection between natural and management science, educators should look for literature outside the management domain (Gunderson & Holling, 2002). Telling new stories that connect business processes with systems in nature could prove to be quite powerful in forming new social contracts (Huntjens, 2021; Muhar et al., 2018). Connectedness with nature or human–nature connection is an ample avenue worth exploring (Zylstra et al., 2014, 2019).

Commitment from HEIs authorities, administrators, and faculty would be necessary for the long-term survival of this initiative. International agencies such as World Wildlife Fund (WWF), Greenpeace, World Bank, United Nations, and others could support strategic alliances toward common sustainable goals. As promoted by other researchers (e.g., Baird et al., 2022), we believe that incorporating nature-based courses in business programs would foster connections to nature and help sustain life on our planet. There is growing awareness among businesses of the connection between nature and business in the form of initiatives such as the Taskforce on Nature-related Financial Disclosure (TCFD). The TCFD was established based on the idea that financial markets need to understand the impacts of climate change further. This includes risks and opportunities presented by rising temperatures, climate-related policy, and emerging technologies, which would improve reporting of climate-related financial information. With increased attention of policymakers and legislation, we will further engage in vital dialog, such as the COP15 UN biodiversity summit, which is crucial to strengthen the interests of nature.

References

Allen, K. E. (2019). *Leading from the roots: Nature inspired leadership lessons for today's world*. Morgan James.

Atchley, R. A., Strayer, D. L., & Atchley, P. (2012). Creativity in the wild: Improving creative reasoning through immersion in natural settings. *PLOS ONE, 7*(12), e51474. https://doi.org/10.1371/journal.pone.0051474

Baird, J., Dale, G., Holzer, J. M., Hutson, G., Ives, C. D., & Plummer, R. (2022). The role of a nature-based program in fostering multiple connections to nature. *Sustainability Science, 17*(5), 1899–1910. https://doi.org/10.1007/s11625-022-01119-w

Barney, J. (1991). Firm resources and sustained competitive advantage. *Journal of Management, 17*(1), 99–120. https://doi.org/10.1177/014920639101700108

Barragan-Jason, G., Mazancourt, C. de, Parmesan, C., Singer, M., & Loreau, M. (2022). Human-nature connectedness as a pathway to sustainability: A global meta-analysis. *Conservation Letters, 15*(1), e12852. https://doi.org/10.1111/conl.12852

Berman, M. G., Jonides, J., & Kaplan, S. (2008). The cognitive benefits of interacting with nature. *Psychological Science, 19*(12), 1207–1212. https://doi.org/10.1111/j.1467-9280.2008.02225.x

Berman, M. G., Kross, E., Krpan, K. M., Askren, M. K., Burson, A., Deldin, P. J., Kaplan, S., Sherdell, L., Gotlib, I. H., & Jonides, J. (2012). Interacting with nature improves cognition and affect for individuals with depression. *Journal of Affective Disorders, 140*(3), 300–305. https://doi.org/10.1016/j.jad.2012.03.012

Capaldi, C., Passmore, H.-A., Nisbet, E. K., Zelenski, J. M., & Dopko, R. (2015). Flourishing in nature: A review of the benefits of connecting with nature and its application as a wellbeing intervention. *International Journal of Wellbeing, 5*(4), 1–16. https://doi.org/10.5502/ijw.v5i4.449

Chiu, P.-Ch., Teoh, S. H., & Tian, F. (2013). Board interlocks and earnings management contagion. *The Accounting Review, 88*(3), 915–944. https://doi.org/10.2308/accr-50369

Davis, G. F., & Mizruchi, M. S. (1999). The money center cannot hold: Commercial banks in the U.S. system of corporate governance. *Administrative Science Quarterly, 44*(2), 215–239. https://doi.org/10.2307/2666995

Explore the Shore (2022). Ghost crabs - What's down that hole in the sand? https://www.youtube.com/watch?v=khJKFe04o54

Ferns, G. (2022). Businesspeople must reconnect with nature to save the planet. *MIT Sloan Management Review*. https://orca.cardiff.ac.uk/id/eprint/149275/

Gayed, S., & El Ebrashi, R. (2023). Fostering firm resilience through organizational ambidexterity capability and resource availability: Amid the COVID-19 outbreak. *International Journal of Organizational Analysis, 31*(1), 253–275. https://doi.org/10.1108/IJOA-09-2021-2977

Gil, M. (2017). Could fish social networks help us save coral reefs? https://www.ted.com/talks/mike_gil_could_fish_social_networks_help_us_save_coral_reefs

Gokkaya, S., Liu, X., & Stulz, R. M. (2023). Do firms with specialized M&A staff make better acquisitions? *Journal of Financial Economics, 147*(1), 75–105. https://doi.org/10.1016/j.jfineco.2022.09.002

Grant, M., Nilsson, F., & Nordvall, A.-C. (2022). Pre-merger acquisition capabilities: A study of two successful serial acquirers. *European Management Journal, 40*(6), 932–942. https://doi.org/10.1016/j.emj.2022.10.006

Gunderson, L. H., & Holling, C. S. (2002). *Panarchy. Understanding transformations in human and natural systems*. Island Press.

Hill, S. A., & Birkinshaw, J. (2012). Ambidexterity and survival in corporate venture units. *Journal of Management, 40*, 1899–1931. https://doi.org/10.1177/0149206312445925

Huntjens, P. (2021). *Towards a natural social contract: Transformative social-ecological innovation for a sustainable, healthy and just society*. Springer eBook Collection. Springer International Publishing. https://doi.org/10.1007/978-3-030-67130-3

Hutchins, G. (2022). *Leading by nature: The process of becoming a regenerative leader*. Wordzworth Publishing.

Hutchins, G., & Storm, L. (2019). *Regenerative leadership: The DNA of life-affirming 21st century organizations*. Wordzworth Publishing.

Ingulli, K., & Lindbloom, G. (2013). Connection to nature and psychological resilience. *Ecopsychology, 5*(1), 52–55. https://doi.org/10.1089/eco.2012.0042

Ives, C. D., Abson, D. J., Wehrden, H. von, Dorninger, C., Klaniecki, K., & Fischer, J. (2018). Reconnecting with nature for sustainability. *Sustainability Science, 13*(5), 1389–1397. https://doi.org/10.1007/s11625-018-0542-9

Ives, C. D., Giusti, M., Fischer, J., Abson, D. J., Klaniecki, K., Dorninger, C., Laudan, J., Barthel, S., Abernethy, P., Martín-López, B., Raymond, C. M., Kendal, D., & Wehrden, H. von (2017). Human–nature connection: A multidisciplinary review. *Current Opinion in Environmental Sustainability*, *26–27*, 106–113. https://doi.org/10.1016/j.cosust.2017.05.005

Marselle, M. R., Warber, S. L., & Irvine, K. N. (2019). Growing resilience through interaction with nature: Can group walks in nature buffer the effects of stressful life events on mental health? *International Journal of Environmental Research and Public Health*, *16*(6), 986. https://doi.org/10.3390/ijerph16060986

Mitchell, M. L. & Mulherin, J. H. (1996). The impact of industry shocks on takeover and restructuring activity. *Journal of Financial Economics*, *41*(2), 193–229. https://doi.org/10.1016/0304-405X(95)00860-H

Muhar, A., Raymond, C. M., van den Born, R. J., Bauer, N., Böck, K., Braito, M., Buijs, A., Flint, C., Groot, W. T. de, Ives, C. D., Mitrofanenko, T., Plieninger, T., Tucker, C., & van Riper, C. J. (2018). A model integrating social-cultural concepts of nature into frameworks of interaction between social and natural systems. *Journal of Environmental Planning and Management*, *61*(5–6), 756–777. https://doi.org/10.1080/09640568.2017.1327424

Nisbet, E. K., Zelenski, J. M., & Murphy, S. A. (2009). The nature relatedness scale: Linking individuals' connection with nature to environmental concern and behavior. *Environment and Behavior*, *41*(5), 715–740. https://journals.sagepub.com/doi/pdf/10.1177/0013916508318748

Nisbet, E. K., Zelenski, J. M., & Murphy, S. A. (2011). Happiness is in our nature: Exploring nature relatedness as a contributor to subjective well-being. *Journal of Happiness Studies*, *12*(2), 303–322. https://doi.org/10.1007/s10902-010-9197-7

Oppezzo, M., & Schwartz, D. L. (2014). Give your ideas some legs: The positive effect of walking on creative thinking. *Journal of experimental psychology: Learning, memory, and cognition*, *40*(4), 1142–1152. https://doi.org/10.1037/a0036577

O'Reilly, C. A., & Tushman, M. L. (2008). Ambidexterity as a dynamic capability: Resolving the innovator's dilemma. *Research in Organizational Behavior*, *28*, 185–206. https://doi.org/10.1016/j.riob.2008.06.002

Palanica, A., Lyons, A., Cooper, M., Lee, A., & Fossat, Y. (2019). A comparison of nature and urban environments on creative thinking across different levels of reality. *Journal of Environmental Psychology*, *63*, 44–51. https://doi.org/10.1016/j.jenvp.2019.04.006

Park, B. J., Tsunetsugu, Y., Kasetani, T., Kagawa, T., & Miyazaki, Y. (2010). The physiological effects of Shinrin-yoku (taking in the forest atmosphere or forest bathing): Evidence from field experiments in 24 forests across Japan. *Environmental Health and Preventive Medicine*, *15*(1), 18–26. https://doi.org/10.1007/s12199-009-0086-9

Pasanen, T., Johnson, K., Lee, K., & Korpela, K. (2018). Can nature walks with psychological tasks improve mood, self-reported restoration, and sustained attention? Results from two experimental field studies. *Frontiers in Psychology, 9*, 2057. https://doi.org/10.3389/fpsyg.2018.02057

Scharmer, O. (2018). *The essentials of Theory U: Core principles and applications*. Berrett-Koehler Publishers.

The Bio-Leadership Project. (2023, January 30). The Bio-Leadership Project. https://www.bio-leadership.org/

The Nature of Business. (2022). The necessary evolution from machine to living-systems L&OD. https://thenatureofbusiness.org/2022/09/02/the-necessary-evolution-from-machine-to-living-systems-lod/

The World Commission on Environment and Development. (1987). *Our common future*. Oxford: Oxford University Press.

Travers, J., & Milgram, S. (1969). An experimental study of the small world problem. *Sociometry, 32*(4), 425–443. https://doi.org/10.1515/9781400841356.130

Weinstein, N., Przybylski, A. K., & Ryan, R. M. (2009). Can nature make us more caring? Effects of immersion in nature on intrinsic aspirations and generosity. *Personality and Social Psychology Bulletin, 35*(10), 1315–1329. https://doi.org/10.1177/0146167209341649

Wernerfelt, B. (1995). The resource-based view of the firm: Ten years after. *Strategic Management Journal, 16*(3), 171–174.

Wiltermuth, S. S., & Heath, C. (2009). Synchrony and cooperation. *Psychological Science, 20*(1), 1–5. https://doi.org/10.1111/j.1467-9280.2008.02253.x

World Economic Forum. (2023). Global Risks Report 2023. https://www.weforum.org/reports/global-risks-report-2023/

Yu, C.-P., & Hsieh, H. (2020). Beyond restorative benefits: Evaluating the effect of forest therapy on creativity. *Urban Forestry & Urban Greening, 51*, 126670. https://doi.org/10.1016/j.ufug.2020.126670

Zelenski, J. M., & Nisbet, E. K. (2014). Happiness and feeling connected: The distinct role of nature relatedness. *Environment and Behavior, 46*(1), 3–23. https://journals.sagepub.com/doi/pdf/10.1177/0013916512451901

Zhang, J. W., Piff, P. K., Iyer, R., Koleva, S., & Keltner, D. (2014). An occasion for unselfing: Beautiful nature leads to prosociality. *Journal of Environmental Psychology, 37*, 61–72. https://doi.org/10.1016/j.jenvp.2013.11.008

Zylstra, M., Esler, K., Knight, A., & Le Grange, L. (2019). Integrating multiple perspectives on the human-nature relationship: A reply to Fletcher 2017. *The Journal of Environmental Education, 50*(1), 1–10. https://doi.org/10.1080/00958964.2018.1497582

Zylstra, M. J., Knight, A. T., Esler, K. J., & Le Grange, L. L. L. (2014). Connectedness as a core conservation concern: An interdisciplinary review of theory and a call for practice. *Springer Science Reviews, 2*(1–2), 119–143. https://doi.org/10.1007/s40362-014-0021-3

10

TEACHING SUSTAINABILITY ACROSS BORDERS

Looking Back to Look Ahead

Subhasis Ray

Abstract

In this chapter, I share the story of my journey as a sustainability educator over the last decade. Teaching sustainability-related topics around the world has been an enriching and rewarding experience. Issues and challenges of teaching in developed and developing economies are quite distinct and different. Students in developed countries are more engaged and aware when compared to their peers in developing countries who are cynical about the future and constrained due to their financial conditions. Beyond teaching, several structural and systemic issues plague the teaching of sustainability in emerging markets. As individual faculty members we still have the toolkit to work toward inside-out changes, leveraging our course, classroom, and system.

Landing in Academia

After eight years leading multinational businesses, I switched to an academic life in 2003. I was accompanying my father for an eye operation in Chennai and a local newspaper advertisement looking for corporate executives willing to switch to academics caught my interest. My company was being taken over by a global IT services company and I was training my colleagues on a version of the Balanced Score Card. I enjoyed the work: reading, preparing content, and speaking about what I read. I decided to make the jump and have no regrets. The chance

DOI: 10.4324/9781003457763-10

timing of these events made me realize the role of serendipity in our professional journey. Another serendipitous event occurred years later, when someone sitting in front of me at a Harvard Business School conference, turned around and asked me about a case I wrote on Shell's Corporate Social Responsibility (CSR) activities in the Sakhalin project. This led to a long sustainability teaching assignment for European students.

This book of "stories of pioneers" made me think of first settlers in a new land or the first climbers of Mount Everest. The newness of the terrain has all shades of beauty, enigma, and danger that only a few embraces. Sustainability teaching in the early years of this millennium had the same charm and feel. The land was new with no maps and little or no record of previous arrivals and adventures. We knew that things are broken but not sure how the future world will evolve. Nowhere has the sustainability teaching journey been more dramatic than the emerging markets of the world. I spent most of the last two decades in creating new curriculum and teaching sustainability-related courses in India and around the world.

Teaching sustainability is no longer an option but a necessity to prepare future generations for living on a warming planet. However, teaching sustainability in business schools has remained a challenge. The situation is more complex in emerging markets precisely for their "emerging" nature. Striving for economic growth has led to a demand for managers who look for a quick return on their investment in highly priced management programs. Students seek degrees that can give them a job with a fat pay package. Anything that does not sound "job worthy" (ethics, CSR, sustainability) becomes a lesser priority for students and business schools. As I write this chapter, two of my sustainability electives were dropped due to poor subscription, crowded out by more job-oriented courses. The college does not have enough rooms to run multiple electives in the school so there is a required minimum enrollment. I now must teach two mainstream marketing courses to fulfill my minimum workload. I am disappointed but not disheartened. I will continue to respond to the urgent need for sustainability teaching in emerging market business schools. Sustainability is yet to be integrated well into core, functional courses and, giving in to market pressure, we even reduced the credits in a core course on sustainability!

Since 2010, I have the benefit of teaching in many countries and can share my experience of teaching sustainability-related courses at leading business schools in two *emerging* economies (India and Russia) and two *developed* economies (Japan and Ireland). My intent has been to bring sustainability into business school classrooms to create managers with triple bottom-line thinking. Perhaps my experience will help other colleagues who are trying to change academic discourse within business schools in a meaningful way to achieve a sustainable, net-zero world. Some structural and systemic barriers for faculty colleagues are highlighted as institutional opportunities to improve.

First Steps

Early in my academic career, I started teaching marketing-related subjects based on my experience in the corporate world. The relationship between business and society always attracted me and I began my PhD in CSR. CSR was not part of Indian academia in the early 2000s and I had to teach management subjects because there was no inclination for new emerging topics like sustainability or CSR to be offered as electives. By 2011, in my second job, we were approached by a leading hydropower producer to develop a 10-month long certificate course of CSR, Resettlement, and Rehabilitation. To my knowledge, this was the first such certificate program for executives in India. The 10-month program was successful, but I found very few resources in local content and examples (Ray, 2016).

Personally, the program provided an impetus and inspiration to continue working in the field of CSR and sustainability. I established the Centre for Resettlement, Rehabilitation and Corporate Social Responsibility in our business school to better organize activities around CSR and sustainability. In 2012, I organized one of the first CSR conference in India that brought together several academicians and practitioners. The conference was supported by my school, but I found the efforts to organize conferences disproportionately high. The government introduced a voluntary CSR policy for corporations that later became mandatory in 2014 so interest in CSR from stakeholders was high. While discussions with CSR colleagues were inspiring, nothing much changed within my own school.

Overall Teaching Experience

Over the last decade, I taught several sustainability-related courses: *Sustainable Development and Corporate Sustainability* (core course); *Sustainability Marketing*; *Responsible Innovation for Circular Economy*; *Strategies for Sustainable Business*; *Sustainable Enterprise*; *Corporate*

Social Responsibility; and *Social Entrepreneurship*. These were mostly postgraduate courses. Courses, talks, and workshops were offered in 25 countries to students of 36 nationalities. As one would expect, the experience of such work is rich, varied, and rewarding.

Of the many countries and programs I taught, a few are significant for their duration or context. In Russia (2015–2020), I taught exchange students from top European business schools (e.g., Copenhagen Business School, HEC Paris) as part of their CEMS dual degree program (www.cems.org). In Japan (2015), I taught sustainability to undergraduates. In Ireland, I designed, developed, and delivered an online module on Sustainable Enterprise for Irish executives. These opportunities revealed the global need and interest in sustainable course material.

At my home university in India, I have been teaching courses related to sustainability for the last nine years. This includes courses on *Sustainable Development and Corporate Sustainability; Sustainability Marketing; Socially Responsible Business*; and *Responsible Innovation for Circular Economy*. I have also taught sustainability-related courses in some of the leading, triple accredited business schools like Indian Institute of Management Calcutta and Indian Institute of Management Indore. I have been able to see first-hand the interest and need for sustainable teaching and business practices while recognizing the high demand among developing countries to pursue growth and profit. I believe that emerging economies hold the key to a low carbon future.

Teaching Students in Developed Countries

Japanese students at Soka University enrolled in my undergraduate course on Sustainability. Given Japan's postwar resource crunch and innovativeness, the Japanese government and companies have progressed far ahead on the sustainability curve. However, true to the Japanese culture and spirit, and unlike their western counterparts, not much publicity is given to such work. Only a few global companies like Sony or Hitachi are showcased in case studies. Even Japanese small- and medium-sized enterprises (SMEs) were active in the sustainability front. It is clear to me why Japan had the largest number of old companies in the world. To sustain for centuries, companies must adopt sustainability as the core value (Funabashi, 2009). We as faculty and global citizens need to learn more about sustainability mindset, culture, policy, and practices in Japan. And we need to share and utilize sustainability lessons from Asia, Africa, and South America, and reflect on their interconnections.

During my stint as a Visiting Professor at the Graduate School of Management in St Petersburg State University, Russia, I taught exchange students (in the CEMS – Community of European Management Schools – dual degree program) courses on *Sustainability Marketing; Sustainable Business Strategies;* and *Social Entrepreneurship.* Most students came from leading European business schools like Rotterdam School of Management, BI School of Management Norway, Copenhagen Business School, HEC Paris, EM Normandie to name a few. There were also a few Russian students enrolled.

It was encouraging to see increasing interest and conviction about sustainability among developed country students. In the early days, I would try to convince them *why* sustainability and climate change matters for business. About two to three years later (particularly following the Paris agreement on SDGs in 2015) I was able to shift focus to *how* climate change could be a lever for change in business and many students wanted to start their own sustainable enterprise. In one class, two students from Austria developed a business plan to rehabilitate ex-prisoners and went on to raise funds for their startup. A student from the Czech Republic started a business where women inmates of old age homes started stitching quilts and blankets for new-born babies to replace low-cost products imported from China.

Many students followed sustainable practices at home and in their community like waste segregation and consuming green products. Government policies in the EU and progressive business leaders created a suitable context for sustainability teaching in developed countries. A social security system and growing impact investing ecosystem emboldened students to participate meaningfully in the course and plan beyond it. In fact, some of the questions from my French students were focused on a post-sustainability scenario. They asked questions such as: How can companies scale up? How not to greenwash? Is it possible for big companies to walk the talk when they were operating in a short-term gain oriented economic model? What business models will work?

In 2019, along with a colleague, I incorporated live projects and gamification to sustainability courses. In collaboration with IKEA Russia, students developed a sustainability game that the company could use for its new and existing employees as well as walk-in customers. It was a great success – students liked the approach and IKEA found it useful for adoption.

In 2021–2022, I designed, developed, and delivered an online module on *Sustainable Enterprise* for Irish executives. Corporate students were quite receptive to the idea of sustainable business and interested in finding working models to use in their business. Corporate sustainability practice evolved considerably as the Irish government was aggressively pushing for carbon neutrality by 2030. Government actions helped me curate content. In talking to officials from different Irish counties about helping their regional businesses move toward net-zero targets, it was clear that in certain industries, like heavy commercial vehicles or food coloring industries, there were not enough international benchmarks or proven technology for companies to use. Students were mostly unaware of sustainability initiatives and challenges in developing countries. My Irish experience mirrored previous classes with European students and led me to believe that teaching must move toward implementation, policy-practice nexus, technology adoption, and the more granular aspects of corporate sustainability.

Teaching Students in Developing Countries

I now have a decade of experience teaching Russian and Indian students. As I mentioned earlier, a chance meeting with a Russian colleague at Harvard Business School led to an invitation to teach CEMS students in Russia. I found that many Russian and Indian students were cynical and skeptical about the potential of sustainable business. In a conversation with a Russian student about how water scarcity is becoming a big issue for business and governments, the student argued that water scarcity would be impossible because Russia had the largest freshwater lake in the world! Consumption of natural resources are critical to those in developing nations that face pressing needs to grow their society and provide for all citizens. In class, students share opinions that corruption is widespread in business. Most actions from big business are seen as an indirect way to appropriate resources and exploit communities, and often government is seen as complicit. It has been difficult to counter such arguments purely from a societal and cultural perspective.

Negative beliefs about business and government behavior or corruption gets in the way of discussions on responsible consumption: *"When businesses act like this, why should we care?"* With large numbers of people struggling to put food on the table for their family, responsible consumption comes down to simply getting things done. I use cases of Unilever's Project Shakti in India to help students understand that there *may be* a sustainable solution while acknowledging that systemic barriers and institutional structures are big bottlenecks.

Another common debate relates to the politics of sustainable development. They challenge how colonized countries, such as India, have been exploited for the growth of the west/UK and now these countries want to grow and prosper. We may not have perfect answers for these questions, but the daily occurrence of climate change–related events (flood, draught, pollution) supports the need to act for the sake of all countries and humans. Recent governmental efforts like Circular Economy helps bolster the case for sustainable business. Just like my students, I too changed by teaching sustainability. I realize the importance of bringing more emotions, spirituality, and philosophy into my teaching. It is still a work in progress.

Challenges beyond Classroom

Although my sustainability courses received positive feedback, for colleagues interested in sustainability teaching there remain several challenges. In developing countries like India, sustainability is still a new topic in business schools. Within the marketing area, I found it difficult to introduce new courses related to sustainability and climate change because the marketing discipline has not engaged with such topics until recently.

Systemic and Structural Issues: In developing countries, business management education is driven by assurance of good jobs at the completion of the program. India has more than 5,000 institutions offering a postgraduate degree in management and the top 50 schools offer "100% placement" for their students. Fees range around $30,000 for a two-year course and most students take loans for studying. An intense focus on jobs for graduates leads to disinterest for any subject that does not cater to a job market where there are few jobs in sustainability.

Business school leaders are not keen to experiment with a proven success formula in terms of courses and outcomes (jobs). University-based business schools, as opposed to autonomous business schools, are often caught in an administrative bind in deciding which schools should lead the initiative to introduce new sustainability courses.

Number of students or enrollment often becomes a criterion for continuing a course rather than institutional obligation and responsibility to expand new thinking and knowledge. Common sense may expect that institutions that were early in the sustainability teaching journey will improve and benefit from their experience over time. However, my experience is to the contrary. Schools that were pioneers have been a victim of market forces that require high volume, high revenue generating courses. They have reduced the focus on sustainability.

Business schools may choose between including sustainability in the core curriculum or offer it as an elective course. Core course offerings are driven by different functional areas like finance, marketing, HR. If sustainability is not embedded in those core disciplines, it is often omitted from core business curriculum. I was able to offer a core course on *Corporate Sustainability and Sustainable Development* for two years, but it was canceled due to such administrative reasons. Offering an elective course on Sustainability is the other way of making it available for students. When the Corporate Sustainability course was canceled, I tried this route with two electives: *Sustainability Marketing* and *Responsible Innovation for Circular Economy*. Both have been running for the last five years.

Interdisciplinary Issues: Sustainability is, by its very nature, interdisciplinary. In general, existing processes for introducing new courses within academic institutions do not encourage faculty collaboration, though I have heard that some of our prestigious India Institutes of Technology (IITs) taking that route. In addition, older faculty members grew up studying and working on traditional business areas and do not have knowledge to introduce dynamic areas like sustainability. A colleague in the business law department at a Portuguese university once told me that a very senior and respected colleague of hers believed that the field of law stopped developing in the Roman era!

Course Curriculum Design: Given the dynamic and expanding nature of sustainability knowledge it has now become impossible to draw pedagogical boundaries while designing a course. This has created a challenge for individual faculty members and administrators to determine curriculum structure and organization. Lack of local content is another serious issue. Companies in developing countries are reluctant to engage in collaborative sustainability research and that makes it difficult to provide scientific evidence to students about the critical and practical aspects of sustainability practice in corporations.

Pedagogic Issues: Much has been written about a new pedagogy of "passion" to teach sustainability (Shrivastava, 2010). I find it challenging to teach sustainability within the existing paradigms of business and business schools. I tried to overcome this obstacle through intense engagement with practitioners who speak to my class about how they are steering their companies/departments toward sustainability. Using a systems perspective helps me in creating context. For example, linking rampant urbanization and consequent natural (man-made) disasters like flooding in Chennai or landslides in the Himalayas helps me impress upon the students the embedded nature of business in society. I often take students out to experience nature, audit our campus, or do a "walk" through the large slum opposite to our business school. I also admit that this continuous search for new ways to teach takes a toll on my research. One technique that helps me is slow, mindful reading of the daily newspaper. During these readings, I often take photos of important news articles and later print and file them for use in different courses. Students seem to love these connections between sustainable business and the world around them.

Individual motivation (teacher and student level): Why should I teach/study sustainability? The academic ranking system pushes faculty members around the world to focus on publications. In a publish-or-perish and university-ranking dominated culture, it is difficult to lead an initiative that is small, innovative, teaching-focused, and not necessarily (job and student) market-oriented in the traditional sense. Monetary incentive structures, wherever in place, do not acknowledge and value sustainability-related teaching and research unless specified by ranking agencies like AACSB. Even after designing a new course on sustainability, it may not be offered for various reasons including lack of student interest/time. Dedicated sustainability pioneers can overcome these barriers by thinking of our primary stakeholders, students. We can help make them better (corporate) citizens in a greener world. I also feel we need mass education programs for faculty – to train them about various aspects of sustainability.

Students are our hope for building an equitable, just, and sustainable society in the coming decades. However, they are trapped by a system that asks them to take huge loans for management courses, effectively restricting their choice of courses and activities in the campus. Mere intention is not enough for them to learn and execute sustainability in their careers. A small number of students have intrinsic interest in climate and sustainability issues, and our hope lies with them for a just transition in developing countries. As discussed above, unless sustainability is made a mandatory course by regulators and/or institutions, it will remain difficult to build sustainability-sensitive managers in emerging markets.

The Way Forward

The world is facing an unprecedented crisis in terms of climate change and sustainable development. All stakeholders need to act now. As faculty members, we have the responsibility to integrate sustainability in all aspects of our teaching (Leal Filho et al., 2019). Even when creating new courses seems difficult, we can bring in relevant examples and assignments in our own traditional courses and enable students to see the systemic connection between people, planet, and profit. There is an urgent need to highlight that caring for man and materials and consciousness of human unity are the emotional/spiritual foundations of sustainability (Leal Filho et al., 2022). Using systems to our advantage, grabbing serendipity when it happens, and focusing on inside-out change are our strategies. We cannot wait for institutions to change. Rather, as Gandhi said, we need to be the change we want to see in others.

Conclusion

Teaching sustainability is still a leap of faith for faculty members in developing country business schools. In this story, I shared my personal experience to show the typical journey path of an academic interested in teaching sustainability. The journey so far has been rewarding and exciting. My personal interest in business as a force for good has given me the energy to develop new courses. Serendipity has played its role in creating new opportunities. In 2023, teaching sustainability enables us to shape a managerial viewpoint built on triple bottom line. Such approaches are critical as developing country economies are grappling with rising inequality, balancing growth with just transition and the need for sustainability innovations.

Not all schools, students, or faculty members will be enthused by sustainability until there is a clear signal from the job market about the need and value of sustainability. The lag between real world events and academic world is a professional hazard for teaching sustainability.

Change is often brought about by individuals and small groups who act as the trigger and lighthouse for the masses. I am happy to walk this less-traveled path even as other curious academic travelers join in making the path a highway for human prosperity.

References

Funabashi, H. (2009). *Timeless ventures: 32 Japanese companies that imbibed 8 principles of longevity.* Tata McGraw Hill.

Leal Filho, W., Salvia, A. L., Ulluwishewa, R., Abubakar, I. R., Mifsud, M., LeVasseur, T. J., ... & Farrugia, E. (2022). Linking sustainability and spirituality: A preliminary assessment in pursuit of a sustainable and ethically correct world. *Journal of Cleaner Production, 380,* 135091.

Leal Filho, W., Vargas, V. R., Salvia, A. L., Brandli, L. L., Pallant, E., Klavins, M., ... & Vaccari, M. (2019). The role of higher education institutions in sustainability initiatives at the local level. *Journal of Cleaner Production, 233,* 1004–1015.

Ray, S. (2016). Innovation in sustainable development and management education in India. In *Human Centered Management in Executive Education. Humanism in Business Series.* Palgrave Macmillan. https://doi.org/10.1057/9781137555410_8

Shrivastava, P. (2010). Pedagogy of passion for sustainability. *Academy of Management Learning & Education, 9*(3), 443–455.

11

HOW AN INNOVATIVE ENTREPRENEURIAL EDUCATION DEVICE FOSTERS SUSTAINABLE ENTREPRENEURSHIP AMONG STUDENTS

Christel Tessier Dargent

Abstract

Facing urgent worldwide challenges and a necessary transition toward a regenerative environmental, social, and economic framework, entrepreneurship might be a key driver toward these changes. This chapter demonstrates that tailored entrepreneurship modules in higher education can be a major lever to provide students with necessary competencies and postures. Some of those competencies include collective intelligence, systemic vision, autonomy, empowerment, taking decisions in complex and uncertain environments, work in group projects and debates with experts in a renewed approach. We chose an innovative pedagogical device, a *learning expedition*, to enable students from engineering schools to confront the difficulties and opportunities of setting up a responsible, sustainable venture, displacing them from their usual benchmarks. The experience was challenging and extremely positive in its outcome. We share the process, results, and experiences in hopes of motivating other faculties to undertake the same experimentation, because our programs need to swiftly adapt to address global problems.

Context

As a scholar, teacher, and mother, I feel the urge to contribute to the transformation of our society and I believe our position is a privileged one to convey critical thinking, tools, networks, and knowledge to students. To encourage "behavior change and action" (Riordan &

DOI: 10.4324/9781003457763-11

Klein, 2010), I share a pedagogical innovation we developed to embed sustainability, environmental and social responsibility in the Entrepreneurship curriculum at French engineering schools. The context is an optional Entrepreneurship module that I renovated to actively integrate environmental, social, and governance (ESG) concerns, as expected by students and required by contemporary challenges (Berthault, 2020; Laplatte et al., 2010). About 200 students are enrolled each year in this 40-hour entrepreneurship program, during the second year of five major engineering schools at a southeastern French university.

I embarked on a journey to identify research papers, concepts, resources, and tools to rejuvenate the courses and include ESG considerations at each step of the entrepreneurial process that would support our learning-by-doing classes. I soon found that academic literature is still under development and mostly focused on theoretical concepts and considerations: "Green entrepreneurs have been identified as agents of change that can challenge environmental, social and ethical transformation of society" (Affolderbach & Krueger, 2017). They are described in research articles as ecopreneurs, green, responsible, engaged, sustainable, social, and impact entrepreneurs, which shows that the concept is still nascent and polymorphic.

As I searched for proven operational tools, I reviewed actions and organizations in the business world such as *Shift Project, Réseau Entreprendre, Ronalpia, Grenoble business angels, Pépite*. I also joined academic initiatives like the task force of the *Confédération des Grandes Ecoles* (CGE) assigned to developing teaching materials and innovating pedagogies on Sustainable Entrepreneurship and precursor groups like *Enseignants pour la transition* and *Campus des Transitions*. These resources enabled me to assemble materials that I adapted, put in coherence, and tested before rolling them out at full scale to meet the urgency of students' expectations. I received full support from the institution, but no additional resources. I also conducted "competitive intelligence" to check what other institutions were setting up. Overall, I collected research articles, videos, podcasts, and relevant media about responsible entrepreneurship and entrepreneurial education that I sorted in a structured database using categories like climate change, engineers of the future, sustainable finance, and green marketing.

The objectives of the renovated curriculum and pedagogical innovation are twofold: (1) provide space for engineers to take control over the challenges they are currently facing, that often feel huge and un-achievable, (2) familiarize students with the concept of Social and Solidarity Economy, and its related ecosystems, which seem to be the most structured option for responsible entrepreneurship. Indeed, entrepreneurship is rightly considered by scholars, governments, and practitioners as a powerful tool to bring large scale, drastic, and rapid changes to processes and societies.

The pilot I developed, a "Learning Expedition for Sustainable Entrepreneurship" was a success, and I received valuable feedback from professional stakeholders and students. I strongly believe that empowering students with pragmatic tools, successful examples, and an understanding of existing ecosystems will enable them to overcome their fear and move to taking actions and feeling in control to positively influence their future.

Entrepreneurial education can be used to gain a deeper understanding of the complexities and intricacies of the world and even change it (Neck & Greene, 2011). The Freirian approach supported by Fayolle (2021) draws on the development of critical consciousness, where learners identify, interpret, criticize, and eventually transform their unsustainable values and practices, while collectively working toward a sustainable course of actions. This approach implies the ability to make the connection between experience, knowledge construction, and transformation to bring about personal and social change: once there is awareness, action must take place (Freire, 1974). As Foliard et al. write (2022), researchers and pedagogues must rethink the entrepreneurial process to provide "explanations, knowledge and teaching materials to help build new entrepreneurial processes and practices based on solidarity and energy saving."

The literature in this domain underlines the importance of learning by doing, teamwork, interdisciplinarity, and project engagement (Fayolle et al., 2021). That is why I identified learning expeditions as an adequate tool to convey the key elements of a sustainable entrepreneurship education: it means learning with an authentic purpose that uses real-life experiences from the local context as a pedagogic medium to develop knowledge, skills, and character. Learning becomes more engaging, meaningful, and personalized. It includes interdisciplinary, in-depth investigations, individual and group projects, field studies, debates, and presentations of student work, in a holistic approach.

Being responsible for an Entrepreneurship module at five engineering schools, I considered it a pertinent curriculum to renovate from an academic viewpoint, because it is intrinsically interdisciplinary and already embedded in an experiential hands-on project pedagogy. Building on my 15 years of experience in entrepreneurship and my network among the local entrepreneurial ecosystem, I contacted potential stakeholders at incubators, business angels' groups, and other entrepreneurship support institutions and I received massive and enthusiastic support.

I hope this story of creating the Learning Expedition for Sustainable Entrepreneurship will engage and inspire other colleagues because it is a very extraordinary, exciting, intimate, and rewarding journey to share with professionals and students.

Description of the Process

Upon taking responsibility for Entrepreneurship initiatives, I was given *carte blanche* to align the entrepreneurship curriculum with the environmental and societal challenges. Students have demanded such change. As described earlier, I set up a new approach and needed to test it before a major roll-out to all students. To test, adjust, and complete the program developed, I resorted to a *beta* Learning Expedition, during a special week-long event called *Semaine Kaleidoscope*. During that week, students were allowed to pick optional courses in an extended catalog, including creativity, entrepreneurship, innovation, ethics, transition.

Our creative pedagogical initiative, a Learning Expedition, allows students to have a clear vision of innovations, trends, and gaps concerning Sustainable Entrepreneurship "in the real world." My approach is very similar to that developed by Fayolle (2021) in a Freirian approach: "in a very counter-intuitive process, learners are encouraged to develop an awareness of the power and freedom they have (and will have) in the choice (or design) and use of management tools." Based on the literature, it seemed obvious that direct inquiries and debates with experts were important. Students also needed time to discuss and ponder entrepreneurial concepts in all their complex dimensions: how can entrepreneurs combine their freedom to set up a venture and put their creativity at the service of higher common goals?

Many local entrepreneurs responded enthusiastically, and we welcomed start-uppers, incubators, Social and Solidarity Economy actors to our project. We also traveled to an innovative community project led by a charismatic serial entrepreneur. Each encounter enabled students to ask questions, exchange and discuss the lessons learned, sources of amazement, ethical questioning. Those extraordinary meetings allowed students to reflect and propose materials, list questions, develop new business canvas. Business leaders also provided invaluable material to further design our new class. Students worked on a group project, thus improving their communication and persuasion skills, which is critical. The program lasted for an intensive 35-hour week and included a mix of 30 students from different engineering and management schools.

The objectives of the module were to:

- motivate and engage students,
- increase awareness of current environmental and social challenges,
- develop understanding of social and solidarity economy and the associated entrepreneurial ecosystem,
- make students feel empowered and discover the possibilities of entrepreneurship.

The Learning Expedition is structured to allow students to:

- get "into the field" as a group to explore an important theme,
- shift from usual academic context, location, and conditions,
- meet and discuss with inspirational personalities they would not have met otherwise,
- develop collective intelligence to tackle a thorny issue and develop innovative and tangible plans for action,
- understand that issues must be explored in-depth as they are more complex than first thought,
- develop a desire to act and a clear conscience of their capability to do so,
- refine their professional project experience.

The program is structured as follows. Each morning students encounter guest speakers – experts from entrepreneurial structures, incubators specialized in social and solidarity economy or impact/responsible/sustainable entrepreneurship, business angels, and of course actual entrepreneurs. There is a short formal presentation relating to "ESG constraints and opportunities," followed by an informal, open dialog between students and experts. This casual discussion is key to the process, as it allows experts to be very transparent and open on their experience and students to feel authorized to ask all questions they have in mind. It allows for an in-depth exploration of ethical, economic, and political issues related to developing a responsible entrepreneurial project. During lunch, students and businesspeople network and hold personal meetings.

In the afternoon, students work on their group investigation. They use resources that I compiled for over a year, including videos, podcasts, books recommendations, and research articles on topics related to responsible entrepreneurship. Students choose a specific topic, develop it, ask questions, and make proposals for actions. At mid-module, we hold an expedition, or fieldtrip in "real-life environment," to visit an innovative, responsible business initiative; for instance, this time a "living lab," an open innovation ecosystem that uses iterative feedback on an innovation to create sustainable impact. It focuses on co-creation, rapid prototyping, testing and scaling-up of innovations and businesses, and providing joint-value to the involved stakeholders.

At the beginning of the Learning Expedition, I use roundtable presentations and icebreakers to build a positive group dynamic. I facilitate a brainstorm module so that students have time to express, share and develop their beliefs about entrepreneurship, responsibility, sustainability, the role of engineers, their hopes, and frustrations. This step is critical as it creates a common ground of understanding and propinquity. Students are provided with an "expedition notebook" to remember what they learn, what surprises or concerns them, which item they want to delve into, and action they plan on taking. At the end, we have a time for feedback and roundtable discussions about how the curriculum help them reflect and evolve.

In finale, students present their group project to all experts invited during the week. Students are required to attend the module, but we have decided not to grade it, as we do for creativity sessions. Indeed, the whole point is to ensure students feel responsible, empowered, and willing to deliver with no "opportunistic" objective. Goal of the program is "higher and further" than gaining a good grade. Also, to feel free to express themselves, to obtain self-efficacy, they need not to feel judged. This requires, however, a huge investment on the part of the professor, who needs to give regular and detailed feedback, question, clarify, and challenge the students, their questions and group work. It requires solid knowledge and competencies, but the results are extremely rewarding. Participants are highly engaged, their presentation very creative and professional.

Successes and Failures

We gathered very useful verbatims and information from students through the roundtable at the end of the module. We also obtained data via an individual digital questionnaire that students completed at the end of the week. Feedback from the experts and professionals who contributed to the module were also gathered and analyzed.

Since most of the students did not choose the module and were not interested in entrepreneurship to start with, their feedback is unexpectedly highly positive. All students stated the training module was very useful, enjoyable, efficient, and expert presentations were extremely well received. Students especially appreciated time for interpersonal discussion with experts and entrepreneurs in a very intimate atmosphere, which allowed for more personal and in-depth relationships with key-note speakers, compared to a classical lecture in an auditorium. They overwhelmingly appreciated the format and content.

They also expressed that they developed their own point of view, thanks to the rich gathering of experiences, topics, and experts. They felt they could now propel themselves in an environment unknown to them and felt empowered doing so. They enjoyed the pedagogical format: debates and speakers in the morning, roundtables for feedback, and group project in the afternoon, with access to a rich database of information. The small class size was key to the success and the quality of the debates. Based on attendance, verbatim, individual questionnaires, and group presentations, we can confirm that students:

- felt highly motivated and engaged,
- deeply increased their awareness of current environmental and social challenges,
- developed a clear understanding of social and solidarity economy and the associated entrepreneurial ecosystem,
- felt empowered and discovered the possibilities offered by an entrepreneurial project.

However, their intention to set up a responsible venture remained low by the end of the module and was a bit disappointing. When signing up for the experience, they were not motivated by intent to become entrepreneurs. During the Learning Expedition they were exposed to unvarnished testimonies of entrepreneurs and understood the complexity of running a responsible business. Nevertheless, they proved more positive and equipped to transform their personal environment in a manner they can envision and endorse.

They developed a deep understanding of (a) the way to measure the environmental and social impacts of a venture setup (product life cycle assessment, eco-conception, greenwashing, triple bottom line, and CARE accounting), (b) the ways to integrate a responsible stand toward sustainable development in an entrepreneurial process (social business canvas, inclusive employment), and (c) the opportunities of transformation provided by responsible entrepreneurship. Students acknowledged entrepreneurship is an accessible, efficient tool, required to transform society. I am thus positive that this innovative pedagogical device contributes to developing answers to students' discomfort and questions and empowers them with means to think and act autonomously. In doing so, we confirm that active and critical pedagogies (Fayolle, 2021; Freire, 1974) appear key to this transformation journey.

The structure and content of the Learning Expedition proved very powerful to effectively *move from awareness of the issues toward awareness of one's capability to act*. We identified some key success factors.

- The future is unknown and under construction. Questions raised do not always find answers and this is uncomfortable both for facilitators and students, but transparency and humility are crucial to the process.
- Faculty and experts present facets of problems and controversies and complexity of challenges to develop understanding and critical thinking. But they must stay clear from ideology and ready-made thinking.
- Students build their own autonomy, goals, and free will to act based on resources offered. They gain knowledge from a diversified and structured knowledge transfer database about responsible entrepreneurship and sustainable development. It encompasses research articles, videos, podcasts dealing with social and solidarity entrepreneurship, including thematic in-depth inputs in sustainable finance, green marketing, social business models, and regulations.
- We clearly define guiding questions to structure reflection, so students do not feel overwhelmed and helpless.
- We examine critical thinking tools (i.e., controversy analysis) that can be used at each step of the entrepreneurial process to ensure a responsible approach; what are the constraints and limitations observed in the "real world"?

- The "outdoor" or field trip visit is a critical "hook" of the module.
- To ensure pertinent experts are invited, strong and diversified relationships with the local entrepreneurial ecosystem are key.
- Class size or audience must be limited to ensure the length and quality of debates. If there is high demand, additional classes must be added.
- At the end of the module, students provide traditional oral presentation. We are considering other options that would better represent the hands-on spirit of the module.
- It is important to not evaluate the module with a grade, as part of this empowerment process, but to provide students with detailed feedback on their work on a regular basis.

I would like to stress that this Learning Expedition project allowed our sustainability community to grow by gathering students, researchers, teachers, and business professionals in our entrepreneurial ecosystem. In the process, we also identified and joined wider networks nationally and internationally to share projects and best practices. It is important to note that it sometimes feels bewildering to operate in such a high level of complexity and uncertainty with no guidance and secured clear objectives ahead. On the positive side, working on such a hot topic, linked to high expectations from students and the professional world is extremely exhilarating and rewarding. Our challenge now is to request resources and time allocation in a very constrained environment.

Overall Results and Low Hanging Fruits

Overall, this innovation is very well received by faculty, students, and administrators. Final student presentations dealt with "local money for a green supply chain," "how can responsible entrepreneurs get hold on the triple bottom line," "Eco-design for sustainable entrepreneurs," and "how to green market and not green wash as impact entrepreneurs."

The scope of the transformation and the number of students that beneficiate from it prove its impact. Once completely rolled-out, about 200 M1 engineer students will be reached. The following student verbatim express change and enthusiasm triggered by participation in the program:

- *"I understand now that social and solidarity entrepreneurship is a way to engage in projects to change the world and it can be supported and financed like any other type of entrepreneurship."*

- *Teacher was top notch and prepared a great program for us with many different experts from the responsible entrepreneurship sector."*
- *Strength of the module was the innovative pedagogic device with experts, open and animated discussions and group debates."*
- *This week helped me put into perspective entrepreneurship, which was before a large and indistinct concept to me."*
- *I discovered there is an important ecosystem to support and finance entrepreneurs and I feel more capable of developing a project."*

Faculty members found the initiative inspiring and hopefully they will incorporate ESG concerns in their own curricula. Administrators supported the initiative both from an entrepreneurship and a transition perspective and recognized that these are differentiating competitive advantages for universities. Going forward we will incorporate this program in a wider initiative with colleagues, named *Transition Entrepreneurship School*. It is interesting to note that this program is part of a massive change; for instance, the *Business Angels* recently described themselves as "Citizen finance" and are setting up a sociocracy-inspired governance system, FrenchTech in the Alps had their first "Green Summit," *Réseau Entreprendre* is rolling out an "Impact Entrepreneurs" program.

Eventually, grounded in contemporary academic research and debates, this initiative contributes to this emerging field of research tackling ESG aspects in entrepreneurship education and entrepreneurial processes. This chapter is part of a wider effort of several groups of academics interacting and networking to contribute. Both at the *Research Center in Entrepreneurship Education* (CREE) and *CGE* taskforce levels, we are developing research projects, articles, communications for symposium – *Académie de l'Entrepreneuriat et de l'Innovation*, colloque *Question de Pédagogie dans l'Enseignement Supérieur*-, pedagogical resources and case studies to share.

Several challenges remain. Political issues, power balance, and turf fighting can harmfully delay decisions, budget allocation, and knowledge sharing. Within academia, we operate at a very slow pace while the world is changing dramatically fast, and students' expectations are increasing daily.

Conclusion

There is a widely shared consensus in the academic world on the urgency to act on sustainability and move from inspiring talks to rolling up sleeves and experimenting. Indeed, current debates, reports, and observations on climate and global equity conditions are stunning. Moving on from denial, fear, and demotivation to empowerment and actions requires tools, resources, and energy, since "up is the only way out." Our "Learning Expedition for Sustainable Entrepreneurship" is challenging and rewarding and represents my willingness to move from reflection to action.

Renovation of an existing and praised curriculum, strongly anchored in current economy and processes, such as Entrepreneurship, can be a thorny issue. Learning Expeditions demonstrates a way to bring together professionals, researchers, and students, expert, or novice on ESG topics, to think, debate, propose, constructively criticize, and question. The learning-by-doing approach has been very rewarding and empowering. This process also legitimizes using pilot projects to develop and test overall curriculum changes, which requires a great deal of support because they are time-consuming. Moreover, entrepreneurial education innovation implies a change in posture both from students and teachers.

Most academics are not used to developing courses and research under such a high level of uncertainty and complexity. The effectual reasoning (Sarasvathy, 2001) that I resorted to, which is so relevant for entrepreneurship, is a powerful tool for action that requires humility but offers proven means to act and shape the future. I hope that my attempt, hereby described, will inspire other practitioners, especially at university, who want to transform their curricula. Entrepreneurial modules can raise awareness among students of the environmental and social challenges at stake, their complexities and inherent uncertainty, and empower the future entrepreneurs as well as employees to be decision-makers and doers.

Based on this pilot program, I believe that interacting with practitioners and other academic experts in different fields, that is, economists, sociologists, philosophers, designers, scientists for instance, will help broaden the perspectives, in a renewed design thinking approach. The process used to develop this course and its overall pedagogical approach could be applied to revising other courses, not only business classes like finance, marketing, or logistics, but any type of teaching programs, even in scientific expertise topics like responsible generative artificial intelligence or responsible digital development.

Personal Learning Outcomes and Recommendations

To conclude, I would like to submit a few recommendations to educators and faculty. Firstly, read, learn, question, be curious, and get an in-depth understanding of the issues at stake. Understand the complexity and the intricacies of the challenges, material problems, political difficulties, economical limits, social hindrances, scientific gaps, and promising initiatives. Then, it is important to have an even deeper knowledge on what is done in our field of expertise, even if it is to realize the shortcomings. It is also a good way to start piling up documentation.

As educators, we need to build self-confidence and self-efficacy in a very uncertain environment. The way we teach to empower our students has evolved. Top to bottom academic discourse is not the most efficient way to have them develop their collective intelligence, critical mind, and free will. Not knowing the answers, generating debates, inviting experts to class can be an unsettling experience; but this is also part of a highly rewarding and exciting process. We can provide honest and forthright answers to students, establish a humble but determined posture, and encourage the right to question, ponder, and reflect. Students value such intellectual integrity. We can be role models in helping to draw new mental maps at a larger scale. My own expectations of students have evolved. Most of them enjoy exploring new knowledge and domains, so I consider this energy more important than specific technical expertise in a subject, that can always be gained further down the road when required. While this type of initiative is very time and energy consuming, sharing it with colleagues alleviates the load.

Our bottom-up initiative to co-create and test a pilot curriculum can only be effective if it is part of a wider initiative. Entrepreneurship or project management classes are good entry-points to test and verify new innovative practices. Identify allies and colleagues willing to collaborate and share concerns and interests is a must.

To me, it appears quite useless to try and convince opponents, since "cultural revolution" cannot be efficiently enforced without voluntary assent. However, if only isolated and enthusiastic scholars take initiatives, we cannot face our current challenges and positively influence society. Higher education institutions need to embark on this exhilarating journey willingly and massively, by conducting institution-wide transformations. I share the views of Satish Kumar (2021) that bottom-up and top-down initiatives are both required. Administrators need to send a clear and strong message of support, explain their vision and the strategy, and provide for resources in terms of time, people, space, and training. Deliberate institutional scoping is a must, otherwise projects remain local, limited, and transient (Verzat & Garant, 2021).

Innovative faculties, researchers and lecturers must be valued and publicized by their institutions to encourage others to follow the same experimentation path. To encourage more faculty participation, institutions could provide incentives. I believe most people are ready and enthusiastic to embrace changes to new, more responsible practices and concrete action can be taken with support.

Another important factor is the right timing: syllabus, programs, and pedagogical contents are reviewed on a regular basis, and we must use those cycles to bring changes and create new modules. Whenever we have a chance to recruit faculties or participants to committees, it is important to suggest names of experts in transition, sustainable development, and impact entrepreneurship. Their legitimacy and expertise can enrich classes, help set up conferences, provide material resources and alternative models from "the real world."

One final point that is dear to me is the importance of getting students off-site: to explore actual situations helps them adopt new viewpoints, behave more like responsible actors rather than passive observers and create new relationships with faculty. I see this approach as "head, hands and heart," balancing cognitive, psychomotor, and affective domains, to target "transformative sustainability learning" (Sipos et al., 2008). Equally important is to take our students into nature since it is center stage in our transformation. Our main objective is indeed to keep our planet habitable. Reconnecting students with nature is of critical importance to make them realize we must care for it for our own sake. Nature needs entrepreneurs.

References

Affolderbach, J., & Krueger, R. (2017). "Just" ecopreneurs: Reconceptualising green transitions and entrepreneurship. *Local Environment*, 22(4), 410–423.

Berthault, M. (2020). Projet ClimatSup INSA-Intégrer les enjeux climat-énergie dans les formations du Groupe INSA-Groupe INSA-The Shift Project.

Fayolle, A. (2021). Construire, déconstruire, reconstruire un outil de gestion dans une approche pédagogique freirienne. *Entreprendre Innover*, 51(4), 29–42.

Fayolle, A., Lamine, W., Mian, S., & Phan, P. (2021). Effective models of science, technology and engineering entrepreneurship education: Current and future research. *The Journal of Technology Transfer*, 46(2), 277–287.

Foliard, S., Verzat, C., Dubard Barbosa, S., & Toutain, O. (2022). De la main invisible à la main dans la main. L'esprit d'entreprendre, questions de sens et de dialogues. *Entreprendre & Innover*, 52, 5–15.

Freire, P. (1974). Pédagogie des Opprimés, éditions Maspero, traduction.

Kumar, S., & Cenkl, P. (2021). *Transformative learning. Reflections on 30 years of head, heart and hands at Schumacher College.* New Society Publishers

Laplatte, B., Bourque, F., Granger, F. P., Dery, G., & Berube, M. (2010). The engineer, sustainable development craftsman at the center of the global energy challenge! L'ingenieur, artisan du developpement durable au centre du defi energetique mondial!

Neck, H. M., & Greene, P. G. (2011). Entrepreneurship education: Known worlds and new frontiers. *Journal of small business management, 49*(1), 55–70.

Riordan, M., & Klein, E. J. (2010). Environmental education in action: How expeditionary learning schools support classroom teachers in tackling issues of sustainability. *Teacher Education Quarterly, 37*(4), 119–137.

Sarasvathy, S. D. (2001, August). Effectual reasoning in entrepreneurial decision making: Existence and bounds. In *Academy of Management Proceedings* (Vol. 2001, No. 1, pp. D1–D6). Academy of Management.

Sipos, Y., Battisti, B., & Grimm, K. (2008), "Achieving transformative sustainability learning: Engaging head, hands and heart". *International Journal of Sustainability in Higher Education, 9*(1), 68–86.

Verzat, C., & Garant, M. (2021). L'accompagnement au coeur de l'institution apprenante. In Raucent B., Verzat C., Jacqmot C., Van Nieuwenhoven C. (Eds.), *Accompagner les étudiants. Rôles de l'enseignant, dispositifs et mise en oeuvre* (pp. 497–514). De Boeck, Bruxelles.

12

BACK TO SCHOOL FOR THE PLANET ALUMNI INITIATIVE

Lifelong Learning in Sustainability

Carina Hopper and Johanna Wagner

Abstract

The Back to School for the Planet Alumni Initiative supports higher educa-tion institutions (HEIs) by bringing their graduates back to the classroom alongside current students to update their knowledge and competencies through newly introduced sustainability courses and other learning ac-tivities. The initiative builds on existing relationships between HEIs and their alumni to facilitate post-graduation access to state-of-the-art, updated learning in sustainability. The program accelerates the adoption of sustain-able practices by graduates who are now professionals in their fields and increases their contribution toward societal change and a more sustainable future. Back to School for the Planet creates an opportunity for HEIs to demonstrate their commitment to lifelong learning, develop new bonds with their alumni by updating their sustainability skills, and provide an in-valuable experience for their current students, who benefit from classroom interactions and knowledge sharing with alumni of their program.

Introduction

The Back to School for the Planet Alumni Initiative provides higher education institutions (HEIs) with a straightforward and scalable method for applying lifelong learning in sustainability. It brings alumni back into the classroom to learn about sustainability, a topic often not taught when they were studying, alongside current

DOI: 10.4324/9781003457763-12

students in newly introduced sustainability courses and activities. Back to School for the Planet grew from a teacher-led initiative into a nonprofit to support HEIs' outreach to alumni for sustainability education. By providing instructional guides, alumni recruitment support, participant certificates, a communication toolkit, and access to the Back to School for the Planet network, the nonprofit helps any HEI broaden its impact by extending its sustainability education to graduates.

Lifelong learning is a crucial part of United Nations' Sustainable Development Goal 4 (Quality Education), which aims to "ensure inclusive and equitable quality education and promote lifelong learning opportunities for all" (United Nations, 2023). In business schools, lifelong learning is often offered to a wide audience of professionals, including those who did not graduate from a management program but seek the soft and hard skills necessary to get to the next step of their career. Today, in the context of the climate emergency, the need for companies to change the way they do business calls for greater commitment from business schools to transform the paradigm not only among their current students but also among their alumni.

Description

Many business schools and other HEIs are adding to their programs courses and other learning activities focusing on environmental and social sustainability. Many professionals who are alumni of business programs, and who are currently at the helm of critical business decisions affecting society and nature, did not have courses relating to sustainable business practices available to them when they were students. The Back to School for the Planet Alumni Initiative encourages HEIs that are now offering sustainability education to invite their alumni back to the classroom to take these new sustainability courses and/or other learning activities alongside current students.

The initiative was conceived during an alumni association event at which graduates learned about new sustainability courses and activities that were launched in their former business school program. Responding to this news, several alumni expressed that they "wished these classes had been available to them when they were students" and that they "would love to take these courses now."

In HEIs, a boundary is often set between current students and graduates. When it comes to sustainability learning, however, this boundary should be reconsidered. Indeed, regarding the topic of sustainability, many alumni resemble incoming students: they are new to the subject and curious to discover what it has to offer. Business schools can build on the existing trust with their alumni to offer them an update on their skills in the much-needed area of sustainability.

The Back to School for the Planet Alumni Initiative leverages the existing relationship between HEIs and their alumni and provides critical access to sustainability education in a way that is innovative and straightforward. By considering alumni as potential students for newly introduced sustainability courses, sessions, and activities, this initiative brings alumni back into the classroom alongside current students either online or in person. The positive effects include improved relationships with alumni and expanded awareness and knowledge about critical sustainability practices needed by business.

The Back to School for the Planet Alumni Initiative can be applied in any HEI, including, but not limited to, business schools. It was piloted in 2020 at ESSEC Business School, in two sustainability courses forming part of the MSc in Hospitality Management (also known as IMHI). The courses, titled Sustainability Essentials in Hospitality Management and Sustainable Finance & Law for Hospitality Managers, had been introduced that year together with a sustainability specialization for students of the program. As part of the Back to School for the Planet Alumni Initiative, these courses were opened to a limited number of alumni, who joined alongside current students of the program. Feedback on the pilot was extremely positive both from alumni as well as from current students, who benefited from the sharing of professional experiences from the graduates.

Alumni inclusion in HEIs' new sustainability education offering can take shape in a myriad of ways and is adaptive to school policy, course format, and alumni availability. Schools might invite their alumni to join current students in:

- New courses dedicated to sustainability (e.g., alumni are invited to join a course titled Sustainability Essentials for Hospitality Managers)
- Select sustainability-dedicated sessions (e.g., alumni are invited to join a session on Sustainable Supply Chain Management within an Operations course)
- Specific curricular activities with a sustainability focus (e.g., alumni are invited to act as jury members for final projects relating to sustainability)

- Specific co-curricular activities with a sustainability focus (e.g., alumni are invited to join a Sustainability Leadership Seminar or a volunteer experience)
- Direct learning from students (e.g., student-led sustainability consulting missions are offered to alumni companies).

Beyond the clear advantages for alumni in benefitting from quality education from their institution years, or even decades, after their graduation, their mere presence in the classroom is evidence for current students that this topic has become strategic for companies. It also sends a strong message to students, candidates, and the community at large that the institution is committed to providing lifelong learning on issues that matter as part of its added value.

The Back to School for the Planet Alumni Initiative is highly transferable thanks to the widespread transition to online and hybrid education seen in many regions across the world. Schools that wish to do so can invite alumni to participate in their new sustainability-focused educational offerings in person, or through an online platform if they have one. The only requirement for institutions interested in participating is to have incorporated courses or activities in sustainability, something that is becoming more and more common due to the rise in education for sustainable development (ESD) in recent years (Ssossé et al., 2021).

Context

Surveys show an undeniable shift in student expectations (SOS-UK, 2021) and rising demand for the skills needed to transform companies in an evolving environment. In business, more practitioners are willing to adapt their professional practices with a focus on sustainability but do not have the necessary training to do so. Sustainability teaching began as late as 1992 and has only recently begun to grow in scale (Barth, 2015). As a result (and what is now a defining obstacle to rapid change), most current professionals did not gain during their studies the knowledge and competencies needed to manage sustainable businesses. Many HEIs are already working to remedy this situation for their current students, but they can also contribute to filling this gap for their alumni thanks to the development of new lifelong learning options.

To pilot the Back to School for the Planet Alumni Initiative, we opened four spots each specifically for alumni in two new 25-hour courses on sustainability. We partnered with the alumni association to promote the initiative through email and in a private LinkedIn group.

We received 16 applications from alumni from a variety of countries and age groups. The eight accepted alumni were invited to attend all 25 hours of their assigned course alongside current students. One accepted alumna decided not to participate just prior to the start of class, leaving seven alumni who participated for the duration of the courses.

The admitted alumni participants were all professionals in the field of the program, hospitality management. Given that the courses required a 25-hour commitment over five to ten weeks and during traditional office hours, alumni participants either worked in flexible full-time schedules or were in between employment. During the sessions, graduates were highly engaged, both in asking questions and in sharing relevant corporate experience, while the students were in turn stimulated by the presence of alumni and their active contribution to the discussions. Table 12.1 provides more information on the courses that were opened to the program's alumni.

Results

Six months after the courses ended, five participating alumni answered our impact survey. In their responses, they unanimously agreed that the experience of returning to their former classrooms to learn about sustainability was transformative and had positive impacts both on their personal and professional lives. An alumna summarizes the perception and high potential of the initiative: *"I probably wouldn't have made the decision to take a sustainability course if it hadn't been offered by the program from which I graduated. It was easy to enroll and required no financial investment."*

In standard course feedback, students (i.e., nonalumni) enrolled in the courses shared that having graduates of the program in class with them was overwhelmingly positive and added value to their learning experience. Only positive feedback was received from the 66 participating students (39 students and 27 students respectively in the two courses offered).

Two years after their participation, a second survey was sent to the same seven participating alumni, this time asking about the impact that the initiative may have had on their personal and professional lives in the longer term. We received three replies. Although one student lamented that their current job did not give them the opportunity to apply the sustainability skills gained, the other two respondents did attribute an increase in their professional commitment to sustainability

TABLE 12.1 Sustainability Courses Opened to a Limited Number of Alumni

	Sustainability Essentials in Hospitality Management	*Sustainable Finance & Law for Hospitality Managers*
Course format	Hybrid sessions, with some students online and others in the classroom, as well as online-only sessions	Online-only sessions
Course duration	25 hours over 10 weeks with classes held in the afternoons from 4:30 PM to 7:30 PM	25 hours over five weeks with classes held in the afternoons from 1:15 PM to 7:30 PM
Learning objectives	1 Identify regulatory, economic, environmental, and social factors that lead hospitality companies to invest in sustainability planning and initiatives 2 Make the business case for sustainability in hospitality firms 3 Outline supply chain and production strategies that will help food and beverage operations address sustainability concerns 4 Develop a framework for addressing ethical concerns in hospitality operations, including discrimination and sexual harassment 5 Discuss digital innovation trends that could have an impact on the sustainable development of the hospitality industry	1 Identify opportunities and challenges related to sustainable finance and law for hospitality managers 2 Demonstrate an understanding of the current trends in sustainable finance within and outside of the hospitality industry 3 Describe the regulatory framework, purpose, and role of nonfinancial reporting 4 Understand the corporate regulatory framework at the EU and national levels and its implications for undertaking sustainable business practices 5 Be aware of the issue of policy incoherence that influences business decisions on sustainable business practices and how to harvest the existing incoherence to the benefit of the business 6 Learn to enhance the performance of the business through sustainable business practices while being certain of their compliance with the existing legal framework 7 Understand the different levels of the hospitality business, the corresponding legal frameworks and the sustainable business practices that can be undertaken under those conditions

Type(s) of assignments	Team presentation of a sustainability action plan for a selected company and an individual essay and interactive panel discussion on environmental and social scandals that have threatened the economic sustainability of hospitality companies	Two team projects (one in the field of sustainable finance and the other in sustainable business law) and an individual case study
Number of students enrolled	39	27
Number of alumni admitted	3	4

to the course they attended as alumni two years prior, one respondent expressing that the course helped them to "look at things very differently and feel less ignorant." In terms of an impact on their personal behaviors, one respondent believed that the course did not change their lifestyle given that they were already very eco-conscious. The other two respondents attributed an increase in sustainable practices in their personal lives directly to the course, with one student stating that, since taking the course, they thought twice before traveling by plane, ate more local products, and had begun car sharing.

Back to School for the Planet was registered as a nonprofit organization in January 2021 with the aim of encouraging and supporting the good practice in other HEIs around the world, including, but not limited to, business schools. Dedicated to fostering a new learning environment for students and alumni alike and offering lifelong qualitative education to alumni, the organization provides guidance and tools for higher education programs to help them open their new sustainability-focused classes to their alumni. Its objective is to accelerate change in professional practices by updating the competencies of those who have or will soon have high-level responsibilities in companies and institutions. It creates an opportunity for HEIs to develop new bonds with alumni as they improve their skills. It also provides an invaluable experience for current students, who benefit from classroom interactions and knowledge-sharing with alumni who can discuss current workplace obstacles to sustainable development.

Implementation

Our hypotheses in launching the Back to School for the Planet Alumni Initiative were (1) that alumni were interested in accessing sustainability training from the schools they graduated from and (2) this access could have a positive impact on their personal and professional lives, which could thus drive sustainability in their communities and industries. As faculty who teach sustainability courses, in this case in the MSc in Hospitality Management at ESSEC Business School, we decided to pilot the initiative in our own classes with the support of the program director, who appreciated its innovative nature. Both the number of applications for the initiative and the answers to the surveys we conducted later supported the hypotheses and demonstrated additional benefits.

The initiative is one that can be implemented by any HEI with relative ease and low costs. Benefits for the institution include evidence of a commitment to lifelong learning as well as the added value for students in having diverse professional perspectives in the classroom. Institutions can also use the initiative to attract candidates that may choose institutions committed to updating the skills of their alumni in critical and evolving topics.

Table 12.2 highlights practical advantages to different stakeholders in bringing alumni back to the classroom.

Further case studies or research projects following or inspired by the Back to School for the Planet model are very welcome and, we believe, valuable for the literature on both ESD and lifelong learning.

TABLE 12.2 Ease of Implementation for Diverse Stakeholders

Stakeholder Group	Ease of Implementation
Dean, School Management	• Low consumption consumption of internal resources • Low/no incremental costs of adding a limited number of alumni to already existing activities
Faculty	• Flexibility in number of alumni participating • Flexibility in format
Alumni	• Free of cost • Limited paperwork • Facilitated access thanks to virtual participation options • Existing relationship and contact with the institution • Access to Back to School for the Planet network
Students	• Potential classroom disruptions are curbed by a Back to School for the Planet Code of Conduct for participating alumni
Recruiters, Corporate Stakeholders	• Companies can rest assured that graduates of participating schools have sustainability training available to them and that their skills will be updated by their schools in the future • Adapted to new working habits (flexible working hours and home office)

Opportunities

Bringing alumni back to the classroom has the potential to transform business education for several reasons. It creates a unique intergenerational learning setting where young students share the classroom with more experienced alumni. In this safe environment, where students and alumni learn on equal footing, both groups benefit from a shared space and time where their common objective is to learn about sustainability. While the usual hierarchical structure disappears, different types of bonding can take place, which strengthens the sense of belonging and community.

Through the Back to School for the Planet Alumni Initiative, the student learning experience is enhanced in several ways:

1 First-hand accounts of how the sustainability strategies and concepts may play out – or may have already been executed – in the professional world are integrated into the classroom discussion with alumni.
2 A strong link is created between current students and participating alumni, leading to potential networking and employment opportunities.
3 A new type of collaborative environment emerges that is intergenerational and bridges the academic and professional world in a dynamic way.

The initiative provides an opportunity for alumni to better grasp knowledge and skills on sustainability subjects that may not have been available when they were students. This improves the practice and recruiting skills of professionals who were not trained in sustainability.

The initiative also provides an opportunity for HEIs to raise awareness about existing sustainability initiatives and courses. It can be difficult for alumni who have a limited understanding of the width and breadth of sustainability to achieve this level of awareness another way. As the four stages of learning remind us, "we don't know what we don't know," which explains this difficulty for alumni (Adams, 2021). By offering free access to newly introduced courses and activities to their alumni, business schools are broadening their impact and contributing to change and innovation in the corporate world.

More fundamentally, this puts business education institutions in a place where they include lifelong learning updates as a benefit to joining their programs. It highlights the responsibility they are taking to bridge new skill and knowledge gaps and supports global efforts to address social and environmental sustainability challenges.

With alumni in the classroom, the teaching experience is also transformed. Faculty benefit from the experience of current professionals who can relate real world examples of topics discussed. It enriches the conversation and leads to very practical questions being asked. As the course progresses, professors, students, and alumni work together to solve real challenges and leverage opportunities.

The transformative potential of this initiative is related to the motivations of key stakeholders of HEIs to implement and/or take part in it (Table 12.3).

Though the initiative is straightforward and inexpensive to implement, there are indeed obstacles (Table 12.4). The Back to School for the Planet nonprofit was created to guide schools through the process and address these challenges.

TABLE 12.3 Motivations for Diverse Stakeholders

Stakeholder Group	Motivations
Dean, School Management	• Innovative lifelong learning offering for alumni, which can also aid in recruitment • Expanded reach of sustainability efforts already in place
Faculty	• Spotlight on sustainability teaching already taking place • Enriched classroom experience • Experience in innovative lifelong learning methods
Alumni	• Updated skills from an institution they trust • Strengthened connection with alma mater • Course certificate
Students	• Strengthened links with alumni • First-hand insight from industry professionals within the learning environment • Experience with an innovative lifelong learning method that they can choose to benefit from once they graduate
Recruiters, Corporate Stakeholders	• Trusted sustainability training available for employees who are graduates from participating schools

TABLE 12.4 Obstacles for Diverse Stakeholders

Stakeholder Group	Obstacles
Dean, School Management	• Interference with revenue-generating lifelong learning offerBlurred lines • Blurred lines between students and graduates·
Faculty	• Worries about downgraded class experience for students • Discomfort with potential arguments triggered by alumni experience
Alumni	• Fear of content inadequacy with their needs • Time commitment over several course sessions • Perception of failure risk
Students	[No obstacles were observed from the side of students, but this is an aspect to be explored in future cases.]
Recruiters, Corporate Stakeholders	[No obstacles were observed from the side of recruiters or corporate stakeholders, but this is an aspect to be explored in future cases.]

Conclusion

Dedicated to creating a new learning environment for students and alumni alike, Back to School for the Planet provides guidance and tools for higher education programs to provide alumni access to new sustainability-focused courses and activities. United Nations' Sustainable Development Goal 4 includes the promotion of lifelong learning, and Back to School for the Planet provides a model for its implementation by bringing alumni into the classroom alongside current students to contribute to active learning and community building.

The Back to School for the Planet Alumni Initiative and results of the pilot program serve as a model for HEIs to innovate in the areas of ESD and lifelong learning and provide value for current students and alumni communities. The nonprofit serves as a resource for universities to obtain recommendations on implementing such programs. The full potential of higher education to contribute to change can be achieved when dissemination of sustainability knowledge and competencies extends beyond traditional limits to empower not just current students but also alumni.

Final note: We would like to thank Patti Brown, who at the time of the pilot at ESSEC Business School was director of the MSc in Hospitality

Management (IMHI) program and who strongly supported the initiative from the start, as well as Dr. Lela Mélon, who played a key role in the development of Back to School for the Planet and who with enthusiasm welcomed program alumni into her sustainable law classes. We are grateful to Patti and Lela for their constant encouragement and for the many ways in which they have and continue to support education for sustainability.

References

Adams, L. (2021). Learning a new skill is easier said than done. Gordon Training International. Retrieved January 31, 2023, from https://www.gordontraining.com/free-workplace-articles/learning-a-new-skill-is-easier-said-than-done/.

Barth, M. (2015). *Implementing sustainability in higher education: Learning in an age of transformation*. Routledge.

SOS-UK (2021). 10 years of research on education and sustainability. Retrieved January 31, 2023, from https://www.sos-uk.org/post/10-years-of-research-on-education-and-sustainability.

Ssossé, Q., Wagner, J., & Hopper, C. (2021). Assessing the impact of ESD: Methods, challenges, results. *Sustainability*, *13*(5), 2854, https://doi.org/10.3390/su13052854.

United Nations (2023). SDG Goal 4. United Nations Department of Economic and Social Affairs. Retrieved January 31, 2023, from https://sdgs.un.org/goals/goal4.

13

CREATIVITY FOR MANAGING LIFE IN COMMON

*Fabio B. Josgrilberg, Luciana Hashiba,
and Luís Henrique Pereira*

Abstract

Creativity has been named one of the main skills of our time because it is at the core of every innovation process. Therefore, within creative processes lies the possibility of developing the necessary solutions for a world at the fringes of environmental, social, and, consequently, economic collapse. What follows is a proposition to both improve our students' sensibility to social and environmental issues and creatively seek solutions in a corporate setting. The suggestion is based on two experimental academic activities carried out at Fundação Getúlio Vargas (FGV), one of the most important business schools in Brazil, under the supervision of the Master in International Management (MPGI) and the Innovation Center (FGVInn).

Introduction

If the World Economic Forum (WEF) report is right, how do we teach creativity? How do we use creativity to solve problems in our lives in common with other human beings? And how is **"creativity for managing life in common"** related to business and business education for that matter? Let's break all these issues down and then share our experience.

First, what is creative or creativity? As a working definition, we assume that some output is creative if it is new, original if compared to the current situation, and useful. Some will say that it must be astonishing and evoke some sort of strong emotional response (Runco & Jaeger, 2012; Simonton, 2018; Wilson, 2017). However, we are talking

DOI: 10.4324/9781003457763-13

about urgent environmental and social problems so, let's stick with "new and useful" for simplicity.

By useful, we mean something that is socially accepted and used. That is the key to entering the realm of business management and education. Whatever a company or small business does to make money must be useful so that people want to buy the products or services and the business is successful. No news here, of course. However, things have become very complicated and urgent, especially when it comes to the sustainability of our planet, Earth. It does not suffice to simply sell products or services; they must be sold in a "good way," that is, a way that promotes and protects life – the "good life," "the just life," as ancient Greek philosophy has understood a long time ago. While it may be disappointing for some managers and executives, the "good way" of doing business is not an individual decision. The definition of the "good way" is a social matter. Irony alert: yes, every business is part of society.

Raworth calls attention to the social implication of goals we set for our economy. To aim at selling more products to increase GDP won't be enough to get us all away from the environmental dead end we are heading to as a society (Raworth, 2017). This is not a narrative pushed forward within some sort of ideological bubble. Since 1973 WEF has been promoting a manifesto for a better kind of capitalism that was not solely focused on shareholders but included society (WEF, 1973). Sadly, since then, our economic society has moved more toward inequality and shareholder primacy.

To summarize: business is part of a society, struggling to find a "good way" where profits, social needs, and environmental limits find balance. Such a delicate equilibrium will only be possible if we are able to listen to stakeholders – meaning all people and groups who have a valid interest in our businesses (Freeman et al., 2018). Remember, stakeholders have a face. We must be able to define a few principles and goals to live our lives in common. Today, to manage a business is also to manage life in common.

Prototyping

We propose a path to creatively seek solutions in a corporate setting that enhances student awareness of social and environmental issues. We conducted two experimental academic activities at Fundação Getúlio Vargas (FGV), one of the most important business schools in Brazil, under the supervision of the Master's in International Management (MPGI) and the Innovation Center (FGVInn). Our rationale was rather simple. We focused on two basic problems: (1) there are social and environmental issues that concern every business; (2) because business is not effective in addressing the social and environmental problems we face as a society; we require more creative solutions.

The need for more creative leaders, managers, and, above all, citizens with a creative and sustainable mindset triggered the idea of developing a course on organizational creativity at the International Management Master Program, within The Global Alliance in Management Education's (CEMS) block seminar, worth three credits. The course took place between August 1 and 5, 2022, at FGV's main campus, São Paulo, Brazil. Thirteen students from five different countries (Brazil, Demark, Germany, Netherlands, and France) attended the course. For more context, this was the first course for international students who arrived for a one-semester exchange program. Students stayed together from 8:00 AM to 5:00 PM every day of the week.

The course emphasized the principles and strategies for developing organizational creativity and innovation processes and culture. It was specifically designed to allow students from different backgrounds to understand critical dimensions of how organizational creativity is developed and managed. The course involved applied, activity-based collaboration, and, in partnership with Lello Lab, it included a design sprint on sustainable solutions for managing life in common. Lello is Brazil's largest condominium management enterprise, with over 1.5 million people living in buildings or house condominiums and utilizing its services.[1]

The first part of the course challenged students' perceptions of how creative they are, and how creativity has a political dimension that questions the status quo within an organization or society. The goal was to increase the students' creative confidence by exposing them to several exercises that questioned their assumptions in four dimensions: communication flows, time, landscapes, and methods.

Student reflections on the creative exercises included

- *What I really liked was the mix of theory and the practical approach, especially that we did not just complete activities such as the final assignment when we had to put us in the shoes of such a project in a company but also those "out-of-the-box" activities. (Student A)*
- *A thing I liked was the broad take on creativity. The lecture content, the games, and the circus all taught me about creativity in a different way. (Student B)*

- *But I would like to thank you for the week; it was amazing! All the super experiences related to administration and management – it was super fun and aggregator! There is only "I like it." Ahahah has no negative points! (Student C)*
- *Getting out of my comfort zone and learning things in the circus that I can apply to my professional and daily life like takings risks, learning to be open-minded, and thinking fast/Improv. I loved all the activities as well and how everything was so dynamic. (Student D)*

For the design sprint section of the course at Lello Lab, students developed solutions to produce energy at the gym, a car-sharing children's pick-up system, and a pet support system for owners who needed to travel away for short periods of time. A four-day Life in Common Journey event followed block seminar and expanded to include students from Master's programs, undergraduates, dwellers of a condominium located at the west end of São Paulo city, and Lello Condominiums' professionals. The condominium is home to 3,000 people.

In the Life in Common Journey event, which was a spin-off from the MPGI block seminar, we employed full hands-on activity. The diversity of profiles and schedules involved in the activity forced us to run the meetings only on Saturdays, from October to November. Four sessions were organized as

1 Visit and understand the condominium's social-environmental needs.
2 Benchmarking solutions at CEFOPEA.
3 Brainstorming solutions.
4 Prototype at WeFab, a maker lab.

CEFOPEA is an NGO known for its low-cost solutions to environmental challenges. At the end of the journey, the group came up with solutions for safety, social engagement, and educational programs all targeted at sustainable issues. All four solutions were approved by the local council and are being implemented at the condominium.

Lessons Learned

Lesson 1 – Creativity Must Be Released. Creative Skills and Culture Are Teachable

As previously discussed, society requires more creative processes to devise innovative solutions for environmental challenges. As much as innovation has become a buzzword in business at all levels, creative people and teams are needed to run innovative processes in full gear as the environmental challenges urge us to do. It is not only about having innovation processes but also about having the creative confidence to propose and test new ideas.

Western society promotes culture and business methods that undermine human creative potential in general. Meanwhile, creativity has become a "special gift" that only a few "chosen ones" or experts have. Curious fact: the limitation of the human creative potential was the object of study in the famous research developed by George Land and Beth Jarman (1998) with 1,600 children for 10 years. This work consisted of applying eight different creativity assessment tests through divergent thinking challenges in relation to different stimuli. The first tests were applied to children aged three to five years, and in that first stage, 98% scored what the researchers classified as a "genius" category. Five years later, the percentage of "geniuses" dropped to 32%, and five years later, that percentage dropped to 10%. The same test was applied to 200,000 adults over 25 years old. In this age group, the percentage dropped to 2%.

In the authors' assessment, the main cause of the restriction of natural creativity would be the socialization process about what is good, bad, wrong, beautiful, and ugly, among other values (Land & Jarman, 1998).

In our project, we found student self-assessment of creativity to be very low. When asked to rate their creativity potential from one to five, just one of them rated five; all the others ranged from two to three, probably because people are afraid or shy to say that they are creative. A similar feeling emerged when, at the end of the second activity, the Life in Common Journey, one participant said that she wasn't expecting that we would reach actual solutions to be implemented. Why didn't she have creative confidence from the start?

Lesson 2 – To Run a Business Is to Run Life in Common

The second lesson truly had a significant impact on us. When we planned the Lello Lab activity, we hoped that the focus on sustainability would be relevant. We were aware of the commons approach to business (Deakin, 2012; Ostrom, 2015), and how social issues couldn't be ignored (Raworth, 2017). What struck us was how the idea of managing life in common significantly motivated our students and the participants at Life in Common Journey, even in a simple exercise toward providing solutions to a neighborhood or condominium.

By deploying a full design thinking sprint in both activities, students dealt with both the principles of product design and stakeholder management to propose new solutions and we circled back to the origins of design thinking. In its first edition in 1972, *Design for the Real World: Human Ecology and Social Change*, Victor Papanek problematized the vision of design reduced to material issues or focused on profit and sought to push forward a more humanistic approach that considers social–environmental issues (Papanek, 1973). In 1987, Peter Rowe published the book, *Design Thinking*, which offered the first systematized view of the term (Rowe, 1991). In sum, at its origin, ecology was at the heart of the design movement that ended up on the design thinking approach.

Somehow over the past decades, we left the ecological aspect of design thinking behind, as the emphasis was so much on trying out new ideas and launching new products. A focus on the user overshadowed the more holistic approach that includes environmental concerns. Again, irony alert: the user is a human living in a world with other human beings!

Business Education and Sustainable Solutions

In this section, we attempt to systematize our learned lessons into a replicable model in business education programs. We recommend two approaches:

1 Design sprint – This could be done in a one-week event, in the freshmen welcome week, for instance, or during the academic semester. This would work as a design sprint, but with at least one period used to increase the cohort's creative confidence and students' understanding of what the "life in common" idea is all about. In our experience, we used the mornings to offer theoretical input and afternoons to run group activities inside and outside the campus.
2 Elective course – A course in which one learns key theoretical aspects and techniques that students may apply in projects toward a life in a common related project. We are yet to run a full course, and although this is a proposal, it is feasible. We find it is important to let the students choose their own projects about Managing Life in Common and use their creativity to propose solutions.

Content-wise, the structure is very similar, but the design sprint will focus more on hands-on activities (maker culture) with less theoretical input. The structure and content we propose is presented in Table 13.1.

The following descriptions provide further explanation of core course content.

Liberating Creativity

The first topic is an exercise that promotes the understanding of limits to our creativity and what fosters good creative processes individually and socially. In our approach, we work with four dimensions of creative processes: communication flows, time, landscapes, and processes. We will make introductory remarks about the first three dimensions, while the process dimension is discussed in the next section.

Communication flows are at the core of both individual and social creativity. Therefore, our cognitive capacity to devise creative solutions depends on our brain's ability to activate different neural networks. This ability depends on external inputs, including biological, social, and physical aspects as well as how our bodies engage with the world (Abraham, 2018; Csikszentmihalyi, 2007; Malinin, 2016; Zwir et al., 2021). Throughout history, creative environments were communication-intensive ecosystems that provided psychological safety to propose ideas, fail, collaborate, diverge, and converge, with multiple perspectives on the challenges being faced (Coulton, 2012; Feld, 2012; Howkins, 2009). Students must trust the power of collaboration. A major myth that is addressed is the notion that creativity is a "gift" received by some. On the contrary, creativity is essentially social, and must be socially recognized for creativity to change society.

Beyond lectures, we address the occasional lack of confidence by teaching the students brainstorming techniques and running group exercises to enable them to understand the communicational dynamics of teamwork. In our one-week activity with international students, we went to the art museum (MASP, São Paulo Art Museum) to understand different perspectives on the same subject, and to a circus (Circo Viramundo) where students had the opportunity to discuss how their brains work when facing new challenges. They were asked to do several acrobatics exercises to overcome thinking limits!

Going outside the campus, students had to think about architectural settings and how they impact the flow of communication. Should we opt for an open office setting? What happens when we need to

TABLE 13.1 Introductory Content and Activities

Content	Theory	Introductory References	Activity	Tools
Liberating creativity	Sociocultural approaches to creativity Neuroscience of creativity	(Abraham, 2018; Glaveanu et al., 2020; Kelley & Kelley, 2013)	Group activities that promote different points of view and collaboration	https://www.liberatingstructures.com/
The discipline of creativity	Design thinking	(Brown & Katz, 2009; Rowe, 1991; Sinfiel et al., 2014)	Design sprint	https://www.designkit.org/
Life in common	Commons approach Donut Economics Stakeholder management theory Change management theories	(Deakin, 2012; Elkington, 2020; Freeman, 1984; Galli, 2018; IFC, 2015; Ostrom, 2015; Raworth 2017; WEF, 2023)	Final Project – Managing Life in Common	https://sdgs.un.org/goals, https://www.ifc.org/wps/wcm/connect/topics_ext_content/ifc_external_corporate_site/sustainability-at-ifc/publications/publications_handbook_csms-general

concentrate? Who is next to you? Who is far away? How does all this matter? Different landscapes allow for different communication flows and embodied experiences and, therefore, different creative processes (Mahmoud et al., 2020; Malinin, 2016).

The third dimension are two different aspects of time: the proper time of an idea as well as the time of creativity. History shows that many creative products were recognized long after they were produced. Just think of so many artists who were considered geniuses only after their deaths: Vincent Van Gogh, Emily Dickinson, and Franz Kafka, and the list could go on. This reinforces the power of the social to foster and define what is creative.

The time aspect applies to business as well. There is a need for long-term vision when it comes to new creative processes. In innovation management, for instance, it is highly popular to work with different time horizons (Coley, 2009). In terms of sustainable solutions for business and society problems, the clock is ticking toward an unreversible environmental situation driving the need for short-term solutions with long-term effects.

To conclude this topic, we pose the question: "when are human beings most creative?" Research shows that we can remain creative throughout our lives. In fact, there are different types of creativity – conceptual or experiential – as proposed by Galenson (Galenson, 2006; Weinberg & Galenson, 2019). At a young age, with less social and cultural pressure and fewer strings attached, some artists like Pablo Picasso broke all the rules (conceptual) and inaugurated a new era. Conversely, in his final years, someone like Paul Cézanne painted his masterpiece, *Les baigneuses*, after several attempts, thus drawing on his capacity to connect the dots of what he learned along the way (experiential).

The Discipline of Creativity

To liberate creativity is fun, right? But we are talking business, aren't we? How do we make our organizations more creative? And how do we make our organizations creative enough to find solutions for the "good way" to manage life in common, and make a profit for those who seek profit, or to deliver the best services possible if you are in a not-for-profit institution? We need processes to suggest new ideas, try them out, learn from errors, and improve or pivot in a different direction.

Creativity requires a kind of discipline that is often overlooked (Sinfiel et al., 2014). The "creative genius" myth, the famous eureka moment, and the light bulb metaphor obscure that fundamental to every creative process is disciplined learning, trial, and error processes. Picasso developed 42 preliminary studies for the painting, Guernica. Thomas Edison's famous quote resumes the effort: "I have not failed 10,000 times; I've successfully found 10,000 ways that will not work" (apud DeGraaf & Gates, n.d., pt. 66). In sum, there must be some sort of process in place – which may be formal or not – to reach success.

Given the necessity of creating new processes, businesses need a robust change management plan to foster innovative culture and implement necessary processes for more creative practices. In our first activity with international students, we spent an entire morning discussing change management strategies, where they proposed a plan for a business of their choice based on a template we provided. In the case of managing life in common perspective, the challenge is even bigger, as one must devise a way to promote a full ESG (environmental, social, and governance) agenda.

Despite the availability of different change management frameworks (Galli, 2018; Kotter & von Ameln, 2019), most follow a basic structure as shown in Figure 13.1.

The planning phase includes identification of gaps in soft and hard skills in the organization, and then development of a required process to allow people to propose ideas without fear, try them out, and validate prototypes. Many large companies opt for stage gate models or some variation thereof. There is also a need for proper frameworks to test ideas before going to R&D or pilot projects. Here, Design Thinking (DT) comes in, and offers the opportunity to examine relevant environmental and social issues (Brown & Katz, 2009; Rowe, 1991).

As discussed in *Lesson 2*, DT at its origins requires an ecological perspective. Above all, DT is a human-centered design approach, and humans not only need good products but products that are sustainable by design. The cycle is rather simple: empathy, definition, ideation, test, and evaluation.

The DT cycle starts with empathy, which can be tricky. Originally, the idea of empathy means "fell into" the objects, an aesthetic experience of painting, for instance, with aesthetic elements of nature, or people, when you imagine what it would be like to be in someone's

Identify the change → Plan → Implement → Reinforce the change

FIGURE 13.1 Change management phases.

else situation (Fagiano, 2016). In DT, of course, we are talking about people. If a designer does not have an ecological view, one may fall into the trap of creating products that feed individualistic immediate needs, but that will harm the individual in the long run – that is the brief history of capitalism. Empathy must go beyond the user and requires listening to other stakeholders. This is what we attempt to stimulate in the students in the second activity, Life in Common Journey where we had dwellers of the condominium, employees from Lello, and members of the condominium council, all engaged in understanding, defining, and proposing solutions that benefitted all parties.

Life in Common

The concept of "life in common" offers a strong opportunity to include the ESG agenda into the journey we propose. To live a life in common with other human beings is an ontological condition that is paradoxically refused by many. Western civilization has emphasized the individual to such a great degree that some people live as though the situation of other beings and common resources would not affect their own lives. This tension can even be found in the Declaration of Human Rights, which aims to protect not only individual rights and private property but also the right to have access to scientific development, culture, and a decent living. This is not an easy equation to handle.

If teaching about creativity provides students with the skills to search for solutions, they also need to understand and apply the role of creativity in a business context. To be clear: there is a political dimension of creativity. What is creativity for, for whom, and how it is deployed in a business context? To run a business oriented by a "life in common," one must unavoidably deal with the social needs of society and the limited resources of planet Earth (Ostrom, 2015; Raworth, 2017), and somehow, the COVID-19 pandemic released some sort of wake-up call to many historical social, and environmental problems.

During and after the pandemic, some major capitalists began pushing the ESG agenda, such as Blackrock's CEO, Larry Fink, or the WEF (Fink, 2021; WEF, 2020a). It was not that they had not recognized such challenges before (Elkington & Bakker, 2020; Fink, 2018; WEF, 1973); it is just that the sense of urgency is now stronger, given the no-turning-back point humanity is reaching.

Suddenly, many companies started asking questions such as:

- Environmental issues
  - What is my impact on the planet?
  - What should I do to neutralize it?
  - What do I need to do to regenerate what has already been destroyed?
- Social issues
  - To what extent do I contribute to the development of society?
  - What social problems am I trying to solve?
- Governance issues
  - How do I combat corruption in the company?
  - How do I value diversity in the company, especially at the highest levels?
  - Do I value and recognize people in the company equally?
  - How should I structure governance and compliance systems?

These questions can't be answered individually by an executive or manager, not even by their own peers inside a business. Businesspeople must leave the comfort of their offices to understand what is at stake from a broader perspective when deciding to create and deliver products and services. A more holistic understanding of society is not only right, pointing to the "good way," but also profitable, as we'll discuss in the Conclusion.

For students to have the opportunity to interact with and see the perspective of the community reinforced their sensitivity to social and environmental issues. A similar experience could be achieved in a neighborhood or with an NGO. The second step is to devise a plan that integrates what students learned in the community into a business plan or course of action. In these simple projects, students exercise their observations and creativity to identify what is significant for the communities around them as first steps to developing a business materiality matrix. While there are often other stakeholders, the surrounding community is one of the key ones.

The exercise could even be more sophisticated if the students are asked to understand the socioenvironmental aspects of the community, for example, using the International Finance Corporation (IFC) standards, and only after that to propose a social or environmental project. IFC's toolkit is very straightforward, and it is worthwhile to look at their Performance Standards (IFC, 2015).

Conclusion

Businesses are becoming more aware of socioenvironmental issues for different reasons, and some will adopt an ESG agenda because they think it is the right thing to do. Others are being pressured by investors or by large contracting companies which are themselves pressured by investors and more rigid ESG requirements. Some businesses will eventually realize that a sustainable approach may be profitable (Eccles et al., 2014; Eccles, Ioannou, & Serafeim, 2014). In a study of 180 US companies between 1993 and 2009, Eccles et al. found that organizations that voluntarily adopted sustainability policies performed 10% better than their competitors, and among many aspects, established stakeholder engagement processes were one of the key aspects they had in common.

Evidence of better performance in the stock market is also confirmed by the ISE B3, the corporate sustainability index of the main stock exchange in Brazil. According to data from the B3 itself, since its creation in 2005 until November 2020, the ISE B3 showed a return of 294.73% compared to the 245.06% of the Ibovespa, an index that measures the average performance of a theoretical portfolio composed of most representative shares traded by B3, serving as a benchmark for the market (ISEB3, 2021).

Even during the COVID-19 pandemic crisis in the early months of 2020, 88% of ESG funds performed better than non-ESG funds, according to a Blackrock research note (Marsh, 2020). The issue of ESG resilience and its impact on stock performance in times of crisis and subsequent recovery is a matter of debate because sustainability efforts cannot be identified as the sole factor influencing better performance (Demers et al., 2021). Despite that debate, interesting possibilities exist for aligning value produced by the capitalist system with a sustainable agenda (Friede et al., 2015).

Asking students to go into the community to devise solutions for the "life in common" proved to be an excellent way of introducing several business themes such as the ESG agenda, stakeholder management, and change management. For students to propose more creative solutions, they need soft and hard skills to understand and apply how creativity works as a social phenomenon. Engagement with stakeholders – or with the community for that matter – provides the seeds to perceiving the challenges ahead and developing solutions for businesses to live in common with their respective societies.

Note

1 In Brazil, condominiums are nonprofit legal entities responsible for running a building or a complex of houses, where the properties are individually owned with common infrastructure and areas. The condominium's trustee and its fiscal board are elected by property owners. Every building in Brazil must have a condominium legally established to operate. Lello supports condominiums all over Brazil – some of them with thousands of residents. Lello's innovation approach aims to develop a sustainable life in common, not only within the condominium but also in the neighborhood.

References

Abraham, A. (2018). *The neuroscience of creativity*. Cambridge University Press.

Brown, T., & Katz, B. (2009). *Change by design: How design thinking transforms organizations and inspire innovation*. Harper Collins.

Coley, S. (2009). *Enduring ideas: The three horizons of growth*. McKinsey Quarterly. https://www.mckinsey.com/business-functions/strategy-and-corporate-finance/our-insights/enduring-ideas-the-three-horizons-of-growth.

Coulton, R. (2012). "The darling of the temple-coffee-house club": Science, sociability and satire in early eighteenth-century London. *Journal for Eighteenth-Century Studies*, 35(1), 43–65. https://doi.org/10.1111/j.1754-0208.2010.00351.x.

Csikszentmihalyi, M. (2007). *Creativity: Flow and the psychology of discovery and invention*. Harper Collins.

Deakin, S. (2012). The corporation as commons: Rethinking property rights, governance and sustainability in the business enterprise. *Queen's Law Journal*, 37(2), 339–381. https://search.informit.org/doi/10.3316/agispt.20211230059124.

DeGraaf, E. (2013). *Edison and the Rise of Innovation*. New York: Sterling Publishing

DeGraaf, E., & Gates, B. (n.d.). *Edison and the Rise of Innovation*.

Demers, E., Hendrikse, J., Joos, P., & Lev, B. I. (2021). ESG didn't immunize stocks during the COVID-19 crisis, but investments in intangible assets did. *Journal of Business Finance & Accounting*, 48, 433–462. https://doi.org/10.2139/ssrn.3675920.

Eccles, R. G., Ioannou, I., & Serafeim, G. (2014). The impact of corporate sustainability on organizational processes and performance. *Management Science*, 60(11), 2835–2857. https://doi.org/10.1287/mnsc.2014.1984.

Elkington, J. (2020). *Green swans: The coming boom in regenerative capitalism*. Fast Company Press.

Elkington, J., & Bakker, P. (2020). *To build back better, we will have to re-invent capitalism*. WEF. https://www.weforum.org/agenda/2020/07/to-build-back-better-we-must-reinvent-capitalism-heres-how/.

Fagiano, M. (2016). Pluralistic conceptualizations of empathy. *The Journal of Speculative Philosophy*, *30*(1), 27–44. https://doi.org/10.5325/jspecphil.30.1.0027.

Feld, B. (2012). *Startup communities: Building an entrepreneurial ecosystem in your city*. Wiley.

Fink, L. (2018, January 17). *A sense of purpose*. Harvard Law School Forum on Corporate Governance; The Harvard Law School Forum on Corporate Governance. https://corpgov.law.harvard.edu/2018/01/17/a-sense-of-purpose/.

Fink, L. (2021). *Larry Fink's 2021 letter to CEOs*. https://www.blackrock.com/corporate/investor-relations/larry-fink-ceo-letter.

Freeman, R. E. (1984). *Strategic management: A stakeholder approach*. Pitman.

Freeman, R. E., Harrison, S. J., & Zyglidopoulos, S. (2018). *Stakeholder theory*. Cambridge University Press.

Friede, G., Busch, T., & Bassen, A. (2015). ESG and financial performance: Aggregated evidence from more than 2000 empirical studies. *Journal of Sustainable Finance & Investment*, *5*(4), 210–233. https://doi.org/10.1080/20430795.2015.1118917.

Galenson, D. W. (2006). *Old masters and young geniuses*. Princeton University Press.

Galli, B. J. (2018). Change management models: A comparative analysis and concerns. *IEEE Engineering Management Review*, *46*(3), 124–132. https://doi.org/10.1109/EMR.2018.2866860.

Glaveanu, V. P., Hanchett Hanson, M., Baer, J., Barbot, B., Clapp, E. P., Corazza, G. E., Hennessey, B., Kaufman, J. C., Lebuda, I., Lubart, T., Montuori, A., Ness, I. J., Plucker, J., Reiter-Palmon, R., Sierra, Z., Simonton, D. K., Neves-Pereira, M. S., & Sternberg, R. J. (2020). Advancing creativity theory and research: A socio-cultural manifesto. *The Journal of Creative Behavior*, *54*(3), 741–745. https://doi.org/10.1002/jocb.395.

Howkins, J. (2009). *Creative ecologies: Where thinking is a proper job*. Routledge.

IFC. (2015). *Environmental and Social Management System (ESMS) implementation handbook*. https://www.ifc.org/wps/wcm/connect/topics_ext_content/ifc_external_corporate_site/sustainability-at-ifc/publications/publications_handbook_esms-general.

ISEB3. (2021). *O que é o ISE B3*. http://iseb3.com.br/o-que-e-o-ise.

Kelley, T., & Kelley, D. (2013). *Creative confidence: Unleashing the creative potential within us all*. Harper Collins.

Kotter, J., & von Ameln, F. (2019). Agility, hierarchy and lessons for the future. John Kotter on the legacy and future of Change Management.

Gruppe. Interaktion. Organisation. Zeitschrift Für Angewandte Organisationspsychologie (GIO), *50*(2), 111–114. https://doi.org/10.1007/s11612-019-00461-5.

Land, G., & Jarman, B. (1998). *Breakpoint and beyond: Mastering the future today.* Leadership 2000 Inc.

Mahmoud, N. E., Kamel, S. M., & Hamza, T. S. (2020). The relationship between tolerance of ambiguity and creativity in architectural design studio. *Creativity Studies*, *13*(1), 179–198. https://doi.org/10.3846/cs.2020.9628.

Malinin, L. H. (2016). Creative practices embodied, embedded, and enacted in architectural settings: Toward an ecological model of creativity. *Frontiers in Psychology*, *6*, 1978. https://doi.org/10.3389/fpsyg.2015.01978.

Marsh, A. (2020). BlackRock Joins Allianz, Invesco Saying ESG Outperformed. In *Bloomberg*. https://www.bloomberg.com/news/articles/2020-05-18/blackrock-joins-allianz-invesco-saying-esg-funds-outperformed

Ostrom, E. (2015). *Governing the commons. The evolution of insitutions for collective action.* Cambridge University Press.

Papanek, V. (1973). *Design for the real World: Human ecology and social change.* Bantam.

Raworth, K. (2017). *Doughnut economics: Seven ways to think like a 21st-century economist.* Random House.

Rowe, P. (1991). *Design thinking* (3rd ed.). MIT Press.

Runco, M. A., & Jaeger, G. J. (2012). The standard definition of creativity. *Creativity Research Journal*, *24*(1), 92–96. https://doi.org/10.1080/10400419.2012.650092.

Simonton, D. K. (2018). Creative ideas and the creative process: Good news and bad news for the neuroscience of creativity. In R. E. Jung & O. Vartanian (Eds.), *The Cambridge Handbook of the Neuroscience of Creativity*. Cambridge University Press.

Sinfiel, J. v., Gustafson, T., & Hindo, B. H. (2014). The discipline of creativity. *MIT Sloan Management Review, Winter*. https://sloanreview.mit.edu/article/the-discipline-of-creativity/.

WEF. (1973). *Davos manifesto 1973: A code of ethics for business leaders.* https://www.weforum.org/agenda/2019/12/davos-manifesto-1973-a-code-of-ethics-for-business-leaders/.

WEF. (2020a). *Measuring stakeholder capitalism: Toward a common metrics and consistent reporting of sustainable value creation.* https://www.weforum.org/agenda/2020/10/top-10-work-skills-of-tomorrow-how-long-it-takes-to-learn-them/.

WEF. (2020b). *What are the top 10 job skills for the future?* https://www.weforum.org/agenda/2020/10/top-10-work-skills-of-tomorrow-how-long-it-takes-to-learn-them/.

WEF. (2023). Global risks report 2023. In *WEF*. https://www.weforum.org/reports/global-risks-report-2023/.

Weinberg, B. A., & Galenson, D. W. (2019). Creative careers: The life cycles of Nobel laureates in economics. *De Economist*. https://doi.org/10.1007/s10645-019-09339-9.

Wilson, E. (2017). *The origins of creativity*. Alan Lane.

Zwir, I., Del-Val, C., Hintsanen, M., Cloninger, K. M., Romero-Zaliz, R., Mesa, A., Arnedo, J., Salas, R., Poblete, G. F., Raitoharju, E., Raitakari, O., Keltikangas-Järvinen, L., de Erausquin, G. A., Tattersall, I., Lehtimäki, T., & Cloninger, C. R. (2021). Evolution of genetic networks for human creativity. *Molecular Psychiatry*. https://doi.org/10.1038/s41380-021-01097-y.

14

KNOWING AND ACTING TOWARD SUSTAINABLE CONSUMPTION

Ruth Areli García-León

Abstract

To inspire other scholars, this chapter describes my journey of transforming the course *Consumer Behavior* as it evolved from centering on the behaviors of consumers to incorporating sustainability concepts and related impact on the behavior of students. Further, it describes the introduction of sustainability topics in the course and how this resulted in the development of new didactic techniques for Responsible Management Education (RME). In developing a new course, I considered how the student's knowledge and understanding of their own behavior and consumption are related to the Sustainable Development Goals (SDGs), and how students could develop a strategy to contribute to one of the SDGs or their targets. It finishes with recommendations to those willing to introduce changes in their courses and eventually develop them into new ones.

Introduction

I still remember the first time that I tried to introduce sustainability topics in my courses. I was studying at McGill University in the summer of 2008, when I found the book *Ecoholic* by Adria Vasil (2007) in one of the bookstores close to the university. I was thrilled to find a best-selling book with so many environmentally friendly tips about products and services available in Canada. In that country, the concern for building a better world based on sustainability or sustainable

DOI: 10.4324/9781003457763-14

consumption was not new. Back in Mexico, I tried to introduce some of the topics in my management and marketing courses. Initially, my students showed interest, but it diluted with time. Now, I can see these concepts may have been too early for them.

At that time, my students of the Licentiate in Marketing were focused on becoming competent marketing directors by learning how marketing could successfully position a company's brand and products to reach the company's economic goals by selling more and more goods and services. At that time, and even today, it is contradictory to think that marketing could *reduce* consumption or contribute to sustainable business results. We should not forget that marketing has often been blamed as the main cause of global overconsumption.

Although the documentary *An Inconvenient Truth*, by Al Gore, was already well known at the time, the practice of developing a better world based on sustainable development was still an idea among only a minority of academics and businesses. As Belz and Peattie (2013) explain in their book *Sustainability Marketing*, it was not until 2008 that many began to understand that the way we were doing business and our way of living was economically and environmentally unsustainable. And even though the Brundtland Report established the concept of sustainable development in 1987, it was not until 2015 that the 17 Sustainable Development Goals (SDGs) of the 2030 Agenda for Sustainable Development were formally adopted by the UN state members (Brundtland, 1987; UN, 2015).

Today we know that sustainability marketing can blend economic and technical perspectives with concepts of the sustainable development agenda to build and maintain sustainable relations with customers, the social, and the natural environment (Belz & Peattie, 2013). More marketing journal articles are centered on sustainability topics and more and more marketing scholars are changing the focus of their research to contribute to the SDGs. More management education institutions and scholars believe it is necessary to equip students with the skills and mindset necessary to become responsible leaders of the future, able to balance economic and sustainability goals. Although there is no consensus on how to teach these subjects (Doh & Tashman, 2014), it is becoming highly necessary to integrate new pedagogies into the management curricula to reach the SDG goals (Morsing, 2021b; PRME, 2021).

This is an ongoing process and I, and many other scholars, are now in the process of searching for new ways to integrate sustainable development topics across the management education curricula (Morsing, 2021a). Sharing these processes helps inspire other scholars interested in facilitating Responsible Management Education (RME). Therefore, I have structured this chapter as follows. I begin by explaining how originally the course *Consumer Behavior* was centered on analyzing others. Then I explain how I changed the direction to analyze the consumer behavior of my students. I describe how adding sustainability topics to the course resulted in the development of new pedagogical tools for RME. I also explain considerations for transforming the current course into a new one. Finally, in the conclusions, I offer insights and give recommendations for those interested in transforming a course into a more sustainable-development-oriented one.

Analyzing Others

I taught the course *Consumer Behavior* for over 15 years to different generations of students. Regardless of the university or country, the syllabus of the course offers consistent concepts: to study how consumers make decisions to spend their time, money, and efforts on consumption-related items. That includes understanding *what* they buy, *why, when, where*, and *how often*. The focus is then on identifying and understanding the behavior of consumers and decision processes to exert influence on those decisions. Students learn about consumers' motivations and perceptions, their attitude formation and change, their learning process, the influences of social and cultural settings on consumption behavior, as well as the process of consumer decision-making. These principles are applied by businesses to achieve the goal of increasing profit and market share for stakeholders.

In Mexico, at Tec de Monterrey, *Consumer Behavior* was a compulsory course part of the Licentiate in Marketing program. The focus was on analyzing the behaviors of different consumer groups. To help my students better understand these topics, I developed a portfolio of activities and used different exercises or activities depending on the number of students, their mood, the time available, or other considerations. Students were happy to apply standard theories related to the behavior of consumers, particularly Mexican consumers, as they worked through exercises that analyzed the behavior of others.

In retrospect, I see that my first shift in transforming the course occurred in 2010 when I was invited to teach *Consumer Behavior* at Universidad de la Sabana in Bogotá, Colombia. There, the course was an elective summer course. During my days in Bogotá, I analyzed radio and TV commercials, visited local markets, convenience stores, supermarkets, and shopping centers, identified regional and international brands, and talked with different persons about brands and consumption activities. I used this information to adapt some examples and activities for my students.

However, Colombian students in my classroom were highly interested in knowing the differences between Mexican and Colombian consumers. Students avidly asked me about differences in brands, advertising, behaviors, etc. They shared their own buying processes from problem recognition until final disposal and post-purchase evaluation. The course was then transformed into a conversation of comparisons of different cultural experiences that enriched the theory and the course in general. Interviews outside of class and shared observations complemented the activities in the classroom.

Back in Mexico, I used student experiences and observations from Columbia to shift attention from analyzing general consumer behavior to analyzing the personal buying experience of students in comparison to those in other countries.

Analyzing My Behavior

Following the positive student response to comparing personal student buying decisions in Columbia and Mexico, I started to shift the course to include analyzing student buying behavior. I relied on the motto: *"To analyze buying behavior of others, one must first understand their own consumption behaviors."* This marked a fundamental change in the dynamics of the class. I realized that it was easier for students to talk about abstract buying experiences of people in other countries than it was to talk about their own behavior as consumers in their own country. By comparing different buying decisions with their own, students were able to see the decision process more clearly.

At first, it was difficult for students to analyze themselves. They struggled to understand and articulate why they were buying something, and why they were following tendencies or brands. It was not compulsory for students to share their activities or their reflections with the class, but some students chose to do so to know more about themselves and enable other students to learn from their experiences. By the end of the semester, some of them were able to share more comments like: "My mother was using this brand when I was a child, that's why I think it is the best," or "We couldn't buy this brand when I was little, that´s why it is aspirational for me."

Later, traveling and teaching in other countries allowed me to adapt and improve the course by sharing and discussing first-hand examples of consumers' purchasing decisions in multiple countries.

In 2013, I started teaching in Germany at Ostfalia University of Applied Sciences. At Ostfalia, *Consumer Behavior* is an elective course in two faculties: the Brunswick European Law School (BELS) for the Bachelor's Degree in Business and Law; the Bachelor's Degree in Law, Human Resources, and Personnel Psychology, and part of the International Program. In the Faculty of Business Administration it is offered for the Bachelor's Degree in Business Administration, and it is part of the courses offered for the International Academic Year, and the Certificate in International Business. As an elective course, taught in English in both faculties, students come from countries like India, the United States, Russia, Mexico, Colombia, Australia, France, Poland, etc. The diversity of student experience enabled my portfolio of activities to grow. I continued to ask students to analyze and compare their own buying behavior and the behavior of other consumers. Incoming students shared their cultural shock during their first days in Germany and how they managed to acquire products from their home countries when they felt homesick. At this stage, I was also introducing sustainability topics in my courses, but not extensively or as a primary topic.

My Un/Sustainable Behavior and the SDGs

In 2018 the BELS became a PRME signatory, and the relevance of the SDGs increased. After that, adding sustainable development topics into the courses was desirable but not compulsory. I soon started talking about these topics in my courses and felt freer to introduce SDGs and related topics more often in all my courses including *Consumer Behavior*. Without changing the content of the courses, I changed examples and adapted the activities to incorporate the lens of the SDGs.

I can now realize that transforming examples and activities in my courses occurred organically. A few tools that I used before were adopted and I am currently using them to improve RME. For example, the use of news items as a pedagogical tool for RME, and the use of collage to enhance knowledge and reduce prejudices. I have improved these pedagogical tools over the years and have cited their use and benefits for RME in several publications. Some of the publications include the chapter, "The use of news articles as a pedagogical tool for responsible management education" for the book *Business Schools, Leadership and the Sustainable Development Goals* (García-León, 2023), and the paper "The Use of Collage in Multicultural Courses to Enhance Knowledge and Reduce Prejudices" presented at the ninth Responsible Management Education Research Conference in Innsbruck, Austria (García-León, 2022).

The use of collage is interesting since it is a qualitative technique for consumer research and a form of metaphor analysis (Schiffman & Kanuk, 2000). I used this technique as an example in the course *Consumer Behavior* each semester. Students would make collages of images from magazines or other material to represent visual examples of buyer categories such as "busy female parent" or "successful male professional." As I changed the course to emphasize student behaviors, the collages could also reflect "successful college student."

Once, the collage technique became a tool to compare gender assumptions in different cultures. I was teaching consumer behavior to a group of six female students, two from Australia, one German/Kurdish, and three students from India. By coincidence, the day scheduled for the collage activity, the only male student registered in the course did not attend class. Teams were organized by country of origin and used images from magazines to portray "A successful woman in my country." Once finished with the collage, students reviewed all collages, and then each student explained their portrait. In the subsequent question and answer period, a free-flowing and deep conversation emerged about differences, doubts, false beliefs about other cultures regarding the female gender, curiosity about how other cultures regarded women, and how womanhood was lived. The class discussed different life stages for women, what each culture dictates for how women should behave and act, and what students thought being a woman should mean. The conversation ranged from general to very personal and intimate conversations.

Later, students shared that this conversation continued after class and generated additional discussions that allowed students to get to know each other better, share information about their cultures, learn from others, and understand many unwritten aspects that, under other circumstances, could be misinterpreted. I realized that this deep knowledge and understanding regarding unknown realities and mindsets could help to reduce ignorance among cultures, which has been long blamed as a key root of prejudice (Stephan & Stephan, 1984).

Case studies have demonstrated that contact and interaction among people from different countries, races, and cultural backgrounds are essential to creating social links and encouraging mutual respect (JRS, 2017; Orton, 2012; Pettigrew & Tropp, 2006). And, although it is well known that multicultural education can help reduce prejudice against other cultures (Camicia, 2007), sometimes students perceive multicultural education as an illusion of inclusivity with superficial knowledge among students, lacking cultural awareness and open dialogs where diversity is not celebrated (Doucette et al., 2021).

This activity allowed me to discover the potential of collage as a tool to increase knowledge among students from different countries and opened the door to honest and deeper dialogs among them during and after class. I proposed its use as a didactic tool for RME in order to contribute to SDG 10 and the reduction of inequalities within and among countries by empowering and promoting social, economic, and political inclusion for all irrespective of race, ethnicity, origin, religion, age, sex, economic or other status (UN, 2021a, 2021b). This example could also represent several other of the 17 SDG goals such as #4 Quality Education, #5 Gender Equality, or #12 Responsible Consumption.

With these and other experiences, I started thinking about the possibility of using activities developed in this and other courses to design a new course that would enable students as consumers committed to sustainable development and as change-makers able to develop strategies toward reaching the SDGs. My objective is not just that students analyze their un/sustainable behavior, but to help them develop strategies to contribute actively to sustainable development. This is the stage I am in at this moment.

Developing a New Course

Transforming the course into a new one is not an easy process. There are many considerations from determining the objective of the course to establishing how the students will be evaluated. Following, I explain my process and considerations in hopes it inspires other scholars to transform a course into a new one.

The General Objective

The general objective of the course will be that students actively contribute toward one or more SDGs through analyzing their own unsustainable or sustainable consumption behavior and by developing new ideas and introducing positive changes in their lives and the lives of others. The most important goal of the course is to help students find active ways to contribute to sustainable development. The goal is highly ambitious and therefore challenging but can be reached in one semester. I am in the process of developing the syllabus, determining specific objectives, and selecting the topics, examples, and activities.

The Topics of the Course

Even though the course will be centered on SDG 12: Responsible Consumption and Production, I considered whether to include just one or two sustainability topics during the semester. As with the example shared previously, there are 17 SDGs that are interconnected. If we were to address SDG 12, Target 1.3, related to food waste, we may combine it with SDG 2: Zero Hunger. These goals may lead students to not only analyze their behavior regarding food waste and how to avoid it but also lead them to analyze how they could contribute to fight hunger in the world.

It is complex to incorporate a systemic understanding of all sustainability challenges (Figueiró & Raufflet, 2015) while integrating harmonically the economic, social, and environmental sustainability dimensions (Lennerfors et al., 2020), and the actors involved in sustainable development. Therefore, I decided to include topics that are familiar to me due to my research and expertise, which are focused on food and sustainability. For this course, I plan to use examples and activities related to food sustainability and its interconnection with other SDGs.

Although we are enthusiasts about sustainability and we want to share the SDGs with our students, it is practical to lecture from our experience and scientific knowledge in order to be able to answer questions from our students effectively.

The Length of the Course

In Germany, noncompulsory bachelor's courses normally have three credits. That means 90 minutes of class per week during the semester. Depending on the semester, that is 12 to 13 classes in one block and around six in two blocks. I prefer double block sessions because I have time to explain the theory, give my students some activities to work on, and then, I can assign some time for reflection. It also allows students to have more time to talk among themselves. It is very important from the beginning to encourage students to think about the final strategy they will develop as part of the final evaluation of the semester.

The Final Exam

I truly believe in the power of collaborative work. Working collaboratively with others is one instructional model based on social constructivism (Lave & Wenger, 1991). Knowledge, understanding, significance, and meaning are developed with others when learning collaboratively, which is a social process fundamental for the learning development of the individual (Cole & Scribner, 1978). As a final project, students will, as a group or in teams, develop a strategy to help themselves and others achieve one of the SDGs or their targets. I believe that working hands-on toward sustainability will give them a genuine sense of success in this area.

Undoubtedly, one of the main challenges is the evaluation of the course. For me, it is important to have an impactful result from my students, something real that they can apply and from which they can learn by having first-hand results. Nevertheless, every university has its own established and authorized evaluation regulations so students should be evaluated by using one of these types of evaluations.

Another challenge is how to evaluate the unsuccessful strategies of my students. When something works, it is easy to evaluate it positively, but how to evaluate an unsuccessful strategy? I think that I should evaluate the process of analysis, the development of the strategy, and its application but *not* evaluate whether the strategy was successful or not. Failure brings experience and knowledge to the students. A successful strategy will bring confidence to students to know that they are able to develop strategies that could impact the world. Hopefully, they will improve and apply this strategy in bigger dimensions in the future.

Flexibility

I am still in the process of completing this new course. Since this is an elective course, it is indispensable to have enough flexibility to make modifications through the semesters. I hope that in the future the new course could be part of the compulsory courses offered in a marketing or management program.

Conclusion

This chapter describes my journey in transforming a management course into a new course that can make a positive contribution to sustainable development. As scholars, each of us can use the expertise and knowledge acquired during our careers to adjust and then transform the courses that we have been teaching. As you see, this change has been a process. Therefore, I recommend other instructors start by introducing sustainable topics in the courses and observing and talking with their students.

By adding sustainable topics to your courses, you enhance your creativity, bring valuable insights, and expand options for developing a new course. It is important to be open and not be afraid to try new activities. You are not alone. Many scholars are researching and developing didactic tools for RME. Institutions and communities of scholars are actively contributing to this transformation. In addition to the PRME Chapters and Working Groups, scholars are leading groups and initiatives like the Global Movement Initiative (www.globalmovement.net) and the Aim2Flourish program (aim2flourish.com).

Observe and listen to your students. Every generation of students is different, they are exposed to different inputs and information, and their interests change with the times. It is important to connect and listen to them. Sometimes we are very busy trying to finish the content of the course or enforcing time assigned for some activity. I suggest you take time to ask if students are truly understanding the topics or enjoying the activities. Sit with them and hear how they are working to solve the activities. You could discover which tools or information they use to solve their queries when they do not ask you. Or you might uncover interesting information and new ways to use these activities to foster learning.

Allow yourself to hear what students want to say. As a management, marketing, and communication docent, I sometimes use cases, news, TV commercials, information related to price, communication campaigns, or other information to exemplify something. Many times, students say "I have a better example." This is an opportunity and I answer: "I am happy to hear that!" By allowing students to use their examples, I can verify whether they understand the topic and I can also collect a new example that they find more appealing or understandable for them.

Most of the time I do not wait for students to volunteer but I encourage them to tell me if they have a better example about something.

Some students stay at the end of the class and share this information with me, or I receive e-mails where they show me interesting things related to the topic. Others confess: "I do not understand why this company is doing this, can you please explain something about that in the next class?" Others write to me saying: "This is not related to the topic, but I find it interesting." I always thank my students for sharing this information and value their interest and willingness to help.

To finalize, I recommend institutions and scholars encourage docents from the same area to form groups to develop new activities or even programs for RME. This could shorten the time to create something that individually could take months or even years to develop.

References

Belz, F.-M., & Peattie, K. (2013). *Sustainability marketing: A global perspective* (2nd ed.). Wiley.

Brundtland, G. H. (1987). *Report of the World Commission on Environment and Development: Our common future. Document A/42/427.* United Nations General Assembly. https://digitallibrary.un.org/record/139811/files/A_42_427-EN.pdf?ln=en

Camicia, S. P. (2007). Prejudice reduction through multicultural education: Connecting multiple literatures. *Social Studies Research and Practice, 2*(2), 219–227. https://doi.org/10.1108/SSRP-02-2007-B0006

Cole, M., & Scribner, S. (1978). Introduction. In M. Cole, V. John-Steiner, S. Scribner, & E. Souberman (Eds.), *Mind in society: The development of higher psychological processes* (pp. 1–16). Harvard University Press.

Doh, J. P., & Tashman, P. (2014). Half a World away: The integration and assimilation of corporate social responsibility, sustainability, and sustainable development in business school curricula. *Corporate Social Responsibility and Environmental Management, 21*(3), 131–142. https://doi.org/10.1002/csr.1315

Doucette, B., Sanabria, A., Sheplak, A., & Aydin, H. (2021). The perceptions of culturally diverse graduate students on multicultural education: Implication for inclusion and diversity awareness in higher education. *European Journal of Educational Research, 10*(3), 1259–1273. https://doi.org/10.12973/eu-jer.10.3.1259

Figueiró, P. S., & Raufflet, E. (2015). Sustainability in higher education: A systematic review with focus on management education. *Journal of Cleaner Production, 106,* 22–33. https://doi.org/10.1016/j.jclepro.2015.04.118

García-León, R. A. (2022). *The use of collage in multicultural courses to enhance knowledge and reduce prejudices.* 9th Responsible Management Education Research Conference: Societal Impact through Entrepreneurship & Innovation, Innsbruck, Austria, 27–29 September 2022. https://

www.mci.edu/en/university/the-mci/responsibility/9th-responsible-management-education-research-conference

García-León, R. A. (2023). The use of news articles as a pedagogical tool for responsible management education. In L. Moratis & F. Melissen (Eds.), *Business schools, leadership and the sustainable development goals: The future of responsible management education*. Routledge. https://doi.org/10.4324/9781003244905

JRS. (2017). *I get you: Promoting best practices to prevent racism and xenophobia towards forced migrants through community building. Europe.* Jesuit Refugee Service. https://jrseurope.org/en/resource/i-get-you-european-report/

Lave, J., & Wenger, E. (1991). *Situated learning: Legitimate peripheral participation*. Cambridge University Press.

Lennerfors, T. T., Fors, P., & Woodward, J. R. (2020). Case hacks: Four hacks for promoting critical thinking in case-based management education for sustainable development. *Högre utbildning, 10*(2), 1–15. https://doi.org/10.23865/hu.v10.1960

Morsing, M. (2021a). Part I. PRME into the decade of action. In M. Morsing (Ed.), *Responsible management education: The PRME global movement* (pp. 1–2). Routledge. https://doi.org/10.4324/9781003186311

Morsing, M. (2021b). PRME–Principles for Responsible Management Education: Towards transforming leadership education. In M. Morsing (Ed.), *Responsible management education: The PRME global movement* (pp. 3–12). Routledge. https://doi.org/10.4324/9781003186311

Orton, A. (2012). *Building migrants' belonging through positive interactions: a guide for policymakers and practitioners*. Council of Europe. http://www.coe.int/t/democracy/migration/Source/migration/EnglishMigrantBelongingWeb.pdf

Pettigrew, T. F., & Tropp, L. R. (2006, May). A meta-analytic test of intergroup contact theory. *Journal of Personality and Social Psychology, 90*(5), 751–783. https://doi.org/10.1037/0022-3514.90.5.751

PRME. (2021). *About: What is PRME?* Retrieved 10 April 2022 from https://www.unprme.org/about

Schiffman, L. G., & Kanuk, L. L. (2000). *Consumer behavior* (7th ed.). Prentice Hall.

Stephan, W. G., & Stephan, C. W. (1984). The role of ignorance in intergroup relations. In N. Miller & M. B. Brewer (Eds.), *Groups in contact* (pp. 229–255). Academic Press. https://doi.org/10.1016/B978-0-12-497780-8.50017-6

UN. (2015). *Resolution adopted by the General Assembly on 25 September 2015: Transforming our World: The 2010 Agenda for Sustainable Development*. United Nations General Assembly. https://www.un.org/en/development/desa/population/migration/generalassembly/docs/globalcompact/A_RES_70_1_E.pdf

UN. (2021a). *Goals. 10 Reduce inequality within and among countries.* United Nations. https://sdgs.un.org/goals/goal10

UN. (2021b). *Take action for the sustainable development goals.* United Nations. https://www.un.org/sustainabledevelopment/sustainable-development-goals/

Vasil, A. (2007). *Ecoholic: Your guide to the most environmentally friendly information, products and services in Canada.* Vintage Canada.

15

MARKETING PRINCIPLES FOR SUSTAINABLE BUSINESS SURVIVAL

Linda Irwin

Abstract

During the past several decades, marketing doctrine provided by business schools has largely supported business practices of creating "more": more products, more promotion, and more profit for corporations or stakeholders. University marketing courses teach marketing tactics that support personal data collection and analysis, expand advertising and promotion to promote consumption, and refine processes used to exponentially expand the volume of product choices pushed to buyers. Create more and sell more. No wonder some see marketing as a nasty pursuit of greed. More importantly, current marketing doctrines are not sustainable in a finite-resource world.

Inspired by Regis University Anderson College of Business efforts to enhance how business education can serve as stewards of society, I had the opportunity to develop three new Master-level marketing courses to incorporate concepts that are economically, environmentally, and socially more sustainable than standard "sell everything" pedagogy. The three-year journey and subsequent implementation of these courses provide ideas for systemic change and transformation of business curriculum.

Context

By 2016, I had written and taught marketing and strategy courses at Regis University for nearly 20 years, while also running a consulting firm specializing in strategic planning and marketing strategies for

DOI: 10.4324/9781003457763-15

organizations. Although I used classic texts and principles from Per-rault, Senge, Kotler, Drucker, and others, I gravitated toward an in-terdisciplinary and humanistic approach in my consulting practice and teaching. In business ventures, I always chaffed at the assumption that marketing was "just" sales and product-pushing because I had a differ-ent view of marketing as creating value. That year, 2016, a new dean was brought to Regis University's Anderson College of Business. Dr. Timothy Keane brought with him the concept of business as stewards and established a vision for the College: "*to help business become stewards of society with the goal of improving the quality of life on earth.*" Frankly, when I first heard this phrase, I thought it was quite lofty. But after volunteering on task forces, conducting research, and talking with Dr. Keane and others he connected me to, I became a passionate convert in the effort to change business education for sustainability and survival. I realized that my professional disciplines of strategy, marketing, and communications could be gateways to a better way of doing business.

To put my new passion into practice, I changed activities and cases for the graduate marketing courses that I was teaching both online and in-person, to highlight sustainability and stewardship concepts. Then in 2019, our Marketing Department Chair, Dr. Abigail Schneider, asked that I re-write three Master-level marketing courses to reflect business practices for a sustainable future. At Regis, "re-writing" a course meant researching and writing eight weeks of content, learning outcomes, ac-tivities, citations, and resource materials that were assembled and then published in modules to be used by *all* faculty teaching that course. While faculty could make modest changes when they taught the ma-terial by adding their expertise or examples, the core course material was designed and standardized to align with college and accreditation standards and to ensure students received core information when they enrolled in a course.

Revision Process

The Department Chair and I met with other marketing faculty mem-bers to discuss how dramatically the content of the new courses should be changed to incorporate sustainability concepts. These colleagues helped to identify core marketing concepts that were deemed essential and would fit with the college vision of "stewards of society." Our goal was to ensure students would become familiar with new marketing management concepts that they could apply for long-term benefit to society. Since these were graduate level courses, most of our students were working professionals that often implemented what they learned in class at their work. To that end, we mapped sustainability principles and examples, validated by our research, to align with existing marketing theories and practices. I was given support to start fresh in identifying which marketing principles should be included in each course so that students would understand the complexity of marketing decisions made in a dramatically changing world.

With that permission, the first course I tackled was titled "Marketing Mix Decisions" and it focused on traditional "4P's" of marketing or "marketing mix," Product, Place, Price, and Promotion (Perreault et al., 2017). Ironically, while I had permission to fully revised the courses, I could not change the title of a course because it was published as part of degree listings in the college catalog.

My first step involved researching foundational texts or academic papers that could serve as the resource for new course principles. I quickly learned that no current textbooks define what marketing for a sustainable world might mean or how it should be practiced. I resorted to using an existing text but augmented it with a significant number of journal articles and videos that explicitly incorporated sustainable theories such as social marketing (Kotler & Zaltman, 1971), humanistic marketing (Varey & Pirson, 2014), and demarketing (Kotler & Levy, 1971). I even included an activity that featured "The Lorax" by Dr. Suess! Since we were taking the first steps in transitioning a course to feature sustainable concepts, we built on a traditional marketing strategy model that has been used for decades and was familiar for faculty and students. We then incorporated new sustainability concepts and activities. Some call this approach "saddle bagging" by adding sustainability topics with known pedagogy.

The revised marketing mix course was first taught in 2019 and we immediately assessed learning outcomes and reviewed student comments. Excerpts of student feedback are provided later in this chapter. The department concluded that a "saddlebag approach" of adding sustainability topics to existing principles seemed to help students become *aware* of environmental and social considerations related to marketing mix decisions but did not provide a *process* or key framework for them to change marketing practices in the workplace. We also recognized that faculty unfamiliar with sustainability concepts might revert to emphasizing traditional rather than transformative practices. We decided we needed to do more with the next course revisions.

To truly transform marketing practices, I recognized that we needed to create a new definition of the *purpose and role* of marketing in business. Why or how did I decide that I should be the one to audaciously just change the very definition of the business discipline that I had practiced throughout my career? Since the current marketing definition contributes to over-production, over-consumption, and environmental destruction, I felt it was necessary to forge ahead. If not me, who would? I collaborated with the Department Chair to publish a paper offering a new *definition* of marketing that changes the purpose of marketing from pushing product sales to creating value (Irwin, Schneider 2020). Our marketing definition did not throw out all prior research or theory. However, it intentionally *flipped* the current emphasis from "product-pushing-to-target-customers" approach to a practice where marketing creates *value* for the business, customer, *and* society by solving a valid problem. Embracing our new core marketing principles of creating value while solving valid problems generates business practices that create value for the long term.

With our new definition of marketing as a foundation, I moved on to develop the second course, "Marketing Opportunity Assessment," a companion course to the "Marketing Mix" course, focused on strategic assessment of a market opportunity. Together, the two courses provide necessary content and analytical processes to create a complete strategic marketing plan for an organization. In changing a market opportunity assessment from "targeting *buyers*" to our "value-*creation*" definition of marketing (Irwin & Schneider, 2020), I quickly realized that I would need to change the entire analytical *process* to focus on vital problems people share rather than products. Starting "fresh" is an opportunity to re-examine and recreate everything!

Our new method of assessing market opportunities is based on identifying valid problems that exist and then determining whether solving the problem can create value for the customer, the company, **and** society. This assessment is a significantly different process than practiced by many companies. Many create a product or service because they have some capability to do so and then they *target* customers to get them to buy.

In this course, we introduced a new problem assessment process that requires students (and faculty) to change their embedded or unrecognized assumptions about marketing practices and business opportunities. Why does the product or service need to be developed – does it solve a valid problem? Is marketing just about selling stuff? What products and services should be created in a resource-restrained world?

How much consumption is necessary for a thriving and just society? How are decisions to develop and promote products balanced with the cost of consuming natural resources? These are among the questions students examine to validate market opportunities that deliver real value to the company, customers, and society. They follow an analytical process with cohort teams that explores these difficult questions as they relate to a specific problem and potential product solution.

Since no text covers these concepts in a way that also met the course definition listed by the university, I curated resources to demonstrate how leading organizations are successfully implementing value-creation marketing and why it is important. We stressed there is no single recipe or model for success but rather each market opportunity must set criteria to examine multiple factors and make decisions. This was a challenging concept to students who were just looking for the "right" answer. As a final project, students work in teams to build a market assessment around a specific problem defined by each team. Ensuring that a market opportunity can deliver value to the satisfaction of potential customers, the benefit of the company, and the benefit to society builds critical thinking and problem-solving skills. And it is challenging!

The market opportunity course was first taught in a hybrid online format during the pandemic in Fall 2020. A benefit of this modality was that student comments and online meeting interactions were recorded and could be used to assess student comprehension and reaction to new concepts. A review of the results told me that I initially tried to pack too much into one eight-week course. Students responded positively to the concepts of long-term value-creation for a sustainable world but found it difficult to also understand how to apply those ideas as they assessed a market opportunity. Using this feedback, I immediately modified the course to refine the analytical processes. Since each student team develops their own problem scenario, we cannot provide answers. Rather, we provided more specific processes that help them ask questions and analyze the situation for themselves. After making these changes, students positively supported the new definition of marketing, and sustainability concepts, and there were fewer problems in understanding how to apply these ideas in practice.

One typical student reflection from the course was:

- *Creating value for the business, customers, and society not only leads to business success but the ripple effects better our world. If companies lead with sustainable solutions to problems, long-term success is achievable."*

I next revised a core Marketing Strategy course in the MBA program, following the same pattern or process we used with the Marketing Opportunity course. We built on our definition of marketing that emphasizes the role of creating benefit for society as well as benefit for the company and its customers. We used curated resource material to provide foundational information, and we structured the activities and final output of the courses to be team-developed projects. Assessment of student work was focused on how well they worked together to attempt to solve problems and face changing situations while integrating concepts to create value. We did not attempt to teach *about* sustainability but helped students learn to assess interrelated business decisions and consequences that could achieve goals for a business and create a sustainable, survivable world. Perhaps the most important learning outcome was that students recognized the need to change business practice and the challenge to balance a full spectrum of stakeholders beyond mere profit.

Since this was a required "basic" marketing course for MBA students, our goal was to help students that would be business leaders in *all* parts of an organization understand the strategic value of sustainable marketing decision-making. We wanted them to see that it is possible, but challenging, to create value for the company, customers, and society. And we wanted to give them tools to ask the right questions, set decision criteria, and form consensus.

This is a significantly different premise and process than those used by many current CEO's or entrepreneurs and significantly different from what is taught in most MBA programs. Many assume marketing is only needed to push product and profit. In this course, whether they have an interest in finance, human resources, or supply chain management, students must work in teams to create a high-level strategic marketing plan for an organization that creates sustainable value. They attempt to solve a stated problem, assess the market of those who share the problem, and then develop product, price, distribution, and promotion strategies necessary to deliver value to the company and customers without harming (or by benefitting) society.

All newly revised courses were taught in 2020 and 2021. Due to the pandemic, most were initially taught online, but that format offered the benefit of student participation from different geographic areas in the United States. The initial Marketing Mix course was then revised again to go beyond "saddlebag" sustainability and embed the new marketing definition with sustainable marketing processes and practices for the course content and activities.

Reflections and Outcomes

Reflecting on the process of transforming these marketing courses and their outcomes, I have a few general observations that other business education transformers may wish to consider.

- My experience in developing and teaching these courses showed me that adding-in or saddle-bagging sustainability ideas to existing content does not change how students *use* their education for good. Teaching *about* sustainability does not transform embedded perceptions and practices in businesses. Instead, we must boldly look at whether the principles we have become comfortable with over decades are valid in today's business world. Use what works, and discard ideas that hold us back. Find new resources that students can relate to and apply to create a better business future. Help students learn how to research and *apply* rather than Google-and-regurgitate facts and philosophies.

- Like housework, the course revision process is never done. This is especially true as new philosophies, examples, and materials dealing with a dynamically changing social and environmental world evolve. Our colleges, departments, and faculty must be prepared to continually evolve with change and know that change is constant. Collectively, universities must practice rapid prototyping and adaptability-to-change skills we hope to impart to our students.

- During these revisions, I had many conversations with our Department Chair and other faculty who may teach the course in the future. I wanted to ensure that core learning objectives were consistent with their professional and research experiences, that they accepted the basic concepts, and that they saw the value of changing our approach. I also prepared a comprehensive facilitator guide for each course that explained the theory and logic behind each assignment, the purpose of different readings or resources, and set expectations for the challenge of teaching new and revolutionary concepts. I tried to stress the excitement of creating real a-ha moments for adult learners who may not expect to learn innovative ideas.

- We don't know what we don't know, but we can ask! Building feedback and communication loops within the courses was essential to understanding whether a concept or a process is resonating with students, especially when we are learning new ideas together. Are we building awareness of issues or are we giving students tools to analyze a situation and develop their own solutions? I included multiple exercises with students to see what they were understanding or struggling with. End-of-course surveys were not standardized forms but confidential open-ended questions about how the students really felt. In my opinion, the most important part of any survey is to genuinely *listen and use* the responses to improve. I often tell market research clients they should not impose on their customers' time by asking questions unless they are fully prepared to *act* on the answers. I feel the same about student surveys.

- Students and faculty must recognize that there is no one expert or perfect answer in an uncertain world. Instead, we need to encourage and build our human skills in analyzing situations, weighing choices, setting decision criteria, working with fewer resources, and within difficult conditions. For me personally, uncertainty is very uncomfortable. But the only way to address the uncertainty of the future is to build my ability to be informed, try to integrate new information and processes to solve problems, and remain dedicated to being a steward of society.

In addition to my thoughts, here are some unedited comments from students upon completion of the revised courses. Their voices may provide motivation or inspiration to attempt transformation of your curriculum or programs.

Marketing Mix – Student comments from a course taught in Fall 2019 with sustainability content added on (saddle-bagged) rather than integrated. Most post-course student comments focused on traditional marketing topics with only a few mentioning sustainability. Awareness was generated but not transformation.

- *This course really helped flesh out the science behind work that I had engaged in previously based solely on intuition. I also really liked learning about the sustainability movement. Nobody wants to be the Lorax.*
- *In marketing people rush to make the product and then try and make their customers fit into their plan. I have learned to take a step back and explore all of the addressable market instead of getting too targeted.*
- *This class brought insight to the issue of sustainability, avoiding spray and pray tactics, and focusing on the importance of green marketing with social and environmental focus being a priority to the firm and to alerted to the fact that we are all dealing with finite resources and to use them wisely.*

- *Understanding the essential needs of a customer and who they are is vital in delivering the 4P's. This is applicable in what I do as I need to know the profile of my vertical.*

Market Opportunity Assessment – Student comments from courses taught in Fall 2020 and Spring 2021, with the new definition of marketing that creates value for society embedded in the course content and an expectation that final projects created value for the company, customer, *and* society. Responses indicate a deeper understanding and impact on changing practices.

- *The fundamental role of marketing is to identify and satisfy needs within the industry as well as to contribute to business growth and sustainability efforts. This means that we will eliminate waste by reducing overproduction and focus on the need of customers. Additionally, we are going to solve problems based on need rather than for-profits, which only brings short-term gains. I will always look at the big picture and try to look for a real need of the population. This will create sustainability for me and save the planet for future generations.*
- *It is also good to be shown and held responsible for how your decisions effect other people as well as the environment. We need to setup the future generations for success.*
- *I found it insightful on how much knowledge, action, and voices can be found as defendants of sustainability practices. Many would assume that, especially in America, companies do not care or consider how their practices affect the economy but converting to a completely sustainability business model cannot happen overnight and involves an extraneous amount of research and consideration before a company could begin big changes (although small changes can be made immediately).*
- *The sole fact that there is a new definition of marketing being discussed is exciting to me. In undergraduate in my classes I was so underwhelmed by the discussions, lack of innovation, and missing link of critical thinking and connection to society.*
- *What struck me is the necessity to intentionally create real, sustained value for the customer and society. Previously, I viewed the value to the business as paramount and if society or customers derived long-term value, that was a bonus. I now see how the new definition of marketing requires a healthy triple-bottom line as a true measure of success.*

Marketing Strategy – Student comments from courses taught in Fall 2020 using the new definition of marketing that creates value for society embedded in the course content. Responses recognize potential opportunities for organizations to be stewards of society if they change strategic marketing practices.

- *I was surprised by the idea that marketing should not follow the consumption increasing ideals that the world seems to have run by my entire life. The idea of taking responsibility for our use of natural resources, and for the economy at a microlevel seems so responsible, and right now that I know about it.*
- *I know that if we do not make a shift from product pushing to creating real sustained value for our customers, the business, and society, we will become obsolete. I know now that if we do not make the hard changes to create value and stop product pushing, in a few years there will not be a need for the type of service and products we offer today. We need to refine our business model to have the customers at the center, not profits.*
- *Stepping back from the "growth at all costs" mentality doesn't mean forsaking profit or growth of the business. Sometimes you have to take a step back to take two steps forward which is difficult with the expectation of constant growth from stakeholders. Find a way to show a long-term goal that allows for a step back when necessary to create more value to society, and that will inevitably bring greater value to the business and to customers over time.*
- *I will leave this course constantly asking myself how a product or service benefits either the consumer, society, and/or the company. The company, the consumer, and society are all intertwined and interconnected in a much more comprehensive and complex way than I had originally ever thought.*
- *Leaders must understand that a reduction in consumption can actually be the best company strategy. Sometimes, it is necessary for companies to reduce consumption for the benefit of society. While traditionally, any reduction in consumption was considered a business decline, we now know that certain businesses can benefit from strategies that incorporate reduced consumption with their products.*
- *Thinking in a new way is harder than imaginable. I was surprised at the power of habit; creating different thought patterns takes real effort. Every business I have ever worked at has been driven by pure profits. It is interesting to see how futile and empty chasing money on a wheel is for*

so many people. As I reflect on the pursuit of cash I can think of many focuses that are more important than money.

Conclusion

Inspiration can arrive when you least expect it. After years of managing businesses and teaching core strategy and marketing principles, I was comfortable, but not inspired, to become an "activist" for change and sustainability. However, when Dr. Tim Keane challenged our college to do more and *be* more, I was launched out of complacency and inspired to become a steward of society. If you are a dean or University leader, you may not realize how much power you have to inspire transformation in your organization. Be the change that business and business education needs!

My Department Chair, Dr. Abigail Schneider was pursuing research relating to sustainability issues, and she encouraged me to learn more about emerging environmental and human challenges. She introduced me to a network of those who were attempting to transform business education. The more I learned, the more my "engagement" turned to panic. It seemed business faculty in general were not aware enough or doing enough to help people survive and thrive in the short-term, let alone the long term. Networking with other pioneers who have been working on transforming business education for decades gave me hope and help. The opportunity to revise these courses helped transfer inspiration and panic into action and allowed me to step out of comfort into creation. In retrospect, the opportunity to chart an entirely new approach to teaching marketing seems a bit daunting. But it did not feel that way during the process. It was actually very exciting to be able to innovate with a purpose.

Thanks to these and other colleagues I found collaboration is critical to generating change. If you can create change, I encourage you to find collaborators, either within your college or among the many organizations that have sprung up to encourage sustainable business development.

When we look at climate news, business news, and social changes we know we cannot keep following the same business practices for profit at the expense of our planet and society. If marketing practitioners are going to be able to create real value for society, college faculty and courses need to help them understand why and how. If we keep teaching the same old practices, we will not give students the tools they need to meet future market needs or solve urgent and critical problems essential to human and ecosystem survival. The new courses I created are not a panacea. Rather, they are a first step to encourage students to ask the right questions, set the right criteria and goals, so that they can make sustainable decisions in an uncertain future. Together, we can all take a few steps forward in being stewards of society.

References

Irwin, Linda, & Schneider, Abigail B. (2020, December). A paradigm shift in marketing, creating value for a more sustainable future. *The Solutions Journal*, *11*(4). https://thesolutionsjournal.com/a-paradigm-shift-in-marketing-creating-value-for-a-more-sustainable-future/

Kotler, P., & Levy, S. J. (1971). Demarketing, yes, demarketing. *Harvard Business Review* 49, 74–80.

Kotler, P., & Zaltman, G. (1971). Social marketing: An approach to planned social change. *Journal of Marketing* 35, 3–12.

Perreault, W. D., Cannon, J. P., & McCarthy, E. J. (2017). *Basic marketing: A marketing strategy planning approach*. McGraw-Hill Education.

Varey, R. J., & Pirson, M. (2014). *Humanistic marketing*. Palgrave Macmillan.

16

21ST CENTURY LEADERSHIP PRACTICE

Building Reflection into Sustainable Purpose

Jed Lindholm

Abstract

Changing how the world creates solutions to sustainability issues require teachers to embody the change we need to see. Creating new awareness, new perspectives, and new tools needed by society that addresses the climate crisis and using this learning to act on sustainability issues, requires teachers to see, teach, and lead in new ways. This chapter presents one teacher's experience in using personal reflection, community networking, a Sustainability Mindset, and the United Nation's Sustainable Development Goals (SDGs) as critical elements in building departmental, campus-wide, and management education change. Personal examples are provided from departmental meetings, organizational changes in mission and operational partnerships, the integration of ideas from *The Sustainability Mindset Principles* (2021) and the UN's SDGs as a new model for leadership, and a view that the universal challenge of protecting this planet must be addressed through the universal recognition of our mutual care for each other and all that is on this planet.

Introduction

Look beyond your screen and what do you see? What is in your immediate view? A light, a shelf, through the window, a bush, building, tree, sidewalk, or a car? What is connected to the light, what's on the shelf, what's the bush look like and where are its roots planted? Where are the trees in relation to the bush and what's the name of the trees you are looking at? Are there walkers on the sidewalk and what's the condition

DOI: 10.4324/9781003457763-16

of the sidewalk? Are there cars in your view? Are they parked or moving? Are the cars e-vehicles, hybrids, or powered only by fossil fuel? I see multicolored light exposing pale green walls between casement windows allowing morning sunlight to warm indoor plants. Through the windows is a dogwood bush growing in the corner of a house with chickadees feeding from its bark. Beyond the bush is stately black chestnut tree balanced by its over-arching, symmetric limbs. A bicycle rests on the tree's trunk.

Seeing sustainability begins with noticing what you can touch, what is just a little further from your reach, and what is beyond your immediate reach but within your view. Everything within my view is connected somehow and is changed by my actions. My journey to becoming a sustainability champion began with a quiet moment wondering how I can become sustainable. Really! My quiet moment began in the process of recognizing my intentions on teaching leadership within the challenges of the climate crisis. Seeing how one thing leads to another and the interconnectedness of our personal and public lives was the first eureka moment in my journey toward sustainability. My journey sees concern for multiple levels of sustainability as examples of updated content in responsible management, and business issues of the climate crisis need leadership models and practices that connect a person's living, working, and teaching to supporting sustainable ecosystems.

Steps in my journey to teaching sustainability began by changing my teaching methods and content, which was accelerated by the COVID pandemic as the background for climate change. In 2023, the pandemic is still ground zero in impacting how students learn and engage others. Looking back, my steps in creating increased awareness between the climate crisis and my leadership course began in 2016 with early discussions in Worcester Polytechnic Institute's (WPI's) Business School and throughout the campus. The immediate shutdown of in-person teaching and working caused by COVID, the multiyear continuation of masking and testing, and the personal loss that we all felt from the pandemic brought increased student interest in student's developing their own leadership for themselves and others. The isolation of people felt during COVID has brought new student interest leading via virtual and in-person environments. COVID highlighted the importance of teaching leadership as an active, real-time process that provides learning material to a student at both the personal and group levels. As a teacher of leadership and organizational change at WPI in Worcester, MA, I use personal reflection assignments so that students learn the importance of designated time and routines where they practice being still and reflect on leadership, ecosystems, personal balance, as well as broader thoughts of their group and organization's business needs.

As I see my journey, I began by recognizing the global, social, and economic changes of the climate crisis and the post-COVID impact on local, regional, and global communities. That led me to talk with other faculty at WPI and others to learn how they see the climate crisis and how they are including climate crisis issues in their research, teaching, and outreach activities. Locally, WPI provides volunteer support to a regional recycling center called Wachusett Earthday. This center provides a recycling service to seven surrounding towns, which provides a point for students to experience how sustainability actions begin at the local collection level, then to the regional distribution level. Wachusett Earthday Services collect items such as textiles, mattresses, construction debris, e-waste, metals, household hazardous materials, mixed paper, and batteries, and is a hands-on environment for learning the interconnectedness of recycling from a personal to a global level.

My experience in using sustainability as a core leadership challenge and goal can be used to teach other concepts and initiate broader educational change. Broad, systemic change is closer than we think. As I began this chapter, WPI announced two significant changes: as a new energy operating system and partnership, as well as a new research initiative, the Institute for Research in Sustainable Systems. Both these campus environmental changes can be seen as key actions for in WPI shifting operationally to a sustainable institution.

In April 2021 my personal sustainability journey in changing the way I teach leadership began with talks between myself and other teachers who share a concern for sustainability. We met to share ideas on how the climate crisis is being presented in our courses. Our conversations began with sharing experiences and passions in teaching about sustainability, and quickly expanded into ideas on how teaching sustainability and leadership might be a way to connect with others inside and outside our department. We also thought it might be possible and important to change how management education connects individual corporate goals to global concerns.

These conversations grew into developing a new shared community and new connections with people interested in sustainability. One of those connections was Isabel Rimanoczy whose teaching, research, and collaboration work developed into a "Sustainability Mindset," which fit nicely into my leadership course and became part of my course readings. This new community shared thoughts on events connected to sustainability, ideas we are seeing that might be connected to sustainability, and general teaching challenges and victories. My focus for leadership is seeing sustainability as a driving concern in teaching marketing, supply chain management, finance and profitability, and management, leadership, and organizational behavior. My view of management education has always been a systems view that began from working on a dairy farm in western Connecticut into the commercial credit market of New York, by way of seeing changes in financial technology of Worcester, MA. My leadership system's view is broadly shared by others at WPI where new thoughts on sustainable innovation are encouraged.

My first opportunity to share ideas about sustainability issues was with other faculty who teach leadership and organizational behavior. Teaching in the Post-COVID/New COVID environment required new approaches in how students see and use their learning and student excitement or apprehension for getting back into classrooms. I proposed that concerns for sustainability could be a way we update our teaching materials with business processes that address the changing nature of learning that is changing as quickly as semester health reports. Through this first meeting, and subsequent discussions with other teachers, my view of using sustainability content became an opportunity for me to increase my intention to help student mental well-being by using the practice of daily reflection, models of dynamic and inclusive leadership, and the UN's Sustainable Development Goals (SDGs) as a new framework for my teaching.

My discussions with others on how to include sustainability within my leadership course began by using personal reflection as key leadership practice. Reflection is not a novel approach to teaching leadership, and the practice of daily reflection is well known to help students identify their leadership strengths, development areas, group connections, and the contextual nature that leadership occurs within. (Clapp-Smith et al., 2019; Wamsler, 2020; Whalen & Paez, 2021; Woiwode et al., 2021). I use guided reflections to encourage students to recall experiences with leaders, view themselves externally and observe how they engaged others, and consider what effective leaders do? I ask them to reflect on their preferred leadership styles within different contexts. Do they see themselves feeling most comfortable within Autocratic, Participative, Servant, or Entrepreneurial style of leadership? Do they see effective leadership as a relationship with others or a task to be accomplished? Can they see themselves moving between a leading or following role?

To add sustainability principles to these leadership questions, I suggested that students view themselves and the world at multiple levels. My objective of teaching leadership as a multilevel thinking process was complemented by Rimanoczy's book, *The Sustainability Mindset Principles* (2021). Ideas from the book offered an effective framework for students to visualize the dimensions of sustainability, the interrelationships that promote sustainability, and help students organize issues as a 21st century leader.

Rimanoczy's four domain, 12-principal sustainability framework is organized in a comparable way to leadership behaviors, styles, and approaches, but also provides focuses on environmental sustainability as a product and goal. The Principles of the Sustainability Mindset, as a leadership tool, gives students a visual and operational map for effective 21st century management. Personally, I see the domains and principles of sustainability in a similar way to my passion for agriculture, low-input production practices, farm-level profitability, and care for the Earth. In my youth, I became interested in farming through working on dairy farms in Sherman, Connecticut. Milking cows, raising pigs, picking up

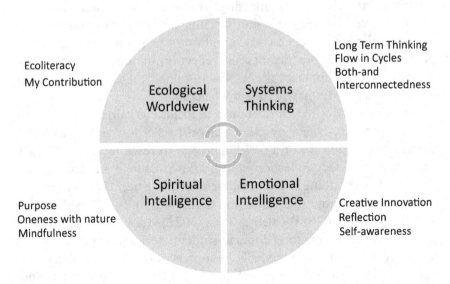

FIGURE 16.1 The 12 Sustainability Mindset Principles and the four content areas.

hay, cutting wood, and working in an entrepreneurial way is how I saw and still do see life. My family was connected to larger production farming by my uncle Keith's beef and hog farm in Hooper, NE, which I drove to over two days and learned the enormity of the United States. Thinking back, I believe my experience of driving half-way across the United States and seeing both the expanse of land, as well as congested urban areas, helped me see sustainability as a multilevel, integrated, complex, and living relationship.

Seeing the ecology of humanity is a global leadership view. Ecological, Emotional, Spiritual, and Systems views of the sustainability mindset is reflective of my passion for agriculture, low-input production, profitability, and care for the Earth. Connecting my personal passions to the idea of a sustainability mindset has provided me a teaching platform to express my wonder, curiosity, and excitement for new leadership models. New 21st century leadership requires teaching to each student's purpose and passion in a process of critical thinking for creating sustainable solutions that are targeted by environmental, economic, and social goals. My classes of 50 to 60 students are challenged by seeing how the four domains fit together, but students are excited to share ideas that are developed through Systems Thinking and Emotional Intelligence. The Ecological and Spiritual views require more time and more direction on how student can develop these views so that they are comfortable in sharing in meaningful ways.

In addition to incorporating the Sustainability Mindset Principles, I have a passion to use the UN's SDGs as 21st century global business challenges. The SDGs support business leadership principles because of the breadth of global issues they address. In faculty discussions we noted changes in student engagement and thought it would be timely to connect environmental sustainability as a business leadership challenge. Not long after, our university announced all departments would begin using SDGs to organize student Independent Qualifying Project (IQP) and Major Qualifying Project (MQP) topics.

What began as a departmental discussion of using SDGs to create links among our disciplines has grown into a campus-wide activity to categorize research. I see students' eyes light up and heads nod when they realize how their research and ideas are connected to larger, regional, national, and global thoughts and goals. Using SDGs as business issues is a way to develop new awareness of current problems and offers the possibility of broad-based change on sustainability through interdepartmental and university collaboration.

One example of the change is in our updated mission statement. WPI's Business School previous mission statement of: *Taking theory to practice to impact, preparing business students for innovative leadership in a global technological economy.* It was presented through the acronym: INSPIRE

Inspiring leaders at the
Nexus of
Science, Engineering, and Business with
Project-based, purpose-driven learning and
Innovative research to achieve impactful
Results and to pursue
Excellence that drives progress.

WPI's Business School new mission statement:

The WPI Business School develops adaptive leaders who create <u>sustainable solutions</u>, deliver globally responsible impact, and conduct transformative research at the intersection of business, technology, and people.

Management education at WPI is changing. New thinking regarding on-line learning, financial services, health care technologies, customer needs, environmental concerns, and the global view that change is framed through are the drivers for WPI's Business School's new sustainable solutions mission statement. Beyond the WPI Business School, WPI employs a Director of Sustainability for the university operations around the WPI Sustainability Plan. I use WPI's Sustainability Plan as a working leadership tool in my class. WPI's sustainability plan was created in 2014. The plan was updated in 2020 and organized around three operational pillars:

1 Developing our campus as a living and learning laboratory,
2 Establishing WPI as a hub for innovation in sustainability, and
3 Reaching out beyond our campus (locally, regionally, and globally).

Students want to know how ideas are put into action, how measurements are used to direct change, and how leaders communicate how well their ideas and management processes are working. I've heard students talking about what WPI is doing to become sustainable.

In January 2023, a new research initiative dedicated to sustainability research was launched that highlights the second pillar by creating the Institute for Research in Sustainable Systems. In addition, WPI also entered a new partnership with the companies Harrison Street and Co-gen Power Technologies to reduce WPI's carbon footprint by expanding energy-conservation measures, improving WPI's power plant, and developing sustainable energy technologies for the WPI campus (Worcester Polytechnic Institute, 2023). Explaining these efforts to leadership students helps them understand how organizations put intention toward sustainability into practice in a framework they relate to.

The UN's SDGs provide a foundation among peers in the business school and WPI programs. At WPI, the 17 SDG goals provide a common framework for groups to orient work and objectives that bring students, faculty, alumni, businesspeople, and community leaders together. Students are not as familiar with SDGs as many teachers think. When I ask my classes of 50 students how many students have heard or used the UN's SDGs, I usually get only five to seven students raising their hands. This means that we face a first task of helping build awareness of these goals.

These 17 goals provide a deep, broad, global platform for interdisciplinary research, teaching, and outreach. Using these business and social challenges to explain the business environment in my leadership course generated innovative ideas about changing WPI and management education.

SDGs provide each person, each student, each project team, a framework for connecting individual leadership to a global community goal. By using them in my course students began to identify with global challenges that required deep thinking and reflective imagination to see how their personal passion and vocation could be linked to a bigger global goal. But 17 goals are too many for any person to manage. The SDGs and five P's were built on MDGs developed by the UN in 2000. The UNs Development Group makes them more manageable by re-organizing the 17 goals into five project areas. These five Ps are described by the as: People, Planet, Prosperity, Peace, and Partnerships.

Over the past three years that I've used sustainability challenges as leadership challenges, I've found that student's interest in the SDGs grows and becomes more personal when student areas of interest are framed within SDGs and grouped into People, Planet, Prosperity, Peace, and Partnerships. These groupings also help organize the class into working groups.

People – Goals one, two, three, four, and five can be combined into the category for meeting the fundamental needs of all people around the world. The first two goals addressed the most basic sustenance. Goals three and four assert the access to fundamental goals of health, well-being, and education. Goal five pose to focus on one of the key social issues of asserting equal opportunity and empowering girls and women around the world.

Planet – Goals six, twelve, thirteen, fourteen, and fifteen reflect the global community's common concern for the critical importance of ensuring our planet supports life and the importance of responding to the climate crisis. These goals focus on access to clean and safe water for all people, appropriate and proportionate consumption and production, all environmental protection policy and targets start from climate action, protection of our ecosystem, and we must achieve these goals systematically and simultaneously.

Prosperity – Goals seven through eleven provide targets for the international community to achieve appropriate and sustainable balance of energy utilization and ensure fair, equitable, and just systems both in public and private communities and national entities.

Peace – Goal sixteen shows how the international community must come together to promote and protect peace around the world, not with military actions, but through strong institutions of justice.

Partnership – As we saw in goal eight of the Millennium Development Goals (MDGs, 2000), SDG goal seventeen promotes a global partnership that constitutes an important factor in all the 17 goals.

As I use SDGs and the five Ps in my teaching, I developed a sense of adaptive change and consideration for how sustainability is being communicated. As a teacher and sustainability champion, my intent is to use them to improve human and planet well-being. SDGs are intended to help economic development, peace and prosperity, planet, and human well-being. The UNDG describes SDGs this way:

> *The intended design objective of the SDGs understands and appreciates the critical importance of the sustainability side to economic development. In all developmental agenda or processes, the attaining energy source and energy utilization are indispensable for achieving the successful outcomes. At the same time, the environmental complications and destruction that can arise from energy utilization must become an important priority for us to managing and resolve to reach sustainable solutions.*

Concluding Thoughts

Each person's story in becoming more sustainable changes the people around them. How each of us sees our ideas, our behaviors, our words, and our actions as connections and contributions to the global community is the heart of systems thinking and the path toward sustainable solutions. In honesty, I don't know how systemic change toward climate change or other SDGs happens, but I do know from my teaching and work experience in leadership that good, effective, positive change happens when people thinking critically share openly, and work together toward identified goals. I changed my leadership teaching pedagogy, began using personal reflection in assignments, identified new content that shows newly identified competencies of sustainability thinking, and used the UN's SDGs as a way for students to personalize and prioritize global concerns.

My discussions about sustainability in and out of the department also changed WPI's Business School by updating our mission statement and engaging new faculty members in becoming involved in sustainability topics. By using WPI's Sustainability Plan as part of my teaching content, inviting students to share their stories of sustainability, and encouraging students to talk with other professors about SDGs and sustainability, additional sustainability change is spreading throughout the campus. WPI's new partnerships for energy use will lessen WPI's carbon footprint and provide a case study on how concerns for sustainability are changing operational decisions that helps students see how global goals can be applied locally.

How can my story help you initiate departmental, organizational, and disciplinary change that is directed by concerns for sustainability? I believe the first step to take is developing clarity of your purpose and how you link your passion for sustainability to actions you are taking. Effective change for sustainability begins with knowing your own personal passion and purpose. As a leadership teacher, I took for granted that knowing purpose is a natural part of being a leader, which, surprisingly, has not been a significant element in writings on leadership behaviors. (Rune, 2021). My foundational leadership and management thought leader is Peter Drucker. Peter Drucker's writings on effective management uses systems thinking, social concern, and attention to the customer as core elements of effective management but doesn't write on the importance of personal purpose to effective management.

In my experience in championing sustainability, I believe it is critically important for each of us to identify and share our passion, purpose, and what we value. How do you purposefully use your passions in your work, teaching, and way of being? How does your interest in sustainability relate to your passion so that you are living in a passionate, purposeful, sustainable way? In her book, *Reimagining Capitalism in a World on Fire* (2020), Rebecca Henderson highlights the importance of purpose in addressing the climate crisis. Her six steps to making a difference are:

1 Discover your own purpose
2 Do something now
3 Bring your values to work
4 Work in government
5 Get political
6 Take care of yourself and remember to find joy

These steps and broader business management practices of identifying customer, employee, and investor connections with sustainability issues are solid steps toward creating solutions for the climate crisis. These steps combined with personal reflection and public action are 21st century leadership practices. I used elements of these steps as a guide for students in their personal reflections on their leadership behaviors. In addition to using personal purpose as the first step in creating change, I learned from others that our mindsets provide us with the "how" and our goals provide us with the "what" to change. The *Sustainability Mindset Principles* provide a tool for students to about sustainability issues. The UN's SDGs give students a way to see the "what" in sustainability. The three areas of a person's Purpose, Mindset, and Goals focused on becoming sustainable are teaching elements that can become a 21st century leadership model. Can your passion, purpose, and concern for the people and planet help identify and meet needs with valuable solutions? How can your business interests and personal passions help you be a purpose-driven leader?

Your perspective on change is the second step a person can take in helping them lead sustainable change. Creating sustainable change happens in phases and evolves. Each person, each teacher, each group, uses their passions and purpose to identify their strengths and weaknesses. In my case, I use the four domains of a sustainable mindset to help students recognize and build from their strengths, see personal areas to develop their weaknesses, and explore how to partner with others to create sustainable change. Thinking sustainably is deep, high-level thinking and is created over time but aided by focused steps. Professor Ban Ki-moon at Yonsei University's Institute for Global Engagement and Empowerment explains the evolution from MDGs to SDGs this way:

> *SDGs are more expansive and ambitious in that in that both the plans (MDGs and SDGs) require continuous progress to achieve their goals. However, the SDGs include more specific goals, and at the same time, a broader range of goals than the MDGs. This helps the scope of achieving goals to be clearer and wider. The SDGs represent the hopes of those who are ready to take action to improve the world.*
>
> (Ki-moon, 2023)

To be sustainable we need to evolve and adapt our ideas and actions to improve the health and well-being of both people and planet.

Lastly, and most importantly, we need to be courageous in sharing our passion for innovative approaches and ideas for sustainability. We need to strengthen and expand our current networks for change toward sustainability. Our models for living, learning, leading, listening, and loving this planet are changing and becoming more integrated through new data, technology, and global concerns. The universal challenge of protecting life on this planet must be addressed through the universal recognition of our mutual survival. We have new technological tools for measuring, analyzing, and knowing how the health of our people and planet is changing both positively and negatively. We have many pockets of success to share that use new mindsets and tools.

One email about starting a conversation on sustainability led me to meet others who helped change my teaching materials with new ideas and new approaches to thinking and working toward sustainability. These people have shared ideas and contacts with other people who share their ideas with others, and share with others, and others, and others. We are all sharing ideas on sustainability to create an uplifting momentum for sustainable change. The story of one can become the story of many when we share our purpose for creating sustainable solutions for people and planet. Look beyond your screen, your tablet, your window. What do you see? What do you want to see, and how have you shared that today?

References

Clapp-Smith, R., Hammond, M. M., Lester, G. V., & Palanski, M. (2019). Promoting identity development in leadership education: A multidomain approach to developing the whole leader. *Journal of Management Education, 43*(1), 10–34.

Henderson, R. (2021). *Reimagining capitalism in a World on fire: Shortlisted for the FT & McKinsey business book of the year award 2020.* Penguin.

Ki-moon, B. (2023). Yonsei University. From MDGs to SDGs. Retrieved Online: https://www.coursera.org/learn/sustainable-development-ban-ki-moon/lecture/fNX2N/from-mdgs-to-sdgs

Rimanoczy, I. (2021). The sustainability mindset principles: A guide to developing a mindset for a better world. Routledge, Taylor & Francis Group.

Rune, T. (2021). Leadership: In pursuit of purpose. *Journal of Change Management, 21*(1), 30–44.

United Nations Foundation. (2019). The sustainable development goals in 2019: People, planet, prosperity in focus. https://unfoundation.org/blog/post/the-sustainable-development-goals-in-2019-people-planet-prosperity-in-focus/

Wamsler, C. (2020). Education for sustainability: Fostering a more conscious society and transformation towards sustainability. *International Journal of Sustainability in Higher Education, 21*(1), 112–130.

Whalen, K., & Paez, A. (2021). Student perceptions of reflection and the acquisition of higher-order thinking skills in a university sustainability course. *Journal of Geography in Higher Education, 45*(1), 108–127.

Woiwode, C., Schäpke, N., Bina, O., Veciana, S., Kunze, I., Parodi, O., ... & Wamsler, C. (2021). Inner transformation to sustainability as a deep leverage point: fostering new avenues for change through dialogue and reflection. *Sustainability Science, 16,* 841–858.

Worcester Polytechnic Institute (WPI) (2023, January). Power play: New partnership accelerates WPI's efforts to reduce its carbon footprint. https://www.wpi.edu/news/power-play-new-partnership-accelerates-wpis-efforts-reduce-its-carbon-footprint

INDEX

Note: **Bold** page numbers refer to tables; *Italic* page numbers refer to figures and page numbers followed by "n" denote endnotes.

Printed in the United States
by Baker & Taylor Publisher Services